New ENTERPRISE

B1

Student's Book

Jenny Dooley

Express Publishing

CONTENTS

In Character

Vocabulary: character & appearance; clothes & accessories
Grammar: present simple, present continuous; action/stative verbs; adverbs of frequency; relatives – relative clauses
Everyday English: deciding what to wear (suggesting – agreeing/disagreeing)
Writing: an article about an inspiring person

Vocabulary

Character & Appearance

1 In a minute, think of as many adjectives as you can that describe character. Compare with your partner.

Study Skills

Using a dictionary

Dictionaries present words in alphabetical order. They contain information about what part of speech each word is, how to pronounce it, meaning(s) of the word and example sentences. Some dictionaries also include synonyms and antonyms.

2 a) Choose the correct word. Check in your dictionary.

1 Tom likes telling others what to do. He's very **bossy/calm**.

2 Pam's so **cheerful/kind**! Her smile lights up the office.

3 Joe's **confident/jealous**; he never doubts himself.

4 Alan's a **gentle/clever** person; he wouldn't hurt a fly!

5 Jean hurts people's feelings all the time. She's extremely **cruel/lazy**.

6 Greg likes learning all about people he meets. He's very **honest/curious**.

7 Glenda is so **generous/reliable**; she loves buying presents for people!

8 Jeremy doesn't mind waiting for things; he's very **friendly/patient**.

9 Paul's **sensible/funny**; he makes reasonable decisions.

10 People find Olga **brave/rude** because she behaves in an impolite way to others.

11 Angela's **sociable/serious**; she rarely laughs at things.

12 Max is really **charming/careful**; he's pleasant to everyone he meets.

b) Which of the adjectives in Ex. 2a best describe: *you*? *your friends*? **Give reasons.**

3 **Look at the people in the pictures.** *Who's in his/her early/late twenties? middle-aged? elderly? in his early/late thirties? a teenager? Who's got thick eyebrows? big ears? small round ears? a long nose? bottom lip fuller than the top lip? a big forehead? a curved forehead? blue eyes? brown eyes?*

Tony is middle-aged with a big forehead and blue eyes.

It's written all over your FACE

*You shouldn't **judge** a book by its cover, right? Well, maybe you should! Face-reading is an ancient art, still **popular** with people today, which says that you can tell a person's personality from looking at their face. And now, even scientists agree that there is some truth in it! For example, in 2008, a pair of Canadian scientists found that ice hockey players with wide faces are usually more violent, and in 2013, a study at Glasgow University found that people with chubby cheeks are often more anxious. So, what else do our faces say about our personalities?*

EYEBROWS

Does the friendliest person in your class have thick dark eyebrows? People with this **feature** are often very sociable, while bushy eyebrows often mean that a person is bossy. Also, arched eyebrows usually belong to funny people.

EYES

We can tell a lot from a person's eye colour. Calm people often have blue eyes, while green-eyed people **tend** to be quite jealous! The most common eye colour, brown, often shows a confident personality.

Listening & Reading

4 a) Guess what someone's facial features might say about their character. Write down one thing for each feature.

Listen to and read the text to see if your guesses were correct.

b) Where do you think the text is from: *a personal blog? a serious newspaper? a light-hearted magazine?*

Amira

Sam

Ann

Sue

EARS
Interviewing people for a job? Then look for people with rectangular ears! This shows the person is honest and hard-working. People with round ears are reliable and make good friends. On the other hand, people with big ears and large earlobes are sometimes cruel.

NOSES
Noses come in all shapes and sizes. People with small noses are often very generous, while a long nose is a sign of a patient person. People with a hooked nose often make good actors because they are very confident.

LIPS
Is your bottom lip fuller than your top lip? Then, maybe you have a curious and **adventurous** personality. People whose top lip is fuller, on the other hand, tend to be a bit rude. What about people with lips which are the same size? You might guess that they are fair people who make very good teachers!

FOREHEADS
People with big foreheads are often quite clever, though this has nothing to do with the size of their brains! A **curved** forehead, on the other hand, is a sign of a cheerful person who **brightens up** the room.

 Check these words

violent, chubby, bushy, arched, rectangular, earlobe, hooked, brain

5 **Read the text again and correct the sentences. Then, explain the words in bold.**

1 A person with thick dark eyebrows is bossy.
2 Blue-eyed people are confident.
3 People with rectangular ears are cruel.
4 People with hooked noses are patient.
5 People with lips the same size are rude.
6 A bright happy person often has a big forehead.

6  COLLOCATIONS **Fill in:** *bottom*, *eye*, *curved*, *chubby*, *round*, *ancient*, *thick*. **Use the phrases in sentences of your own.**

1 .... art
2 .... cheeks
3 .... eyebrows
4 .... colour
5 .... ears
6 .... lip
7 .... forehead

7 PREPOSITIONS **Choose the correct preposition. Check in your dictionary.**

1 Bob is very kind and friendly **to/for** everyone.
2 Susan's very patient **to/with** even the naughtiest children; she stays calm all the time.
3 Little George shouldn't be rude **for/to** grown-ups.
4 Helen is jealous **by/of** what other people have.
5 Mary is curious **about/for** the world around her.
6 John can be very cruel **to/with** others.

8 WORDS EASILY CONFUSED **Fill in** *popular* **or** *famous*. **Check in your dictionary.**

1 Which .... actor would you most like to meet?
2 Light-hearted magazines are .... with teenagers.
3 Adrian is .... for telling funny jokes.
4 It's such a .... book that they're making it into a film.

9 PHRASAL VERBS **Fill in the correct particle(s).**

look after: to take care of sb/sth
look for: to try to find sb/sth
look forward to: to expect sth with pleasure
look up: to try to find a word, name, etc in a reference book

1 I've forgotten the number – let me look it ....
2 Julie looks .... our children while we're at work.
3 Jane is looking .... her graduation.
4 Helen is looking .... a good book to read.

Speaking

10 THINK **Think of someone you know well. Describe him/her to your partner and then say whether or not the person's character matches the description in the text.**

Grammar in Use

Bill: Hello, Bob. Do you have a moment?

Bob: Hi, Bill. What's up?

Bill: I *want* you to meet our new receptionist, Sally French. Sally, this is Bob Grant.

Bob: Pleased to meet you, Sally. Is this your first day?

Sally: Actually, I**'m starting** work next Monday. I**'m doing** a computer course this week. Mr Kent **is** just **showing** me around at the moment.

Bob: I'm thinking of updating my computer skills, too. I think they're getting a little out of date!

Bill: And here comes Mary Boylan! She **works** in sales, but she often **comes** over here to discuss results with Bob.

Sally: Oh, I have experience in sales. That's a hard job!

Mary: Well, it's never slow! In fact, I have to be quick, Bob. My department meeting **starts** at 10:30.

Bill: Let's leave them to it, Sally. Now, over here ...

Present simple – Present continuous ▶ pp. GR1-2

1 Identify the tenses in bold in the dialogue. How do we form each tense? Match the verbs in bold to their uses:

- actions happening at the time of speaking
- habits/routines/repeated actions
- fixed arrangements in the near future
- timetables/schedules (future meaning)
- permanent states
- temporary situations

Look at the circled adverbs of frequency in the dialogue. How do we use them in a sentence?

2 Read the theory. Then, look at the highlighted verbs in the dialogue. Do they have a continuous form? Why/Why not?

Action verbs – Stative verbs ▶ p. GR2

Action verbs describe an action. They have simple and continuous forms.
*He **goes** to work by bike. He **is going** to the cinema now.*
Stative verbs are verbs which describe a state rather than an action and do not usually have a continuous form.
*I **feel** exhausted.* (verbs of the senses)
*I **know** who he is.* (verbs of perception)
*He **wants** to have pasta for dinner.* (verbs which express feelings and emotions)
*Who **does** this bag **belong** to?* (other verbs)

3 Put the verbs in brackets into the correct tense. Give reasons.

Steven **1)** .... **(work)** as a director. When a film is in production, he **2)** .... **(get)** up very early every day to work with his crew. He's in the studio now. He **3)** .... **(direct)** a scene from his new film *The Lost Treasure*. He **4)** .... **(stay)** in London at present, but he **5)** .... **(fly)** to Morocco tomorrow to shoot some scenes. His flight **6)** .... **(leave)** at 6:00 am and although he **7)** .... **(love)** travelling, he **8)** .... **(dislike)** early mornings.

4 Read the theory. Look at the underlined verbs in the dialogue. How does the meaning differ?

Stative verbs with continuous forms ▶ p. GR2

Some stative verbs can be used in continuous tenses, but with a difference in meaning.

Present simple	Present continuous
*These flowers **smell** nice.* (= have a good smell)	*She **is smelling** the flowers.* (= sniffing)

5 Put the verbs in brackets into the present simple or the present continuous. Explain the meaning.

1 Morgan .... **(see)** his dentist tomorrow.

2 I .... **(see)** a big queue outside the cinema.

3 She .... **(look)** happy today!

4 What's that glossy magazine you .... **(look)** at?

5 The chef .... **(taste)** the stew to see if it needs more pepper.

6 I like this ice cream; it .... **(taste)** of peanut butter!

7 Our neighbour .... **(be)** an extremely kind and polite person.

8 The children .... **(be)** very noisy, today. Tell them to stop, please!

6 Put the verbs in brackets into the present simple or the present continuous. Give reasons.

INBOX   OUTBOX   CONTACTS

Hi Annie!

Hope you're fine! Guess what? Our college **1)** .... **(put)** on a play next month and I've got the main part. The play's called *Mirror, Mirror* and it's a black comedy based on the fairy tale *Snow White*. Rehearsals are three times a week – the next one **2)** .... **(start)** in an hour, actually. Right now, I **3)** .... **(try)** to learn my speech. I **4)** .... **(know)** the director. He **5)** .... **(work)** in the college Drama Department – he **6)** .... **(teach)** us on Mondays. He's very strict and he **7)** .... **(not/like)** it when actors forget their lines, so I'm a bit nervous! For my character, Rose White, I **8)** .... **(need)** to wear a white dress. I **9)** .... **(not/have)** one so I'll have to go shopping! What about you? How's your film project going? **10)** .... **(you/get)** much done on it these days? I **11)** .... **(believe)** the actress you're writing about **12)** .... **(appear)** at the Gate Theatre soon. We can go and see her!

Talk to you later,
Tara

Relatives ▸ pp. GR2-3

7 Look at the words in bold in sentences 1-5. Which are used for *people*? *things*? *time*? *place*? Which shows possession?

1 Daryl is not the sort of person **who/that** expects help without giving anything back.

2 She prefers casual clothes **which/that** are comfortable to wear.

3 She is a complicated person **whose** character has many sides.

4 Mexico City is the place **where** she was born. (= in which)

5 March is the month **when** she usually travels to Spain.

Defining / Non-defining relative clauses ▸ p. GR3

Defining relative clauses give necessary information essential to the meaning of the main sentence. We do not put the clause in commas. *This is the shop **whose** clothes are all made from organic materials.*

Non-defining relative clauses give extra information that is not essential to the meaning of the main sentence. The relative pronouns cannot be omitted and we put the clause in commas. *My next-door neighbour, **who** is quite young, is a very kind and generous person.*

8 Read the theory. Fill in the correct relative pronoun. Which of the relative clauses are *defining*? *non-defining*? Put commas where necessary.

1 I met someone at Jack's house .... was extremely rude.

2 That's the seafood restaurant .... I first tried octopus.

3 Chloe bought a new dress .... really suited her.

4 My cousin Harry .... uncle is a physicist plans to get a science degree.

5 She's the designer .... sportswear is popular with teens.

6 I'll never forget the day .... I started my first job!

7 Mr Bloggs .... is a reliable builder did an excellent job on our house.

8 Sandra is curious by nature .... means that she enjoys exploring new places.

9 Join the sentences as in the example. Use: *who*, *which*, *whose*, *where* or *when*.

1 Ms Brown is a friendly person. She likes meeting new people.
   *Ms Brown is a friendly person **who** likes meeting new people.*

2 James enjoys sailing in summer. The weather is good then.

3 Claire is a model. She has been in lots of fashion shows.

4 The Wilsons live in a big house. The house is near the park.

5 Sheila is wearing a nice dress. The dress fits her perfectly.

6 Steven is a lawyer. His office is in Baker Street.

7 Alfie works in a shop. They sell men's clothes there.

10 **SPEAKING** Complete the sentences so they are true for you. Use relative pronouns.

1 I like people ....

2 I can't stand people ....

3 I like films ....

4 There are times ....

5 I hate places ....

Skills in Action

Vocabulary

Clothes & Accessories

1 **a)**  Match the items in the list with the correct departments in the store directory. Some items can be listed under more than one department.

GOLDEN GATE STORES

5th	ACCESSORIES
4th	BEACHWEAR
3rd	SPORTSWEAR
2nd	FOOTWEAR
1st	MENSWEAR
GROUND	WOMENSWEAR

- leather belt • evening dress • ankle socks
- high-heeled shoes • polo-neck jumper • bow tie
- skinny jeans • silk blouse • swimsuit • pullover
- tracksuit • walking boots • waistcoat • raincoat
- tailored suit • polo shirt • sweatshirt

b) Ask and answer questions, as in the example.

A: Excuse me. Where can I find leather belts?

B: In the accessories department on the fifth floor.

Listening

2 You will hear a fashion designer and one of his clients talking. Listen and choose the correct answer (A, B, C, or D) for each question.

1 David's new line is clothes for

    A older people.   **C** old customers.

    B sports fans.   **D** young people.

2 Where is Claudia's new shop?

    A in Knightsbridge   **C** in Halifax Street

    B in East London   **D** south of the river

3 This is the first time David is selling

    A ties.   **C** shirts.

    B jackets.   **D** complete outfits.

Everyday English

Deciding what to wear

3 **a)** Complete the dialogue with the correct form of the verbs in the list. Who do you think the speakers are?

- suit • prefer • fit • look • match • go with

A: What are you going to wear to my boss's retirement dinner?

B: My new blue jeans and a blue T-shirt to **1)** ....

A: Don't you think jeans are a bit too casual to wear to a retirement dinner?

B: Hmm. Maybe you're right. How about a dress then?

A: Yes. You've got lots of stylish dresses. The black one with the polka dots really **2)** .... you.

B: But I've put on a bit of weight so it doesn't **3)** .... me very well now. I'll wear my brown woollen one. It **4)** .... my brown leather belt. What are you going to wear?

A: I'm thinking of wearing my blue suit with a white shirt.

B: Really? I **5)** .... your grey suit. You **6)** .... very smart in it.

A: OK. I'll wear that, then!

b) Listen and check.

4 Decide with your partner what to wear in the following situations. Use phrases from the language box. Record yourselves.

- a barbecue at your cousin's house
- a cycling trip • a presentation at work

Suggesting	Agreeing/Disagreeing
• How about ...? • Why don't you ...?	• Maybe you're right. • I think you're right. • That's a good idea.
	• I don't think so. • Really? I prefer ... .

Pronunciation: diphthongs /eɪ/, /aɪ/, /ɔɪ/

5 Listen and repeat. Can you think of more words with the same sounds?

/eɪ/ w**ay**, l**a**zy, f**a**mous

/aɪ/ b**uy**, t**ie**, rel**i**able

/ɔɪ/ b**oy**, enj**oy**, ann**oy**

Reading & Writing

6 Read the task and answer the questions.

Articles wanted!

> **Inspiring People**
>
> *Who is someone you greatly admire? What makes them inspiring to you? Is it their appearance, character, achievements or all three? Write an article answering these questions (120-150 words). We will publish the most interesting ones in our magazine.*

1 What are you going to write? Who for?

2 What should you write about? How many words should your piece of writing be?

Word formation

Forming adjectives

- We can form adjectives from **nouns** by adding **-ful** (*wonder – wonderful*) and **-ous** (*danger – dangerous*).
- We can form adjectives from **verbs** by adding **-able/-ible** (*rely – reliable, access – accessible*) and **-ive** (*invent – inventive*).

7 Read the article and fill in the gaps with adjectives derived from the words in brackets.

The Blind OLYMPIAN

The person I really admire is Canadian champion cross-country skier Brian McKeever. He's a **1)** .... **(fame)** international athlete, but suffers from an eye disease. However, being almost blind doesn't stop him from having a **2)** .... **(success)** career!

Starting competitions at the age of 12, Brian is now one of the best athletes in the Winter Paralympics. He regularly participates in 20-kilometre cross-country events with his guide and has won lots of medals!

Brian is fit and **3)** .... **(attract)**. He loves wearing red and white skiing outfits – the colours of Canada! He is always cheerful, confident and **4)** .... **(response)**. He proudly follows in his father's footsteps, who had the same disease.

Brian inspires me because it's not **5)** .... **(accept)** for him to give up. Whatever the difficulties, he believes in doing his best and fair play – the true meaning of the Olympic ideal.

Writing Tip

Linking ideas

Adding ideas

He is tall. He is handsome.

*He is tall **and (also)** handsome.*

*He is tall **and** he is handsome **as well**.*

Making contrasts

*He has a sight problem **but** he's a great athlete.*

*He has a sight problem. **However/Still**, he's a great athlete.*

***Although** he has a sight problem, he's a great athlete.*

8 Join the sentences. Use the words in brackets.

1 Roger is friendly. Roger is caring. **(as well)**

2 John suffers from a disease. He is a champion swimmer. **(however)**

3 Fran looks after old people. She cares for stray animals. **(also)**

4 Becky is very young. She has a successful career. **(although)**

5 Hugo usually has a lot of energy. He gets tired sometimes. **(but)**

Writing (an article about an inspiring person)

9 a) **BRAINSTORMING** Read the task in Ex. 6. Think of a person who inspires you. Make notes under the headings: *name – where from – what famous for – achievements – appearance – character – why inspiring* in your notebook.

b) Use your notes in Ex. 9a to write your article. Follow the plan and give it a title.

Plan

Para 1: name – where from, what famous for

Para 2: achievements

Para 3: appearance & character

Para 4: why inspiring to you

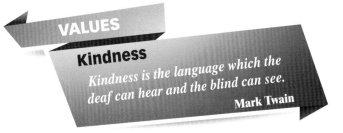

VALUES

Kindness

Kindness is the language which the deaf can hear and the blind can see.

Mark Twain

Culture

The Real Scotland

The Real Scotland

▶ Scot Kirsten McCoy answers readers' questions about Scotland.

Scottish kilts

See more

Is it true that Scottish men wear skirts?

People sometimes ask this, but what they are actually talking about is the Scottish kilt. Scottish men wear kilts on traditional and formal **occasions**, from weddings and funerals to the Highland Games and traditional music **events**. Kilts date back to the 1700s.

The kilt comes down to the knee and is made of a thick kind of **cloth**. It is called twill and it is from high quality wool. It has pleats, or folds in the cloth, at the sides and back, but not at the front. The checked **pattern**, which is called tartan, comes in hundreds of different varieties. That's because each Scottish clan, or family, has its own pattern. The Scottish wear it with a shirt, jacket and tie on formal occasions, as well as hose (knee-high socks) and ghillie brogues (a kind of leather shoe). A sporran, meaning 'purse' in Scottish Gaelic, hangs at the front. This is a small **pouch** to keep things in, since kilts don't have pockets. Finally, a kilt pin holds the kilt together, often at the bottom on the right-hand side.

Unlike some other traditional pieces of clothing, the kilt is very popular. On visits to Scotland, the men of the British Royal Family always put on kilts, which are often made of Balmoral tartan, the Queen's own special pattern. Scottish actors like Ewan McGregor, Gerard Butler and James McAvoy are very proud to wear their kilts. Tartan is also very popular, appearing on hats, scarves, socks and any other item of clothing you can imagine!

✓ **Check these words**

funeral, date back, knee, pleat, hang, clothing

Reading & Listening

1 When do the Scottish wear the kilt?
🎧 Listen and read to find out.

2 Read the text again and match the numbers (1-5) in the picture with the highlighted words. Then explain the words in bold.

Speaking & Writing

3 Use the photo to present the kilt to the class.

4 ICT Collect information about a traditional piece of clothing from your country. Make notes under the headings: *name and where/when it is from – description – present popularity*. **Write a short article for an online travel website about your country.**

Vocabulary

1 Match the adjectives (1-6) with their definitions (a-f).

1 ☐ confident   a not wanting to work hard
2 ☐ generous   b sure about your abilities
3 ☐ cheerful   c enjoying the company of others
4 ☐ sociable   d happy to give what you have to others
5 ☐ lazy   e able to make people laugh
6 ☐ funny   f always in a good mood

(6 X 3 = 18)

2 Choose the correct item.

1 I put on my **waistcoat/raincoat** because it was pouring down.
2 Jim put on weight and now his clothes don't **match/fit** him.
3 Do these trousers look nice with this **bow/polo-neck** jumper?
4 **Skinny/Ankle** jeans are very fashionable at the moment.
5 Those shorts don't **go with/suit** Michael.
6 The campsite is 10 km away, so you need **walking/evening** boots.

(6 X 1 = 6)

3 Fill in: *of, up, after, for, to (x2)*.

1 Ann looks .... a 10-year-old boy on weekdays.
2 He's very friendly .... his colleagues.
3 Bob's jealous .... our new house.
4 What are you looking ....? Your keys?
5 Look .... the word in your dictionary.
6 Don't be cruel .... others.

(6 X 2 = 12)

Grammar

4 Put the verbs in brackets into the present simple or continuous.

1 I .... **(enjoy)** going shopping with my friends on Saturdays.
2 The sales assistants .... **(get)** the department store ready for the sales next week.
3 Carl .... **(not/wear)** formal clothes very often.
4 The fashion editor .... **(not/go)** to the show next week because she's sick.
5 What time .... **(your plane/leave)**?
6 .... **(your daughter/study)** fashion design at college now?

(6 X 4 = 24)

5 Fill in: *who, which, whose, where, when*.

1 This is the college .... I studied fashion.
2 A coat is a piece of clothing .... you wear to keep warm in winter.
3 Muriel is a designer .... hats cost up to £500!
4 Sunday is a day .... most people have a break from their daily routine.
5 Lee's father is the person .... she relies on most.

(5 X 4 = 20)

6 Match the exchanges.

1 ☐ What are you going to wear?   a I'll wear that, then!
2 ☐ How about wearing your jeans?   b I prefer the grey one.
3 ☐ You look great in it!   c Maybe you're right.
4 ☐ Don't you think it's a bit casual? d I'm thinking of wearing a suit.
5 ☐ How about this blue tie?   e They don't fit me.

(5 X 4 = 20)

Total 100

Competences

GOOD ✓
VERY GOOD ✓ ✓
EXCELLENT ✓ ✓ ✓

Lexical Competence

understand words/phrases related to:
- character & appearance
- clothes & accessories

Reading Competence
- understand texts related to character & appearance (read for specific information – sentence correction/meaning from context)

Listening Competence
- listen to and understand dialogues related to clothes & accessories (listen for specific information – multiple choice questions)

Speaking Competence
- decide what to wear (suggest – agree/disagree)

Writing Competence
- write an article about an inspiring person

Vocabulary: types of books; feelings
Grammar: past simple – past continuous; *used to/would*
Everyday English: narrating an event – expressing sympathy
Writing: a story

Reading Time

 VIDEO

Vocabulary

Types of books

1 Which of the following types of books are fiction? non-fiction?

- thriller • science fiction • crime • horror
- textbook • biography • fantasy • travel
- romance • mystery • health • science
- comedy • history • action & adventure

2 List the types of fiction in order of preference. Use the adjectives to discuss, as in the example.

- amusing • interesting • full of action • educational
- complicated • confusing • serious • easy to read • exciting • impossible to put down • scary
- silly • realistic • powerful • dull • difficult to read
- unbelievable • original • clever

A: *I like action and adventure books most of all. They're impossible to put down.*

B: *Oh, really? I prefer fantasy stories. They're full of imagination. I don't like horror stories, though. I think they're scary.*

A: *Well, I can't stand romance novels. I find them dull.*

Listening & Reading

3 Read the descriptions. What books do you think these people like reading?

1 Jake is a programmer who loves stories that move fast. He prefers not to take any chances when buying books, so generally goes for ones he can see are popular or classics.

2 Patsy used to read thrillers, but now she prefers stories about ordinary people trying to solve everyday problems. She loves books that make her laugh and teach her about life.

3 Sam loves amusing stories about strange lands. He likes books to have an interesting main character and, as a student, he wants to learn from what he reads.

4 Aidan loves reading books – the longer the better! His favourites have exciting storylines, kings and queens, and imaginary worlds.

Ⓐ *A Game of Thrones*

"When you play the game of thrones, you win or you die." In the Seven Kingdoms of Westeros, ancient families stop at nothing to rule the land. George R R Martin's 694-page fantasy epic was at the top of the bestseller lists when it first came out. Along with later novels, it is the basis for the famous TV series. **Settle down** for a long thrilling read to find out how this series watched by millions started.

Ⓑ *The Martian*

Mark Watney's spaceship left him on Mars! Most people give up in situations like that, but not Watney. In this science-fiction novel by Andy Weir, Watney decides he is the first Martian, and uses his knowledge to stay alive until help arrives. Very funny at times, extremely educational and **totally** realistic!

Ⓒ *The Snowman*

When the first snow fell, lots of people built snowmen in their front gardens. But only one was wearing a **missing** woman's scarf! This is Jo Nesbø's seventh novel with Norwegian policeman Harry Hole as the main character, solving terrible crimes. A fast clever crime story that's impossible to put down!

4 Look at the titles A-E. What type of story does each title suggest? Listen and check.

Study Skills

Multiple matching

Read the texts and the descriptions of the people carefully. Look for paraphrases (something written using different words) of the information. Do not try to match words as these can sometimes be distractors.

---

5 Decide which book (A-E) would be the most suitable for the people (1-4). Then, explain the words in bold.

BOOKS RECOMMENDED BY JIM ELIOT

D Digital Fortress

The US government call Susan Fletcher, an expert at **breaking** codes. They want her to break into their own computer system! Dan Brown's first novel has everything readers expect from him: action, excitement and secret codes. Like Brown's hugely successful *The Da Vince Code*, this book was a **bestseller**.

E About a Boy

This novel is really about *two* boys. Will's father was rich, so Will doesn't need to work. As a result, even though he is an adult, he never really grew up. Marcus is a teenager living with his mum, who is very **depressed** because she and his dad broke up. Nick Hornby's second novel is a comedy about an unlikely friendship, and how each friend helps the other fix his life.

NICK HORNBY
About a
BOY

✓ **Check these words**

throne, rule, epic, spaceship, main, secret code, unlikely

6 PREPOSITIONS **Fill in:** *by, as, about (x2), at (x2)*.

1 A new novel .... your favourite author came out last week.

2 *The Hobbit* is a story .... stealing a dragon's treasure.

3 The writer is an expert .... creating excitement.

4 Paul's sister prefers mystery books with a woman .... the main character.

5 Her new novel is .... the top of the bestseller lists.

6 This science book taught me a lot .... the moon.

7 COLLOCATIONS **Fill in:** *arrives, break, build, falls, stay, solve, take, wear*. **Use the phrases in sentences of your own.**

1 .... alive
2 help ....
3 snow ....
4 .... a snowman
5 .... a scarf
6 .... a crime
7 .... a code
8 .... a chance

8 WORDS EASILY CONFUSED **Choose the correct word. Check in your dictionary.**

1 Sam **looked/saw/watched** at the open door and knew someone was waiting for him inside.

2 Tony **looked/saw/watched** his friend Martin in the bookshop.

3 I don't **look/see/watch** TV every night.

9 PHRASAL VERBS **Fill in the correct particle.**

break down: (of cars, engines, etc) to stop working
break into: to get into a building, etc to steal sth
break out: (of wars, fires, storms, etc) to begin suddenly
break up: 1) (of schools) to stop for holidays; **2)** to end a relationship

1 Fire broke .... so we had to leave the building.

2 I couldn't wait for school to break .... and the holidays to begin.

3 Jake's car broke .... just as the snow started falling.

4 The men broke .... the building through the back door.

5 Her parents broke ...., but then they got back together!

Speaking & Writing

10 a) 💬 THINK **Imagine a book of your own. Design the cover for it. What will your cover show? Why?**

b) **Write a short paragraph to describe your book for the back cover (50 words). Think about:** *main characters, where they are, why they are there* **and** *what happens*. **Make sure you don't say what happens in the end.**

Grammar in Use

Past simple – Past continuous
> pp. GR3-4

It was a sunny afternoon in July. A light breeze was blowing across the bay. David and his friends were sailing along the coast enjoying the warm weather. They <u>used to be</u> together more often. They <u>would meet</u> every weekend, but that changed after university. That's why they made sure they had this one holiday together every year.

The friends all felt relaxed. Rick and Tyler were helping David as Max and Bill were talking about their summer holidays. Suddenly, the sky went dark, the sea got rough and waves crashed against the boat. David was trying to lower the sails when Rick shouted out, "Where's Tyler?"

1 Read the story. Identify the past simple and past continuous forms. How do we form these tenses? Which tense do we use for:

- actions that happened at a definite time in the past (stated or implied)?
- an action in progress at a specific time in the past?
- actions that happened one after the other in the past?
- two or more actions in progress at the same time in the past?
- a past action in progress when another action interrupted it?
- background information in a story?

2 Put the verbs in brackets into the past simple or the past continuous.

1 A: Where .... (you/be) last night?
   B: Dan .... (fall) down the stairs so I .... (take) him to the hospital.

2 A: .... (it/snow) when you were on your mountain hike?
   B: Yes. It .... (snow) when I set out and it .... (not/stop) until I got back home!

3 A: .... (you/see) the car crash on your street yesterday?
   B: Yeah, I .... (go) to the market when it happened.

4 A: Why .... (Susie/look) so frightened?
   B: She .... (hear) a knock at the front door, but there .... (not/be) anyone there.

5 A: What .... (you/do) while the police .... (search) the house?
   B: I .... (wait) for Mark to come.

3 Put the verbs in brackets into the past simple or the past continuous. Then ask and answer questions about the story, as in the example.

It **1)** .... (be) a cool autumn morning, but it **2)** .... (not/rain) so Paul decided to drive to the river to take a walk. The sun **3)** .... (shine) at first, but later the sky went dark. Soon it **4)** ....(rain) heavily.

Paul waited under a tree, but the rain just got heavier. As he was watching, the river **5)** .... (move) faster and faster. Suddenly, Paul **6)** .... (hear) a shout for help. There was a man in the water – and the river **7)** .... (take) him down past Paul!

Without thinking, Paul jumped in. As the man **8)** .... (go) past, Paul grabbed his arm and **9)** .... (pull) him to the river bank.

Paul **10)** .... (drive) the man to hospital, where they said he was fine. Paul **11)** .... (feel) glad about that, but he was cold and wet. All he **12)** .... (want) was to go home and have a hot shower. Wouldn't anyone?

A: Was it raining when Paul left for the river?
B: No, it wasn't.

4 Join the sentences below using *when*, *while*, *and*, *so* or *because*, as in the example.

The sun was shining and the birds were singing.

1 The sun was shining.
2 Aidan was watching TV.
3 I was having a bath.
4 I heard a noise in the garden.
5 Amy went to bed early last night.

a His brother was getting dressed.
b She was very tired.
c The birds were singing.
d I went to see what it was.
e My doorbell rang.

Avoiding repetition

When there are two past continuous forms in one sentence talking about the same person, you can omit the conjunction *and*, the subject pronoun and the auxiliary verb (*to be*), and use only the *-ing* participle. *The child was looking around and he was crying for his mother.* → *The child was looking around crying for his mother.*

5 Read the theory. Cross out the unnecessary words.

1 He was running down the street and he was carrying a big box.

2 They were standing on the beach and they were admiring the view.

3 Olivia was sitting in front of the TV and she was eating her dinner.

4 Max was sitting in the garden and he was reading a book.

5 Jenny and Ann were drinking coffee and they were talking about their summer plans.

used to – would ▶ p. GR4

6 Read the theory. Look at the underlined verbs in the text on p. 14 and answer the questions.

used to – would

- We use ***used to*** to talk about past habits or states that are no longer true. *I used to ride a motorcycle, but now I drive a car.* We use the **past simple** instead of ***used to*** with no difference in meaning to talk about past habits or states. *Lucas used to live in Bath when he was younger./Lucas lived in Bath when he was younger.*
- We use ***would*** to talk about past habits. *As a child, I would/used to spend my holidays by the sea.*
- We do not use ***would*** to talk about states. *Sally didn't use to feel tired in the morning.* (NOT: *Sally wouldn't feel tired in the morning.*)

1 Which underlined verb is talking about: a past state? a past habit?

2 Can we replace *used to* with *would* in 'used to be'? Why/Why not?

3 Can we replace *would* with *used to* in 'would meet'?

7 Complete the sentences with *used to* or *would*. In which sentences can you use both?

1 Ann .... go horse riding before the accident.

2 You .... be good friends with Max, didn't you?

3 I .... play tennis after school when I was 12.

4 Jack .... love spending time with his cousins.

5 We .... live in the countryside when I was a kid.

6 My friends and I .... hang out together every Saturday while at college.

7 Logan .... have a little dog called Spike.

8 Lily .... get really stressed before her exams.

8 SPEAKING What did/didn't you use to do when you were ten years old? Use these phrases as well as your own ideas to tell your partner.

- play basketball • play video games
- go scuba diving • read comics • chat online
- watch films online • hang out with friends
- share a room with my brother/sister

9 Complete the second sentence so that it has the same meaning as the first sentence, using the word given. Use between two and five words.

1 Tom had a part-time job when he was a teenager. **USED**
Tom .... a part-time job when he was a teenager.

2 Jane started watching TV at 8 pm and finished at 11 pm. **WAS**
Jane .... from 8 pm to 11 pm.

3 My grandma always visited us in the summer. **WOULD**
My grandma .... us in the summer.

4 Did you read a lot as a child? **USE**
Did .... a lot as a child?

5 The ship sank in an hour. **TOOK**
It .... to sink.

10 CHAIN STORY Look at the picture. Continue a story that starts with the sentence below.

It was midnight and Tim was walking back home.

S1: Suddenly he saw a strange man coming towards him.

S2: The man was wearing a black coat.

Skills in Action

Vocabulary

Feelings

1 Check the adjectives below in the Word List. How did each person (1-10) feel?

- relieved • embarrassed • miserable • confused
- nervous • disappointed • bored • annoyed
- amazed • scared

1 Tom's face turned bright red as everyone laughed and pointed at him. *Tom felt embarrassed.*

2 Ann was tired of doing the same things every day.

3 Standing outside the exam hall, Kate realised her hands were shaking.

4 Jake couldn't believe how big the castle was.

5 Liz sat with her head in her hands, close to tears.

6 Sue couldn't understand anything he was saying.

7 Tim couldn't stand her rude behaviour.

8 The hotel looked awful; Kelly hadn't expected that.

9 Bob started screaming when he saw the snake.

10 Steve now knew he had made the right decision.

Study Skills

Descriptive language

You can make a character appear more realistic by describing their feelings. This makes your narration more interesting for the reader.

Listening

2 a) Look at the pictures. Where and when did the story take place? Who was involved in the story? What happened? How did they feel? Think of a sentence for each picture to make a story.

b) Listen to the story and compare it to yours.

Everyday English

Narrating an event – Expressing sympathy

3 Read the dialogue and put the verbs in the correct tense.

Listen and check.

Peter:	Did you hear about Morgan?
Danny:	No. What happened?
Peter:	He 1) .... **(hike)** up a mountain when the weather 2) .... **(change)**. The wind 3) .... **(blow)** and the rain 4) .... **(pour)** down.
Danny:	So what did he do?
Peter:	He 5) .... **(find)** a cave, went in and started a small fire to keep warm. He tried to phone for help but he 6) .... **(can/not)** get any signal.
Danny:	How did he get back?
Peter:	He 7) .... **(stay)** there all night and then made his way back in the morning when the weather was a little better.
Danny:	Oh man, that sounds like a terrible weekend.

4 Use the ideas below to act out a similar dialogue. Use the language in the table.

- holiday abroad • sail in the sea
- fall asleep in the sun • wake up – lost at sea
- drop phone into sea • nearly night/see another boat
- boat/rescue him/her

Narrating	Expressing sympathy
• You won't believe what happened to ...!	• Oh no! • Poor him/her!
	• That's/What a shame/pity.
• He/She was ... when ...	• I'm sorry to hear that.
• Then he/she ...	• That's/How terrible/awful!
• In the end, he/she ...	• That sounds terrible/awful!

Intonation: interjections

5 Listen and match the interjections to how the speaker feels. Listen again and repeat.

1	Eek!	**a**	confused	**b**	scared
2	Ooh!	**a**	interested	**b**	bored
3	Uh-oh!	**a**	worried	**b**	annoyed
4	Aww!	**a**	amazed	**b**	pitying
5	Phew!	**a**	relieved	**b**	disappointed

Reading & Writing

6 Read the story and choose the correct time words. Find all the prepositions of movement.

One cold winter night, Kate and Ann were going home after a relaxing weekend in the countryside. They were driving through a forest **1) when/while** it started to snow.

It wasn't long **2) after/before** the snow was so thick that they couldn't see the road. "Let's wait **3) as/until** the snow stops," said Kate, and pulled over. It was warm in the car and they both quickly fell asleep.

4) A short while later/By that time, Ann woke up. The car was moving from side to side. She looked outside and saw a large bear looking back at her! Terrified, she screamed. Kate woke up and saw the animal. "Uh-oh!" she said. She honked the horn as hard as she could and the bear ran back into the forest.

Kate drove off and they were **5) later/soon** home, relieved to be safe. "I think it just wanted a ride," joked Ann. "Not in my car!" said Kate.

Word formation (-ing/-ed adjectives)
-ing adjectives describe what something is/was like. *It was an amazing experience. (What was the experience like? Amazing.)*
-ed adjectives describe how someone feels/felt. *We were amazed. (How did we feel? Amazed.)*

---

7 Read the theory. Find examples in the story in Ex. 6. Then complete the gaps with adjectives derived from the words in brackets.

1 The view from the top of the mountain was .... **(amaze)**.

2 Gary was .... **(exhaust)** after sightseeing all day.

3 Mia was .... **(worry)** about flying.

4 It was a .... **(terrify)** experience.

✏ Writing Tip

Ending a story
We can end a story with these techniques to make it more interesting to the reader.
• use direct speech *"I'm glad nothing bad happened, but I'll never go back there," said Julie.*
• ask a rhetorical question *Who wouldn't be?*

---

8 How does the writer end the story? Suggest an ending using the other technique.

Writing (a story)

9 Read the rubric. Look at the pictures and brainstorm for ideas with your classmates.

You have decided to write a story for an international magazine short story competition. Your story must begin with this sentence: *Mark and Paul were walking along the beach carrying their surfboards.* Write your story (120-150 words).

Mark   Paul

Mark

10 a) 🎧 Listen and keep notes.

b) Use your notes in Ex. 10a to write your story. Follow the plan. Give your story a title.

Plan

Para 1: set the scene *(who, when, where, what)*
Para 2: events leading to the main event
Para 3: the main event *(climax)*
Para 4: feelings; ending

VALUES

Imagination
The world of reality has its limits; the world of imagination is boundless.
Jean-Jacques Rousseau

A Great Detective

Agatha Christie (1890-1976) is known **1)** .... the Queen of Crime Fiction for her 66 novels and 14 short story collections. One of her most **popular** characters is Hercule Poirot, a short Belgian detective famous for his intelligence and moustache, **2)** .... he describes as "a thing of beauty". He always dresses in the **finest** clothes and is very careful about the food he eats. Working with Captain Hastings, Poirot **3)** .... the mysteries that confuse the police, using only his "little grey cells" – his brain. He first appears in *The Mysterious Affair at Styles*, published in 1920. Mrs Inglethorp, a very rich woman, dies in strange circumstances and Hastings **rushes** to get the great detective.

A few minutes later, I was knocking at the door of Leastways Cottage. A window opened above me and Poirot looked out. I explained the tragedy and asked for his help.

He looked surprised. "Wait my friend. You can tell me everything while I get dressed."

He soon **unlocked** the door and I told him the **4)** .... story. I hoped I wasn't leaving out any important details.

"Take your time, my friend," Poirot said, "When we are calmer, we can arrange the facts, carefully, each in its **proper** place. The important ones, we put to one side; the unimportant ones, we **ignore**."

"But how do you decide what is important and what isn't?" I asked.

He was carefully putting on his jacket. "One fact in the mystery leads to another. Does the next fact fit? No! There is something missing – a link in the chain that is not there. We examine, we search and we find that missing fact. And it is a mystery no **5)** ....!" He was ready. "Now, Hastings, let's start!"

(Adapted from *The Mysterious Affair at Styles*)

✓ **Check these words**

collection, detective, intelligence, moustache, circumstances, tragedy, a link in the chain

Reading & Listening

1 Look at the picture. Who is this character? Who created him? Who does he work with? Read to find out.

2 **a)** Read the texts again and choose the correct word for each gap (1-5).

1	**A** like	**B** for	**C** as	**D** about
2	**A** which	**B** what	**C** where	**D** why
3	**A** answers	**B** replies	**C** gets	**D** solves
4	**A** all	**B** whole	**C** every	**D** lot
5	**A** else	**B** little	**C** more	**D** much

b) 🎧 Listen to check.

3 Match the words in bold in the text with their synonyms.

• correct • not pay attention to • well-liked
• opened • moves quickly • most stylish

Speaking & Writing

4 THINK What do you think makes Poirot a popular character?

5 ICT Collect information about a book character from your country or another country. Make notes under the headings: *who he/she is – where he/she appears – why he/she is a great character*. Present the character to the class.

Vocabulary

1 Choose the correct word.

1 My favourite kind of **fiction/non-fiction** books are biographies.

2 Tony loves action and **adventure/mystery** books.

3 The book became a **bestseller/thriller**.

4 We **watched/saw** Lucy outside the cinema.

5 Shane really enjoyed that **amusing/dull** story.

(5 x 3 = 15)

2 Fill in: *annoyed, relieved, solved, took, confusing, disappointed, stayed, embarrassed.*

1 We .... alive by making a fire.

2 I .... a chance and bought you a book – I hope you like it!

3 The detective quickly .... the crime.

4 The story was too .... for me to follow.

5 Jill was .... with the travel book because it didn't have much information.

6 Jenna felt .... when she spilled coffee on Tony's shirt.

7 Back home, we felt .... we were safe.

8 I was really .... about the way he behaved towards us.

(8 x 2 = 16)

3 Choose the correct item.

1 When do schools break **out/up** for summer?

2 I read a novel **from/by** Stephen King last week.

3 The car broke **out/down** half an hour into the journey.

4 It's a story **around/about** two brothers.

5 This book has a 13-year-old boy **at/as** its main character.

(5 x 2 = 10)

Grammar

4 Put the verbs in brackets into the past simple or the past continuous.

1 Jo was packing while Tom .... **(book)** a taxi.

2 What .... **(you/do)** at 8 o'clock last night?

3 He was asleep so he .... **(not/hear)** anything.

4 The sun .... **(shine)** as we sailed out of the harbour.

5 Paul .... **(close)** the door and left.

6 We .... **(walk)** to the beach when it suddenly started to rain.

(6 x 4 = 24)

5 Fill in: *used to* **or** *used to/would.*

1 My family .... live by the sea when I was a kid.

2 As a child, Luke .... visit his aunt every summer.

3 Kate .... have a huge dog called Charlie.

4 I .... like horror stories, but I don't read them anymore.

5 Carl .... sleep in late on Saturdays, but he's got a part-time job now.

(5 x 3 = 15)

Everyday English

6 Match the sentences.

1 ☐ What did he do?

2 ☐ How was Jenny's holiday?

3 ☐ It was a robbery!

4 ☐ Did he get the money in the end?

5 ☐ How did he feel about that?

a No, he left it all behind.

b Very disappointed.

c He called the police.

d You won't believe what happened to her!

e How awful!

(5 x 4 = 20)

Total 100

3

Vocabulary: travel/means of transport, parts of an airport
Grammar: present perfect – present perfect continuous; past perfect – past perfect continuous; *The*/ –

Everyday English: reporting lost luggage
Writing: an article describing a journey

All around the world

▶ VIDEO

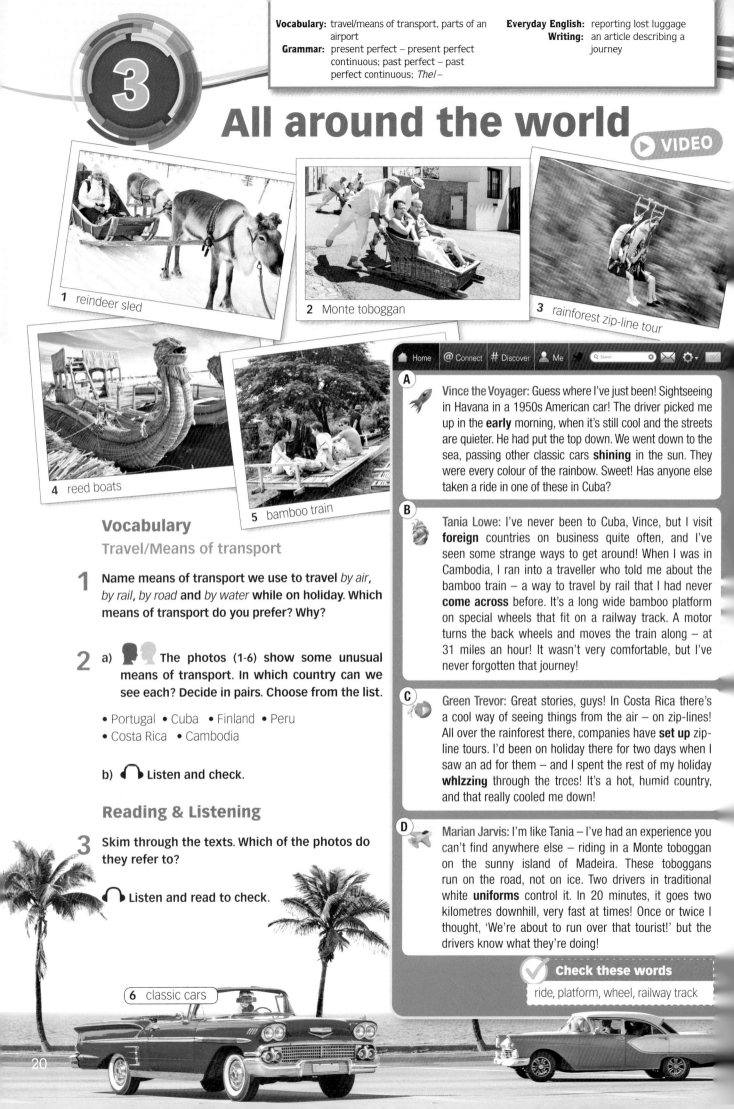

1 reindeer sled

2 Monte toboggan

3 rainforest zip-line tour

4 reed boats

5 bamboo train

6 classic cars

Vocabulary

Travel/Means of transport

1 Name means of transport we use to travel *by air*, *by rail*, *by road* and *by water* while on holiday. Which means of transport do you prefer? Why?

2 a) The photos (1-6) show some unusual means of transport. In which country can we see each? Decide in pairs. Choose from the list.

• Portugal • Cuba • Finland • Peru
• Costa Rica • Cambodia

b) Listen and check.

Reading & Listening

3 Skim through the texts. Which of the photos do they refer to?

Listen and read to check.

🏠 Home   @ Connect   # Discover   👤 Me   🔍 Search   ✉   ⚙

A

Vince the Voyager: Guess where I've just been! Sightseeing in Havana in a 1950s American car! The driver picked me up in the **early** morning, when it's still cool and the streets are quieter. He had put the top down. We went down to the sea, passing other classic cars **shining** in the sun. They were every colour of the rainbow. Sweet! Has anyone else taken a ride in one of these in Cuba?

B

Tania Lowe: I've never been to Cuba, Vince, but I visit **foreign** countries on business quite often, and I've seen some strange ways to get around! When I was in Cambodia, I ran into a traveller who told me about the bamboo train – a way to travel by rail that I had never **come across** before. It's a long wide bamboo platform on special wheels that fit on a railway track. A motor turns the back wheels and moves the train along – at 31 miles an hour! It wasn't very comfortable, but I've never forgotten that journey!

C

Green Trevor: Great stories, guys! In Costa Rica there's a cool way of seeing things from the air – on zip-lines! All over the rainforest there, companies have **set up** zip-line tours. I'd been on holiday there for two days when I saw an ad for them – and I spent the rest of my holiday **whizzing** through the trees! It's a hot, humid country, and that really cooled me down!

D

Marian Jarvis: I'm like Tania – I've had an experience you can't find anywhere else – riding in a Monte toboggan on the sunny island of Madeira. These toboggans run on the road, not on ice. Two drivers in traditional white **uniforms** control it. In 20 minutes, it goes two kilometres downhill, very fast at times! Once or twice I thought, 'We're about to run over that tourist!' but the drivers know what they're doing!

✓ **Check these words**

ride, platform, wheel, railway track

4 **Read again and decide if the statements are *T* (True), *F* (False) or *DS* (Doesn't Say). Then explain the words in bold.**

1 Vince the Voyager used an old means of transport. ....

2 Vince the Voyager can't drive. ....

3 It was Tania Lowe's first visit to Cambodia. ....

4 Tania Lowe loved everything about the bamboo train. ....

5 Green Trevor went zip-lining in Costa Rica more than once. ....

6 Marian Jarvis was worried about hurting herself. ....

5 **Read the paragraph below and replace the words in bold with their opposites from the list.**

• hot • comfortable • cheap • fast • huge • long • modern • wide • amazing

*It was a very **1) short** train and extremely **2) old-fashioned**. When we got on, we saw that it was **3) narrow** inside, too, and the seats were really **4) uncomfortable**. Once we left the **5) little** station, we realised it was a very **6) slow** train! And on top of all that, the weather was **7) cold** and the scenery was **8) boring**. We couldn't believe the tickets were so **9) expensive**!*

6 **COLLOCATIONS** **Choose the correct verb, then make sentences using the collocations.**

1 go/have

a .... on holiday   b .... a holiday

2 go/take

a .... a trip   b .... on a trip

3 go/do

a .... shopping   b .... some shopping

4 go/do

a .... some sightseeing   b .... sightseeing

5 go/make

a .... a journey   b .... on a journey

6 go/take

a .... a ride   b .... for a ride

7 **PREPOSITIONS** **Choose the correct preposition.**

1 We can go to the airport **in/on** my car.

2 His car got a flat tyre in the forest, so he continued **in/on** foot.

3 There's no road – the only way up the mountain is **by/in** cable car.

4 You can get to the city **by/on** rail, but the trains are a bit slow.

5 A jet plane travels **in/at** around 925 kilometres an hour.

6 Ladies and gentlemen, we'll be landing in Rio de Janeiro **in/at** 15 minutes.

8 **WORDS EASILY CONFUSED** **Fill in:** *travel, journey, trip.*

1 Susan's job involves a lot of ....

2 Let's take a .... to the sea this weekend – the weather's so lovely!

3 The .... by car takes five hours; it's exhausting!

9 **PHRASAL VERBS** **Fill in the correct particle(s). Then, try to make up a story using the phrasal verbs.**

run into: to meet sb by chance
run after: to chase sb/sth
run out of: to have no more of sth
run over: to hit sb/sth with a car, etc

1 A bus almost ran .... my dog!

2 The ball rolled down the hill and the children ran .... it.

3 While we were on the way to Paris, the motorbike ran .... petrol.

4 Guess what! I ran .... Bill Garrett, our old car mechanic, yesterday.

Speaking & Writing

10 **THINK** **Imagine you have just got back from one of the places in the photos on p. 20 that is not mentioned in the text. Tell your partner about it.**

11 **Write a comment on Vince the Voyager's blog. Use the other comments as guides.**

Grammar in Use

 KauaiTravel ⊘ @Kauaitravel   8 days ago

Have you ever visited Kauai in Hawaii? Here at KauaiTravel, we've been showing people around this fairytale land for over ten years. We even won an award last year for the most exciting tour from Adventure Tours Magazine. Check out our website for details! #visitkauai

 KauaiTravel ⊘ @Kauaitravel   6 days ago

We've had lots of calls from customers who've booked holidays on Kauai, and those who've already flown there. Please stay calm. The storm that's been travelling towards the island is weakening. They'd been calling it a hurricane up until yesterday, but now it's a tropical storm. #kauaistorm

 KauaiTravel ⊘ @Kauaitravel   3 days ago

The storm's left its mark, no doubt. But by Sunday, it had passed and Kauai has already started to recover. After all, storms have been happening here since records began! We're tired because we've been cleaning up all day, but now we're ready to move forward! #kauaistorm

Present perfect – Present perfect continuous ▶ pp. GR4-5

1 Read the tweets. Identify the past simple, present perfect and present perfect continuous forms. How do we form the perfect tenses? Which tense do we use:

- for actions that happened at an unstated time in the past?
- for actions that started in the past and continue up to the present?
- to talk about a past action that has a visible result in the present?
- to put emphasis on the duration of an action that started in the past and continues up to the present?
- for actions that happened in the past at a specific time?
- for actions that started in the past and lasted for some time and whose results are visible in the present?

2 Choose the correct item. Give reasons.

1 Henry **has flown/has been flying** in a plane twice **yet/before**.

2 Has this pilot **ever/just landed/been landing** a plane during a snowstorm?

3 I haven't **received/been receiving** my new passport **since/yet**.

4 Has the temperature **risen/been rising for/since** last Tuesday?

5 We have **waited/been waiting** for our coach to arrive **for/since** three hours!

6 How many places have you **visited/been visiting recently/so far**?

7 It's so cold this year that the lake has **already/yet frozen/been freezing**.

8 Joan's tired because she's **travelled/been travelling for/since** 6 am.

9 The Smiths called – they've **just/never arrived/been arriving** from El Salvador.

10 I have **read/been reading** this book **since/for** last week.

3 Fill in *been* or *gone*.

1 Have you ever .... abroad?

2 Tom's not here – he's .... to Dubai on holiday.

3 My mum's never .... on a plane.

4 Liam isn't here. Has he .... to the beach?

5 I've .... to Spain at least ten times.

4 SPEAKING 🗣🗣 Read the dialogue. Then, act out similar dialogues using the notes. Think of three more situations to act out.

> **A:** Have you ever been on a plane?
>
> **B:** Yes, many times.
>
> **A:** When was the first time?
>
> **B:** Three years ago.
>
> **A:** What was it like?
>
> **B:** It was a bit scary.

1 be/in a helicopter – two weeks ago/exciting

2 go out/thunderstorm – last autumn/thrilling

3 drive/a car – a month ago/difficult

Past perfect – Past perfect continuous ▶ pp. GR5-6

Past perfect (*had* + past participle)
Affirmative I/You/He, etc **had come**.
Negative I/You/He, etc **hadn't come**.
Interrogative Had I/you/he, etc **come**?
Short answers Yes, I/you, etc **had**. No, I/you, etc **hadn't**.

We use the **past perfect** for:
• an action that **finished before** another **past action** or **before a stated time in the past**. *Sam had gone to the market before Kate arrived.*
• an action that **finished in the past** and whose **result was visible at a later point in the past**. *He had lost his passport, so he couldn't travel abroad.*

Time expressions: *before, already, after, for, since, just, till/until, by, by the time, never*, etc

Past perfect continuous (*had been* + verb *-ing*)
Affirmative I/You/He, etc **had been working**.
Negative I/You/He, etc **hadn't been working**.
Interrogative Had I/you/he, etc **been working**?
Short answers Yes, I/you, etc **had**. No, I/you, etc **hadn't**.

We use the **past perfect continuous**:
• to put emphasis on the **duration** of an action that happened **before** another past action or stated time in the past. *We had been waiting for an hour before the plane landed.*
• for an action that **lasted for some time** in the past and whose **result was visible** in the past. *He was tired because he had been working since 9 am.*

Time expressions: *for, since, how long, before, until, by, by the time*, etc

5 Read the theory. How do we form: the past perfect? the past perfect continuous? Find examples in the tweets on p. 22.

6 Put the verbs in brackets into the correct tense. Give reasons.

1 My aunt only let me use her camera after she .... **(show)** me how.
2 When we got to the station, the train .... **(not/leave)** yet.
3 Sue .... **(travel)** for three days before she reached her destination.
4 Mark was tired because he .... **(walk)** for an hour.
5 How long .... **(you/save up)** before you could buy your car?
6 He didn't come with us to France because he .... **(break)** his leg.

7 SPEAKING Act out exchanges, as in the example.

1 John/tired? study since morning
   A: Why was John tired?
   B: He had been studying since 10 am.
2 Mary/upset? miss her flight
3 you/on foot? my car/break down
4 Kelly's/legs sore? cycle/all day
5 John's parents/late? the snow/delay them

8 Complete the second sentence using the word in bold. Use two to five words.

1 The last time we went fishing was last summer.
   have We .... last summer.
2 She has never eaten Vietnamese food before.
   time It's the .... Vietnamese food.
3 When did he go to Naples?
   since How long has .... to Naples?
4 It was a long time since we last ate out.
   eaten We .... a long time.
5 It hadn't stopped raining for days.
   been It .... for days.

The/– ▶ p. GR6

9 Fill in *the* where necessary. Then do the quiz.
   ICT Check your answers online.

How's your general knowledge?

1 Which of .... London's main airports is bigger, ... Heathrow or .... Gatwick?
2 Is Times Square in .... USA named after .... *New York Times* newspaper?
3 Which is a bridge over .... River Thames, ... Tower Bridge or .... Brooklyn Bridge?
4 Which mountain range does .... longest train tunnel in .... world go under, ... Alps or .... Andes?
5 How long would it take to travel to .... Moon by .... car, six days or six months?
6 Are .... Canary Islands in .... Pacific Ocean?
7 Which month was .... last month of .... First World War, ... July or .... November?

23

Skills in Action

Vocabulary

Parts of an airport

1 a) **Match the signs to what passengers do there.**

a Departures ✈
b Arrivals ✈
c Check-in 🧍
d Passport Control
e Information ❓
f Baggage Reclaim 🧳
g Duty-free 🛍
h Customs

1 ☐ Passengers can buy things here.
2 ☐ Passengers ask questions here.
3 ☐ Passengers flying out from the airport go here.
4 ☐ Passengers landing at the airport come out here.
5 ☐ Passengers check in their bags here.
6 ☐ They search passengers' suitcases here.
7 ☐ Passengers get their bags here after the flight.
8 ☐ They check passengers' passports here.

b) 👤👤 **Say a sentence. Your partner guesses where you are. Use:** *suitcase*, *perfume*, *land*, *fly out*, *flight*, *boarding pass*.

A: How many suitcases can I check in?
B: You're at the check-in desk.

Listening

> **Study Skills**
>
> **Predicting missing words**
> Read the notes. Think about what type of information is missing, e.g. a name, a date, etc. This will help in the task.

2 🎧 **You will hear a conversation at a check-in desk. Complete the passenger's boarding pass.**

✈ *Air Gold* BOARDING PASS

| Name of passenger: | Carrier: | Flight No: | Class: |
| Kylie Banks | Air Gold | **1)**......... | B |

| From: London LGW | Date: | Luggage: | Seat: |
| To: **2)**..........JFK | 23/12/2018 | Y | **3)**......... |

| GATE | BOARDING TIME | |
| **4)**......... | **5)**......... | FZ 34 45 99 |

Everyday English

Reporting lost luggage

3 a) **The woman from Ex. 2 is reporting missing luggage. Complete the dialogue with questions a-f.**

a And what was in it?
b Could I have a contact number?
c And where are you staying?
d Can you give me your baggage receipt number?
e Can you describe your luggage?
f May I have your name and flight number, please?

> **A:** Excuse me. My suitcase never came out at baggage reclaim!
> **B:** **1)** ....
> **A:** Kylie Banks. Flight AG533 from New York.
> **B:** **2)** .... That's on your boarding pass.
> **A:** Erm ... Ah, here it is. FZ 34 45 99.
> **B:** Thank you. **3)** ....
> **A:** It's a large, green, leather suitcase with brown straps.
> **B:** **4)** ....
> **A:** Just clothes, really.
> **B:** **5)** ....
> **A:** At 86, Newton Grove, London W4 1LB.
> **B:** **6)** ....
> **A:** It's 07335 939411.
> **B:** Alright, Ms Banks, your luggage was put on a later flight. We will deliver it to you before 8 pm tonight.

b) 🎧 **Listen and check.**

4 👤👤 **Act out a similar dialogue using the notes.**

Sam Cook
EX147 (Glasgow-London) – ML 45 87 66 – 2 small blue suitcases – clothes and papers – 89, Wood Lane, London E12 6PQ – 733 456 1290

Pronunciation: silent letters

5 🎧 **Listen and underline the silent letter(s). Listen again and repeat.**

1 interesting
2 autumn
3 safety
4 whole
5 foreign
6 Wednesday

Reading & Writing

6 Read the task and complete the sentences.

You see this notice in an international travel magazine.
Send us articles with this title:
A JOURNEY I'VE NEVER FORGOTTEN
The most interesting article goes in next month's issue!
Write your article in 120-150 words.

1 I should write a(n) .... for................... .
2 I must write about .... in .... words.

Word formation (forming adjectives)
We can form adjectives from nouns by adding: *-ly* *(friend – friendly)*, *-ic* *(romance – romantic)* or *-y* *(rain – rainy)*

7 Read the article and fill in the gaps with the adjectives derived from the words in brackets.

A journey I've never forgotten

I've been coming to Scotland for years, and I thought I'd seen everything it has to offer – until I rode the West Highland Line to Mallaig. This train journey has the most **1)** .... **(fantasy)** views I've ever seen.

The train left Glasgow and soon we were passing through a beautiful green landscape with clear blue lakes. Just after Ben Nevis, the UK's highest mountain, was the **2)** .... **(attract)** town of Fort William. Finally, we reached Mallaig, a port with **3)** .... **(taste)** seafood and **4)** .... **(friend)** locals.

My favourite part was the Glenfinnan Viaduct, a 380-metre-long railway bridge across the River Finnan. Thirty metres high, it offers such **5)** .... **(amaze)** views that it has appeared in many films, including four Harry Potter films!

The West Highland line shows passengers a part of Scotland that is not **6)** .... **(access)** by road. No visit to Scotland is complete without taking this **7)** .... **(wonder)** trip.

Using the senses
When you describe a place, give examples of what you see, hear and smell. This brings the description to life.

8 Read the phrases. What does each describe? Use them to complete the descriptions.

- sweet smell • sea birds' cries • only sound
- clear blue sea • perfume of • tall green trees

A
I sat on deck looking at the
1) ...., drinking my coffee, and listening to **2)** ....
As we approached the island, the
3) .... of the pine forest reached me.

B
Our horse ride through the forest was peaceful. There were
4) .... all around us. The **5)** ....
was birds singing in the trees. The
6) .... spring flowers filled the air.

Writing (an article describing a journey)

9 **BRAINSTORMING** Think of the best journey you have ever taken. Make notes under the headings.

recommendation ← **best journey** → place, means of transport

favourite part

description of journey

10 Use your notes in Ex. 9 to write your article for Ex. 6. Follow the plan.

Plan
Para 1: place, means of transport
Para 2: description of journey
Para 3: favourite part
Para 4: recommendation

VALUES

Experience
Don't listen to what they say. Go see.
saying

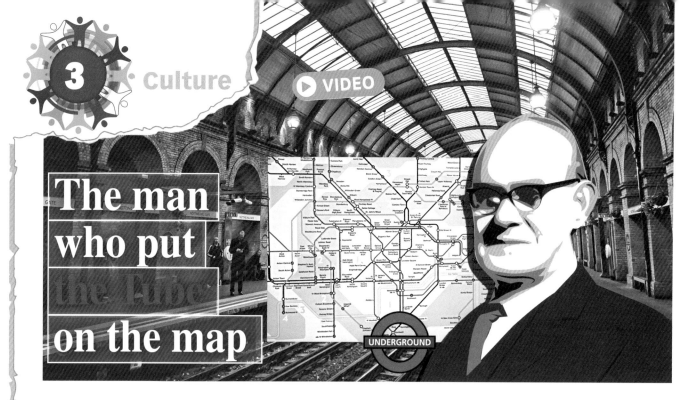

The man who put the Tube on the map

The London Underground – or the Tube, as people have called it for years – is the oldest underground railway in the world. In fact, it has been running since 1863, when its first **line** opened between Paddington and Farringdon. Since then, it has grown to 11 lines with 270 stations, carrying nearly five million passengers a day.

One of the reasons why it works so well is the London Underground map. The first maps of the railway looked like any other map, but by 1931 an employee called Harry Beck had realised that these traditional maps were becoming too **confusing** as the underground grew. Harry also understood that passengers didn't care what point on the streets they were below. They just wanted to understand, quickly and easily, how to get from one station to another.

Harry designed a map of mostly straight lines in simple **bold** colours. The distance between stations was the same, even if it wasn't in real life. Interchange stations (where you could change trains) were at first a diamond, then later a circle. The River Thames was the only geographical feature on the map, but it followed straight lines too, and not **curves**. Harry's employers weren't too sure about his map when they saw it, but passengers loved it.

One **amusing** result of the map's design is the mistakes people make with distances. For example, it is common for passengers to get a train from Chancery Lane to Farringdon, changing twice, when you could walk there in ten minutes! To travel from Mansion House to Bank means **changing** once and going six stops – but you can get there in six minutes on foot!

Generally, however, the map has been helping visitors find their way round London for nearly a century. Along with the red London bus, the black London taxi and the red telephone box, the London Underground map has become a **symbol** of the city. Although Harry Beck didn't get much money for all his work, you can find his name at the bottom of every London Underground map to this day.

✓ **Check these words**

underground railway, straight, diamond, at the bottom of

Listening & Reading

1 Read the text quickly and find the names of five stations.

2 🎧 Listen to and read the text. Complete the sentences. Then explain the words in bold.

1 The London Underground started working in ....

2 The design for the modern London Underground map came from ....

3 He first used a(n) .... to show stations where you could change trains.

4 Mansion House is surprisingly close to .... Station.

5 Other symbols of London are the red bus and the .... taxi.

Speaking & Writing

3 👤👤 THINK Discuss with your partner what design or symbol reminds people of your country/ capital city.

4 ICT Research the design or symbol you decided on in Ex. 3 and make notes under the headings: *who designed it – where you can see it – why it reminds people of your country/ capital city*. **Write a text about it and read it to the class.**

Vocabulary

1 **Fill in:** *uniforms, classic, motor, reed, sled, toboggan, zip-line.*

1 We drove in a(n) .... American car.
2 People on Lake Titicaca use .... boats.
3 The bus needs a powerful .... to move it along.
4 A(n) .... usually goes downhill on snow.
5 The gondoliers wore blue and white ....
6 One way to travel long distances across the snow is by reindeer ....
7 I whizzed above the trees on the ....

(7 x 2 = 14)

2 **Fill in:** *duty, information, baggage, passport, customs.*

1 Wait at .... reclaim for our suitcases.
2 There were lots of people at .... control.
3 A man searched my bag at ....
4 I bought some perfume in the .... -free.
5 John asked about hotels at the .... desk.

(5 x 3 = 15)

3 **Choose the correct item.**

1 Let's go **for/to** a walk in the forest.
2 A car ran **after/over** my cat, but she's OK.
3 Why don't you try going to work **by/on** foot?
4 Let's drive there **in/by** my car.
5 We've run **into/out of** time – back to the coach!
6 Where are you going **on/for** holiday this year?

(6 x 2 = 12)

Grammar

4 **Write** *the* **or** *–*.

1 .... River Nile
2 .... London
3 in .... morning
4 .... Mount Everest
5 .... Hyde Park
6 by .... plane
7 .... UK
8 .... Sahara Desert

(8 x 2 = 16)

5 **Put the verbs in brackets into the present perfect simple or continuous.**

1 It .... **(rain)** all day!
2 .... **(Jim/ever/stay)** in a hotel?
3 I .... **(drive)** for three hours.
4 Jo .... **(be)** in Cuba for a week.
5 Sorry I'm late! .... **(you/wait)** long?
6 Kim .... **(not/visit)** Peru yet.

(6 x 3 = 18)

6 **Choose the correct item.**

1 I had just **left/been leaving** the house when it started to snow.
2 **Had you ever ridden/Did you ever ride** on a motorbike before you came to the USA?
3 It hadn't **rained/been raining** long before I got home.
4 Sally hadn't tasted snails before she **came/had come** to Paris.
5 Gary was red in the face because he had **cycled/been cycling** for an hour.

(5 x 2 = 10)

Everyday English

7 **Match the exchanges.**

1 ☐ What's your flight number?
2 ☐ Can you describe your luggage?
3 ☐ What was in it?
4 ☐ Where are you staying?
5 ☐ Could I have a contact number?

a It's a brown suitcase.
b 892 473 8383.
c 86, Pine Road, York.
d YT355.
e Just clothes.

(5 x 3 = 15)

Total 100

Competences

GOOD ✓
VERY GOOD ✓✓
EXCELLENT ✓✓✓

Lexical Competence
understand words/phrases related to:
• travel
• means of transport
• parts of an airport

Reading Competence
• understand texts related to transport (read for specific information – T/F/DS statements; sentence completion)

Listening Competence
• listen to & understand texts related to transport (listen for specific information – gap-fill)

Speaking Competence
• report lost luggage

Writing Competence
• write a comment on a blog
• write an article describing a journey

Values: Philanthropy

 **VIDEO**

Encyclopedia

http://www.encyclopedia

Biographies.com 🔍 Andrew Carnegie

STUDENTS | EDUCATORS | HELP

Andrew Carnegie
The Father of Modern Philanthropy

Article   Related   Teacher

Andrew Carnegie (1835-1919) was born in Dunfermline, Scotland, into a poor family. They moved to Pennsylvania, USA, in 1848. His first job, aged 13, was in a factory on $1.20 a week, but by the 1860s he was a millionaire, mainly from **investing** money in railways. After 1865, he moved into steel and, in 1892, he created the Carnegie Steel Company, the biggest producer of steel in the world. He sold it in 1901 for $225.64 million, making him the richest man in the world, but he then started giving his **fortune** away. By his death, he had given $350 million, about 90% of his fortune, to different public projects.

Early life ▼

Business ▼

Charity ▲

Carnegie had a rule: spend the first third of your life educating yourself, the second third making all the money you can, and the last third giving the money away to worthwhile causes. He believed that rich people had a responsibility to give back to society. He created museums and concert halls, put money into universities and scientific **projects** like the Hooker telescope, and set up charities all over the world.

Carnegie's real passion, however, was public libraries. He only went to school for a few years in Scotland, but in Pennsylvania, a local man called Colonel James Anderson **announced** that he was opening his 400-book personal library to working boys. Carnegie was able to go there every Saturday and **borrow** a book. He never forgot the chance he got to educate himself, and promised to do the same when he was rich.

By the time of his death, Carnegie had built over 2,500 public libraries in 47 states of the USA, as well as in the UK, Canada, Ireland and many other countries. He also provided books and equipment to many more. The very first public library he created was in Dunfermline, Scotland, the town of his birth.

1 What is the purpose of the text: *to inform*? *to entertain*? *to persuade*? **Read through quickly to check.**

2 🎧 **Listen to and read the text. Write five questions based on the text. Exchange with your partner. Answer the questions. Then, explain the words in bold.**

3 👥 THINK **If you were very rich like Andrew Carnegie, which charities/organisations would you donate to? Why?**

4 ICT 💬 **Collect information about other people who have donated their fortunes to charities. Present them to the class.**

Public Speaking Skills

1 Read the task. What is the purpose of the presentation? What is the situation? Who are you? What will you be talking about?

You are a tour guide. Present a statue and explain its significance to some tourists.

Study Skills

Making descriptions interesting

You can make information more interesting if you use a story. This captures the audience's attention and makes them want to learn more.

2 🎧 Listen to and read the model. What story has Ricky included? How does this make his presentation sound?

Welcome to Kensington Gardens, where we begin our tour today. My name is Ricky Martinez, and I'm going to be your tour guide.

"So come with me where dreams are born and time is never planned." I'm all grown up now, but I've never forgotten the words of my favourite character as a child, Peter Pan. And in Kensington Gardens I never have to, because the character's most famous statue is here! The creator of Peter Pan, J. M. Barrie, paid for the statue himself in 1912. They put it here in the middle of the night, so families taking a walk in the morning would discover it! He didn't even ask for permission, but everyone liked it so much that they let it stay. But why did Barrie choose Kensington Gardens? Well, it was where he met Peter Pan!

One day in 1897, he was walking his dog Porthos there when he met two boys, George and Jack Davies, with their nurse. He made friends with them, their three other brothers, Peter, Michael and Nicholas, and their parents, and became like an uncle to the boys. He often brought them to Kensington Gardens on fine days, and loved playing games, telling them stories and making them laugh. Michael was his favourite, because of his cheeky character, and though Peter gave Peter Pan his name, the character of Peter Pan was all from Michael.

And I think the statue really helps us understand the character of Peter Pan. He's wearing a nightshirt, a long shirt that children used to wear to sleep. His face shows his happy, brave, independent spirit. He is playing on his pipes, standing confidently on the trunk of a tree. And all the way up the tree trunk are little rabbits, a squirrel, a bird, mice and, of course, lots of fairies. They all seem to be listening to the music coming from the pipes, don't you agree?

I'm going to let you have a closer look at the statue now, but if you have any questions about it, please ask me.

ICT Collect information about a statue of a fictional or mythical character in your country or another country. Make notes under the headings: *name of the character – where the statue is – why it is there – description of the statue – who made it – how well it shows the story*. Use your notes to present the statue to a group of tourists. Include a story.

Vocabulary: stressful events; fears & physical reactions
Grammar: future tenses, *will – be going to –* present simple/continuous (future meaning); conditionals type 1; time clauses
Everyday English: asking for/giving advice
Writing: an email giving advice

Hard Times

 VIDEO

Vocabulary
Stressful events

1 Look at the pictures (1-8). Which three of these events do you think are the most stressful? Why?

1 becoming unemployed

2 divorce/separation

3 serious injury/illness

4 moving house

5 starting a new job

6 taking exams

7 having financial problems

8 someone stealing your personal information

Maggie Palmer

Advice Column

No_Luck_Lucy asks:
A few months ago, I lost my job as a tour guide in a museum. The museum wasn't **attracting** enough visitors, so the manager decided to **let me go**. Since then,

I've applied for lots of jobs, but I haven't heard back from anyone. I feel **miserable** waiting by the phone every day, and I'm anxious about the bills which are piling up, too. What can I do?

Hands_Full asks: Last week, I returned to work after having my first child. He's six months old and it's very difficult for my husband and me to leave him in day care every morning. When I'm at work, I can't help feeling that I should be

taking care of my son. But I don't want to **quit** my job. I'm really **proud** of my career, and I've worked too hard to throw it all away. Could you please help me?

✓ **Check these words**

anxious, bill, pile up, day care, retire, cause, afford, promotion, volunteer, CV, professional networking site

Reading & Listening

2 **a)** Match the people in the pictures (1-3) to the problems (a-c).

a How to keep busy after retirement.

b How to combine work and family life.

c How to find employment.

b) 🎧 Listen to and read texts 1-3 to see if your guesses were correct.

Brian_65 asks:

In two months, I'll be 65. For most people, that's a reason to celebrate, but I don't feel very excited about retiring, to be honest. For the last 40 years of my life, I've worked full-time in the same clothes shop, so it's going to be very strange to suddenly have so much free time. I'm an **active** person and it will be impossible for me to just stay at home and relax doing nothing. Also, I'm not interested in golf, or walking in the park. I much prefer doing something **useful**. Any ideas?

This is a common cause of stress for parents – and I'm afraid there's no easy answer. If you can afford to live on less money, you could ask your boss to work part-time so that you could see your son more often – but this might mean **missing** the chance of a promotion. You ought to talk with your partner and make the best decision for you and your family.

You've worked hard all your life, so it's a pity you aren't looking forward to a nice rest! You should realise that there are plenty of ways to keep busy and useful after you retire. Why not volunteer for a charity? How about helping organise **fundraising events**? Or, with your experience, you could work part-time in a charity shop. Hope my advice helps!

Being out of work can be a stressful and scary experience – but you've got to have a **positive attitude**. These days, the best place to look for jobs is online. You can even post your CV on a professional networking site and then employers might get in contact with you. So, don't **give up**. I'm sure you'll find something soon!

3 (THINK) 🎧 **Listen to and read Maggie's advice. Match the people (1-3) with the advice (A-C). Do you agree with Maggie? Discuss with your partner. Then, explain the words in bold.**

4 COLLOCATIONS **Fill in:** *easy, fundraising, positive, day, free, tour.* **Use the phrases in sentences of your own.**

1 .... guide
2 .... care
3 .... time
4 .... attitude
5 .... answer
6 .... events

5 PREPOSITIONS **Fill in:** *about (x2), out of, from, for, at, of (x2), in (x2).* **Then make sentences using the completed phrases.**

1 to apply .... job
2 to hear back .... sb
3 to be anxious .... sth
4 to take care .... sb
5 to be proud .... sth
6 to stay .... home
7 to be interested .... sth
8 to be .... work
9 to get .... contact with sb
10 to be excited .... sth

6 WORDS EASILY CONFUSED **Choose the correct word. Check in your dictionary.**

1 There must be a good **reason/cause** why Bill moved house.
2 We still don't know the **reason/cause** of the accident.
3 If you **believe/think** in yourself you can do anything!
4 What did you **believe/think** of the bank manager's advice?

7 PHRASAL VERBS **Fill in the correct particle.**

> **take after:** to have the same appearance or character as sb
> **take off: 1)** to remove clothes (opp: put on); **2)** (of planes) to leave the ground
> **take over:** to gain control of sth
> **take up: 1)** to begin a hobby, sport, etc; **2)** to fill (time, space)

1 Kate's very anxious about taking .... her family's shop.
2 Phil takes .... his mum – they both get stressed easily.
3 Driving to and from work takes .... two hours of Andy's day.
4 We'd better hurry – the plane takes .... in 15 minutes!
5 You can take .... jogging to relieve stress.
6 You should take .... your hat when you're indoors.

Speaking & Writing

8 **Imagine you have one of the problems in Ex. 1. Write a short email to Maggie.**

9 (THINK) **Swap papers with your partner. Advise him/her what to do.**

31

Grammar in Use

C: Hi, Ollie. Do you have any plans for the weekend?

O: Not really. **I'm going to study** for our business exam on Monday. I think **it'll be** really difficult.

C: I'm stressed about it, too. Actually, **I'm meeting** Brian and Suzie in the library at five today for a group study session. Do you want to come along?

O: OK, but the library **closes** at six today, doesn't it? That doesn't leave us much time. Why don't we meet earlier?

C: Oh, yes. I forgot. OK, **I'll text** Brian and Suzie and ask them to meet at four instead.

O: Great. Then, when we finish, maybe we can go for a walk in the park.

C: No, look at those dark clouds in the sky – **it's going to rain**. Let's get a pizza and hang out at your place instead!

O: Good idea! After we leave the library, I'm sure **I'll be** hungry!

C: Well, see you at the library at four, then. If there's a change of plan, I'll text you.

O: OK, bye, Colin.

Future tenses ▶ pp. GR6-7

1 Read the dialogue. Identify the tenses in bold. Which tense do we use for:

• on-the-spot decisions • fixed arrangements in the future • future plans & intentions • timetables/ programmes • predictions based on what we think or imagine • predictions based on what we can see or know

2 🎧 Jenny is moving from her village to a big city. Listen to the dialogue and tick (✓) what she *thinks, expects, hopes, guesses*, etc. she will do, and add a cross (✗) for things she won't do. Tell the class.

1 ⬜ find a good job   4 ⬜ enjoy living there
2 ⬜ share a flat   5 ⬜ get bored there
3 ⬜ find a place with a garden   6 ⬜ miss her family

Jenny thinks she'll ... .
Jenny expects she won't ... .

3 a) 🎧 Listen and make notes, then tell the class what Stan *is going to* do when he goes on holiday.

Stan is going to stay in a five-star hotel.

b) **Make similar sentences using *be going to* about your plans for your next holiday.**

I'm going to visit Rabat. I'm going to go sightseeing around the city. I'm going to ...

4 Fill in: *will* or *am/is/are going to*. **Give reasons.**

1 A: The dentist's surgery is on the first floor.
   B: I .... take the stairs, then. I don't like lifts.

2 A: What are your plans after graduation?
   B: I .... go backpacking around Asia.

3 A: Be careful! You .... crash into that tree!
   B: Sorry, I'm a bit tired today.

4 A: Will Alice come to the opening ceremony?
   B: No, I expect she .... miss it – she hates crowds.

5 A: Max is afraid of flying, so he .... travel to the USA by ship.
   B: Really? But that's going to take him weeks!

5 Read Paul and Max's notes, then put the verbs in brackets into the present simple or the present continuous.

Monday	Food festival: 11 am – 9 pm
Tuesday	Concert (Singer-Julie Watson): 8:30 pm – 12 pm
Wednesday	Theatre (Macbeth): 7:30 pm – 9 pm
Thursday	Exhibition (Picasso): 9 am – 5 pm
Friday	Book reading (Kiera Patrick): 1 pm – 3 pm

1 Paul and Max *are attending* **(attend)** a food festival on Monday. It *starts* **(start)** at 11 am.

2 Julie Walters .... **(perform)** a concert on Tuesday. It .... **(finish)** at 12 pm.

3 A group of actors .... **(act)** in a production of Macbeth on Wednesday. It .... **(end)** at 9 pm.

4 Paul and Max .... **(visit)** a Picasso exhibition on Thursday. It .... **(open)** at 9 am.

5 Kiera Patrick .... **(give)** a book reading on Thursday. It .... **(begin)** at 1 pm.

6 Put the verbs in brackets into the correct future tense: *be going to, will*, the present simple or the present continuous. Give reasons.

INBOX   OUTBOX   CONTACTS

Hi Bill,

Hope you're well. Any summer plans? **1)** .... **(you/visit)** your friends in Spain again like last summer? Anyway, I need your advice. I bought the tickets, so next Wednesday I **2)** .... **(travel)** to France. I checked the weather forecast and it **3)** .... **(be)** hot and sunny there, so I think I **4)** .... **(have)** a great time there. The only problem is the flight. You see, I have a terrible fear of flying. The flight **5)** .... **(leave)** at 11 pm, so I guess I **6)** .... **(be able to)** sleep for most of the journey, but I'm still stressed about take-off and landing. Anyway, it's getting late, so I **7)** .... **(stop)** writing now.

Talk to you soon,
Sam

Conditionals Type 1 ▶ pp. GR7-8

7 Study the theory. Find an example in the dialogue on p. 32.

Conditionals Type 1

If + present simple → *will/may/can* + infinitive without *to*
(used to talk about real or likely situations in the present or future)
*If it **rains**, we **won't go** to the beach. We **can go** to the beach if the weather **is** fine.*
We can use ***unless*** (= **if not**) with this type of conditional.
*Unless it **rains**, we **will go** to the beach.* (= If it doesn't rain, ...)

8 Join the sentences using *if* or *unless*.

1 The dog won't bite you
2 I can take part in the match
3 I'll pass the test
4 I'll be really nervous
5 I'll buy a new laptop
6 We may go on a picnic

if

unless

a you need me.
b I get stressed in the exam hall.
c there are many people in the audience.
d it rains.
e you bother it.
f I can afford it.

9 SPEAKING   Look at the examples in the bubbles. Then continue these people's thoughts.

If I drive through the city, I'll run into traffic. If I run into traffic, I'll ...

If I don't study, I won't pass my exams. If I don't pass my exams, I ...

Time clauses ▶ p. GR7

10 Read the theory. Find examples in the dialogue on p. 32.

Time words

We don't use future forms after: ***when*** (time conjunction), ***while, before, until, after, as soon as, by the time, if*** (conditional), etc. *I'll go there **when** I finish work.*
BUT when (question word) + **will** *When will he come?*

11 Cross out the word which should not be in the sentence. Some sentences may be correct.

1 I will call you as soon as the plane lands in Amsterdam.
2 If you will feel anxious during the exam, you can take some deep breaths.
3 When will you know the results of your blood tests?
4 After you will finish these reports, will you please come to my office?
5 When the kids will fall asleep, you can turn off the light.
6 By the time we will arrive at the shopping centre, it won't be very busy.

12 THINK   In a minute, complete the sentences.

1 I'll go to the cinema when ....
2 As soon as I finish my homework, ...
3 I don't know if ....
4 I'll go to the library before I ....

Skills in Action

Vocabulary

Fears & Physical reactions

1 a) **Choose the correct word.**

1 Whenever I see lightning or hear thunder, my mouth **empties/goes dry** and I **freeze/stop**.

2 When I have to give a speech, my hands **sweat/wet** and my heart **beats/moves** faster.

3 I know they can't **damage/hurt** me, but I always run a **metre/mile** when I see a bug!

4 Even before I get on board, I **shake/stay** like a leaf and I **feel/smell** terribly sick.

5 When I stepped onto the roof, my hair **stood/sat** on end and I couldn't **control/change** my fear.

6 I know I should **face/look** my fears, but I always **avoid/keep** using lifts.

b) **Match the sentences (1-6) to the fears (A-F).**

A ☐ fear of bugs
B ☐ fear of public speaking
C ☐ fear of storms
D ☐ fear of flying
E ☐ fear of closed spaces
F ☐ fear of heights

Listening

> ### Study Skills
>
> **Predicting content – key words**
> Before you listen, read the sentences and underline the key words. They will help you predict the content of the recording.

2 🎧 **You will hear a conversation between a radio presenter and a woman. Decide if the statements are correct (Yes) or incorrect (No).**

	Yes	No
1 Pam is the first ever caller on Victor's show who has a phobia.	☐	☐
2 Pam still thinks about the moment when she developed her phobia.	☐	☐
3 When Pam sees a balloon, she can't breathe properly.	☐	☐
4 Pam told her best friend about her phobia.	☐	☐
5 Victor says that Pam should start touching balloons straight away.	☐	☐
6 Victor advises Pam to get professional help.	☐	☐

Everyday English

Asking for/Giving advice

3 a) **Read the first exchange in the dialogue. What advice would you give Alan?**

> **Sam:** What's up, Alan? You look a bit worried.
>
> **Alan:** Oh, hi, Sam. It's this presentation I need to give at university tomorrow. I'm really worried about it.
>
> **Sam:** What do you mean? You've been preparing for it for weeks, haven't you?
>
> **Alan:** Yes, the presentation is ready, but I get really nervous when I speak in public – I'm sure I'll freeze up there! What should I do?
>
> **Sam:** Hmm, let me see. Have you thought about practising in front of a mirror? That way, you'll see yourself giving the presentation and you'll realise that you're a better speaker than you think you are.
>
> **Alan:** That's not a bad idea. I'll give it a try. Thanks, Sam.
>
> **Sam:** Glad to help. Good luck with your presentation!

b) 🎧 **Listen to and read the dialogue. Was any of your advice mentioned?**

4 👤👤 **Use the prompts and the phrases in the box to act out similar dialogues. Record yourselves.**

A afraid to go to dentist's for appointment – discuss problem with dentist/ask for music to relax

B nervous about learning how to drive – play driving simulation games/find an instructor you can trust

Asking for advice	Giving advice
• What do you suggest?	• It might be a good idea to …
• What's your advice?	• Why don't you …?
• Do you have any advice?	• You'd better …
• Any ideas (on how to help)?	• You ought to/should …

Pronunciation: /z/, /s/

> In British English, some verbs ending in **-se** form nouns ending in **-ce**. Some of these pairs are pronounced the same, but with others, the verb is pronounced /z/ at the end and the noun /s/.

5 🎧 **Listen and tick the pairs with different pronunciation. Use them in sentences of your own.**

1 advise, advice ......
2 practise, practice ......
3 license, licence ......
4 devise, device ......

Reading & Writing

Word formation (forming verbs)
We can use these prefixes to form other verbs from verbs: **dis-** = not (*obey – disobey*), **mis-** = wrongly (*spell – misspell*), **re-** = again (*use – reuse*)

6 a) Billy has been invited to a barbecue, but he's nervous about attending because he won't know anyone there. He has written to his friend Conrad asking for advice. Read Conrad's reply and fill in the gaps with verbs derived from the verbs in brackets. Use appropriate prefixes.

Hi Billy,

Sorry to hear about your problem, but I completely **1)** .... (agree) that you shouldn't go to the barbecue. My sister **2)** .... (like) meeting new people, too. She used to **3)** .... (appear) when we had visitors to our house! But she learnt how to deal with it, and so can you!

Firstly, why don't you **4)** .... (think) what the barbecue will be like? Instead of being pessimistic, imagine having a good time there. This way, you'll have a better chance of enjoying yourself.

Also, when you get there, you should **5)** .... (consider) how other people are feeling. Maybe they're feeling shy, too. By focusing on other people, you'll forget about your anxiety.

Often people **6)** .... (understand) social anxiety and don't realise how difficult it is to overcome it. But I know what you're going through, and I hope my tips help. Write and tell me how you get on.

Talk soon,
Conrad

b) Is the email formal or informal? Give reasons.

Writing Tip

Giving advice
We need to support pieces of advice with expected results.

7 What advice does Conrad give to Billy? What expected results does he mention?

8 Find the phrases Conrad uses to give advice and the expected results. Replace them with phrases from the box.

Giving Advice	Expected Results
• It would/could be a good idea to ... • You could also ... • I (strongly) advise you to ... • Another idea would be to ...	• If you do this, you'll ... • This would mean that ... • By doing this, ... • Then, ...

Writing (an email giving advice)

9 Read the task. What are you going to write? Who for?

Your English friend Max has been invited to go on a sailing trip with some friends. He's nervous about the trip, though, because he's scared of the sea. Write Max an email (120-150 words). In your email: • sympathise • give him advice • express hope that the trip goes well.

10 a) Listen to a conversation and complete the table.

Advice	Expected result
identify the **1)** .... for your **2)**	understand it **3)** .... and deal with it
4) .... about safety equipment	learn how to stay **5)** .... and feel less **6)** ....

b) Use your notes in Ex. 10a to write your email (120-150 words). Follow the plan.

Plan

Hi (friend's first name),
Para 1: sympathise with friend's problem; offer to help
Paras 2-3: give advice and say expected results
Para 4: express hope that things go well; closing remarks
Write soon,
(your first name)

VALUES

Courage
Courage is knowing what not to fear.
Plato

Join in ...

BUG FEST

▶ VIDEO

If you've got entomophobia, a fear of insects, then this festival is not for you! On an August weekend every year, Drexel University in Philadelphia, USA, hosts Bug Fest – the largest celebration of creepy-crawlies in the USA!

Students and professors at the Academy of Natural Sciences at the university run the festival. So, if anything is 'bugging' you about bugs, these experts will help you! There are over 100 insects from around the world on display – from glow-in-the-dark scorpions to **rare** stick insects – and you can see them up close. Also, the festival has lots of special presentations and exhibitions.

The highlight for most people is the 'Xtreme Bugs' exhibition. Ever wonder what it would be like to be the size of a bug? Well, imagine walking among huge robot insects! There are over 20 of them – from a monarch butterfly to a Madagascar cockroach. Coming face-to-face with these **giant** bugs is an experience you won't **forget**!

But that's not all. If you get hungry during the festival – and are **brave** enough – you can visit 'Bug Appétit'. In this presentation, a **local** sweet maker shows how to make sweets from insects you can eat – and there are lots of samples for visitors to try! Kids will love Bug Fest, too, with insect face-painting and the Roach Races Grand Prix – an **exciting** cockroach race!

Bug Fest celebrates the amazing variety of insects. It's the perfect place for both young and old to get to know the creepy-crawlies that are all around us!

✓ **Check these words**

host, bug, creepy-crawly, up close, highlight, wonder, sample

Reading & Listening

1 **How are these words/phrases related to Bug Fest?**

• creepy-crawlies • see up close • huge robot insects • sweet maker • cockroach race

🎧 **Listen to and read the text to find out.**

2 **Read again and answer the questions.**

1 What is 'entomophobia'?
2 Which section of Drexel University organises Bug Fest?
3 What can visitors see in the 'Xtreme Bugs' exhibition?
4 Who is 'Bug Appétit' run by?

3 **Match the words in bold to their opposites.**

• remember • boring • tiny • common
• afraid • foreign

Speaking & Writing

4 THINK **Is there an annual festival in your country or another country which celebrates something that people are commonly afraid of? Why should people go to it?**

5 ICT **Collect information about the festival in Ex. 4. Make notes under the headings:** *Name – Place – Date – Reason – Activities*. **Write a short text about it for a website's culture column.**

Vocabulary

1 Fill in: *financial, unemployed, injury, retirement, positive, fundraising.*

1 Jane organises lots of .... events for charity.
2 Ann became .... when the factory closed.
3 Steve moved back to his village after ....
4 Kate had to quit her job because of a serious ....
5 We're having some .... problems, so we won't be able to go on holiday this year.
6 People with a(n) .... attitude have less stress.

(6 x 3 = 18)

2 Choose the correct word.

1 I'm really worried about an exam I'm **taking/making** tomorrow.
2 You have to **face/avoid** your fear to overcome it.
3 After he lost his job, Greg couldn't **retire/afford** to pay his rent.
4 Kate's heart was **beating/sweating** fast as she went on stage.
5 If you **think/believe** in yourself, you'll get the job.
6 Don't be afraid – the spider won't **hurt/damage** you.

(6 x 2 = 12)

3 Choose the correct item.

1 Is he interested **in/at/on** going to Bug Fest?
2 Please take **off/over/to** your shoes before you enter the room.
3 She was excited **for/about/in** moving to the big city.
4 He is proud **in/for/of** overcoming his fear of insects.
5 Steve wants to take **on/up/off** a hobby.

(5 x 2 = 10)

Grammar

4 Fill in: *will* or *is/are going to.*

1 I feel scared in the dark – I .... turn the light on.
2 I've just heard the forecast – there .... be a storm later.
3 Steve believes his new job .... be very stressful.
4 This weekend, we .... move into our new flat.
5 I don't think Dennis .... come to the exhibition.

(5 x 2 = 10)

5 Choose the correct tense.

1 The train **will leave/leaves** in half an hour.
2 Look at that dog! It **will/'s going to** attack!
3 Bob **talks/'s going to talk** to a doctor later.
4 I guess it**'ll be/'s being** a very stressful year.
5 He**'s flying/'ll fly** to Oman on Monday.

(5 x 4 = 20)

6 Put the verbs in brackets into the correct tense.

1 If Jane sees that mouse, she .... **(scream)**!
2 We won't start until you .... **(arrive)**.
3 Kate .... **(quit)** if her job becomes stressful.
4 When you move house, I .... **(help)** you.
5 Unless Peter .... **(get)** medical help, he'll never overcome his phobia.

(5 x 3 = 15)

Everyday English

7 Match the sentences.

1 ☐ Thanks for your advice.
2 ☐ You look worried.
3 ☐ I'm worried about the presentation.
4 ☐ What should I do?
5 ☐ You should get more sleep.

a Why don't you talk to him?
b What do you mean?
c That's not a bad idea.
d It's an exam I'm taking tomorrow.
e Glad to help.

(5 x 3 = 15)
Total 100

Competences

GOOD ✓
VERY GOOD ✓✓
EXCELLENT ✓✓✓

Lexical Competence
understand words/phrases related to:
• stressful events
• fears & physical reactions

Reading Competence
• understand texts related to stressful events (read for gist – multiple matching; read for detail – answer questions)

Listening Competence
• listen to and understand dialogues related to fear & physical reactions (listen for specific information – Yes/No statements)

Speaking Competence
• ask for/give advice

Writing Competence
• write an email of advice
• write a short text about a festival

Citizen 2100

Vocabulary

Cities of the future

1 Look at the picture. Which of the features of a future city (A-H) can you see? Which do you think will exist in 2100?

A vertical farms

B self-driving buses

C 3D-printed houses

D solar windows

E drone deliveries

F vacuum tube trains

G floating buildings

H charging stations for electric cars

Reading & Listening

2 Read through the text quickly. How will cities of the future improve people's lives?

3 Read the article and fill in the gaps (1-5) with the headings (A-E).

A Getting around

B A bright future

C Spending your free time

D A place to call home

E Food on your doorstep

🎧 **Listen and check. Then explain the words in bold.**

1 ☐

Today, around 55% of the world's population live in cities, and that number will have **increased** to 85% by 2100. But will cities be able to deal with so many extra people, or will they become even more **crowded**, uncomfortable and unsafe than many of them already are today? Nobody knows for sure, but many experts are hopeful about the city of the future. With the help of modern technology, they could be the **perfect** places to live and work.

2 ☐

In 2100, cities will improve public transport with high-speed vacuum tube trains and self-driving buses. This will **reduce** the number of cars on the roads. Also, we will be driving electric cars – and there will be charging stations on every street. So, there will be less air pollution, fewer traffic jams and people will be able to go from place to place quickly and without stress.

The City of the FUTURE

4 a) COLLOCATIONS Match the words to form collocations.

1 ☐ modern   **a** door
2 ☐ healthy   **b** transport
3 ☐ traffic   **c** power
4 ☐ public   **d** jams
5 ☐ solar   **e** technology
6 ☐ front   **f** food

b) Use the completed phrases in sentences of your own.

3 ☐

As more and more people move to cities, we will need to build more houses. In the future, we will use huge 3D printers to build houses and blocks of flats extremely quickly. Also, to create space, we will construct floating blocks of flats on rivers or off the coast. And a lot of modern buildings will have solar windows, which will **create** solar power for the people who live there.

4 ☐

Today, we spend a lot of time and money transporting food to cities. So, people have begun trying to find ways to produce food close to the people who eat it. Some vertical farms already exist today, but in the future we will build them in every major city. They'll **provide** healthy food to people living nearby.

5 ☐

The city of the future will have a lot of green areas. There won't be space for large parks, but buildings will have green roofs – perfect for relaxing and exercising. Also, less space will be taken up by shops, as people will order almost everything online. Within minutes, drones will **deliver** products to your front door!

✓ **Check these words**

improve, traffic jam, construct, produce, take up space

5 PREPOSITIONS Choose the correct preposition.

1 We will have to deal **with/for** more extreme weather in the future.
2 Lisa ordered a pizza and **inside/within** minutes it was at her door.
3 They plan to build a floating shopping mall **at/off** the coast of the UAE.
4 The professor is hopeful **about/with** the future of our planet.
5 **In/At** the future, we will probably work a four-day week.

6 WORDS EASILY CONFUSED Choose the correct word. Check in your dictionary.

1 In 50 years, robots will help **lonely/alone** older people.
2 The astronaut was happy to be **lonely/alone** on the space station.
3 The ship **delivers/transports** both people and goods to the island.
4 The restaurant **delivers/transports** food to your home.

7 PHRASAL VERBS Fill in the correct particle. Then try to make up a story using the phrasal verbs in the box.

come across: to meet/find sb/sth by chance
come back: to return
come round/over: to visit
come into: to inherit sth

1 My brother came .... a metal object in a field, which had fallen from the sky.
2 Jenny came .... a lot of money when her aunt died.
3 Steve has moved to the USA, but his parents hope he will come .... some day.
4 You should come .... for dinner one evening.

Speaking & Writing

8 💬 THINK Design your city of the future. Where will it be? What will it have? Present it to the class.

Grammar in Use

The Future Forum

Today's question:

How do you think education will be different in 2100?

In 2100, technology will definitely be a big part of education. In fact, it's already starting! For example, later this year, at the school where I work, every student will be receiving a VR headset. We'll be using them in class.
Paul Rans   13:12   08/01

By 2100, we will definitely have changed the way we teach young people – and I'm not just talking about using technology. For example, I think we'll be seeing more project-based work with fewer exams.
Lisa   15:39   08/01

Fewer exams would be great! By the end of this term, I'll have sat over 10 exams, and I find them really stressful. Actually, this time tomorrow, I'll be taking an important business exam. Wish me luck, everyone!
Steve   16:08   08/01

1 Read the theory. Find examples in the forum.

Future continuous
(*will be* + main verb *-ing* form)   ▶ **p. GR8**

Affirmative	I/You/He, etc **will/'ll be** work**ing**.
Negative	I/You/He, etc **will not/won't be** work**ing**.
Interrogative	**Will** I/you/he, etc **be** work**ing**?
Short answers	**Yes**, I/you/he, etc **will**. **No**, I/you/he, etc **won't**.

We use the future continuous for:
• actions which will be in progress at a definite time in the future. *He will be flying to Morocco this time next Friday.*
• actions which will definitely happen in the future, as a result of routine or an arrangement. *They'll be constructing a vertical farm later this month.*

Time expressions with the future continuous: *this time tomorrow, at one o'clock tomorrow, three hours from now, later*, etc

2 Put the verbs in brackets into the future continuous.

1 This time next week, I .... **(visit)** a vertical farm.

2 In 2100, we .... **(not/use)** cars to get around.

3 This time tomorrow, they .... **(install)** solar windows in the building.

4 .... **(you/work)** on your science project tomorrow evening?

5 At 4 pm on Tuesday, Lucy .... **(give)** her presentation on future cities.

6 Three hours from now, the delivery drone .... **(arrive)** outside your house.

7 In the near future, everyone .... **(learn)** from robot teachers.

8 This time next Wednesday, I .... **(move)** to a bigger house.

3 Read Kate's notes. Ask and answer questions, as in the example.

Monday	1 pm - eat lunch with Frank
Tuesday	3 pm - go shopping at the supermarket
Thursday	9 pm - visit robot exhibition
Friday	2 pm - fly to Barcelona

1 Kate and Frank/eat lunch/one o'clock next Monday?
   A: Will Kate and Frank be eating lunch at one o'clock next Monday?
   B: Yes, they will.

2 Kate/shop/supermarket/two o'clock next Tuesday?

3 Kate/visit/robot exhibition/ten o'clock next Friday?

4 Kate/fly/to/Barcelona/two o'clock/next Friday?

4 SPEAKING THINK What trends will people be following in 30 years? Discuss with your partner. One person makes positive predictions, the other negative. Think about *housing, food, entertainment, education* and *transport*.

A: *In 30 years, people will be living in green cities.*
B: *In 30 years, people will be living in tiny flats.*

5 Read the theory. Find two examples in the forum on p. 40.

Future perfect (*will have* + past participle of the main verb) ▷ **p. GR8**

Affirmative	I/You/He, etc will/'ll have left by 5 pm.
Negative	I/You/He, etc will not/won't have left by 5 pm.
Interrogative	Will I/you/he, etc have left by 5 pm?
Short answers	Yes, I/you/he, etc will. No, I/you/he etc won't.

We use the future perfect for a completed action in the future that will take place before a stated time or another action in the future. *They will have reached their destination by this time tomorrow.*

Time words/phrases: *before, by, by then, by the time, until/till,* etc

Note: *until/till* are normally used with future perfect only in negative sentences.

6 Put the verbs in brackets into the future perfect.

1 Some people believe we .... **(move)** to another planet by the year 2100.

2 .... **(you/finish)** your science project by the weekend?

3 By 2100, I think we .... **(discover)** life on other planets.

4 Stan .... **(not/leave)** the office yet, so there's no point calling him at home.

5 George and Sam .... **(not/finish)** their project before the deadline.

6 I think scientists .... **(find)** a cure for hair loss by 2060.

7 🗣️🗣️ Ask and answer questions about Max, as in the example.

Friday **5** **November**	**09:00**	move into new office	🔊
	13:00-14:00	have meeting with sales department	🔊
	18:30	meet Jerry for a coffee	🔊
	21:00	pick up Lisa	🔊

1 move into new office/10:00?

2 finish meeting with sales department/13:20?

3 meet Jerry/18:45?

4 pick up Lisa/20:30?

A: Will Max have moved into his new office by 10:00?

B: Yes, he will.

8 Put the verbs in brackets into the future continuous or the future perfect.

1 A: I can't believe that in few hours, we .... **(travel)** to London.

   B: Yes, it's going to be amazing!

2 A: .... **(underwater cities/create)** by 2080?

   B: No, I doubt it.

3 A: Why don't we go to the theatre?

   B: The play .... **(start)** by the time we get there.

4 A: Are you free at this time tomorrow, Alan?

   B: No, this time tomorrow, I .... **(visit)** a science museum.

5 A: Will the solar windows be ready tomorrow?

   B: No, I'm afraid we .... **(not/finish)** installing them by then.

6 A: Could you give this letter to Mr Franklin?

   B: Actually, I .... **(not/see)** him today. We cancelled our meeting.

Listening

9 🎧 Listen to an author talking about how his life will be different in ten years' time, and mark the sentences *T* (True) or *F* (False).

1 He'll still be writing novels. ....

2 He'll have written five more books by then. ....

3 He'll still be living in New York. ....

4 He'll be working on films then. ....

5 He'll have won the Nobel Prize by then. ....

Speaking

10 ⟨THINK⟩ **Think of yourself in** *five years' time, ten years' time* **and** *twenty years' time.* **What will you be doing/will you have done? Think about education, home, work, travel and family.**

I'll have finished university in five years' time. I'll be looking for a job in ...

Skills in Action

Vocabulary

Future predictions

1 **a)** Read the predictions about life in the year 2080 (1-6) and match them to their reasons (a-f). Which of the predictions are: *positive*; *negative*.

1 ☐ pollution levels in cities/decrease
2 ☐ crime/increase
3 ☐ people/live in cities under the sea
4 ☐ people/live longer
5 ☐ people/go on holiday to other planets
6 ☐ there be/more poverty

a life/become more expensive
b people/use electric cars
c regular cities/become too crowded
d scientists/find cures for serious diseases
e space travel/become affordable
f criminals/use advanced technology

b) Expand the ideas into complete sentences using *because*, *as* or *since*. Use the future continuous or the future perfect.

By the year 2080, pollution levels in cities will have decreased because people will be using electric cars.

Listening

2 🎧 You will hear two friends making predictions about the world in the year 2080. Listen and decide if the statements are R (Right), W (Wrong) or DS (Doesn't Say).

1 Jason hasn't started his project yet. ....
2 Jason mainly wants to talk about the environment in his project. ....
3 Jason thinks that air pollution will be worse than water pollution. ....
4 According to Anna, a bigger population won't mean less food for people. ....
5 Jason finds predicting the future very difficult. ....
6 Anna offers to help Jason's project become more positive. ....

Everyday English

Discussing future plans

3 Read the dialogue between two friends about their summer plans and fill in the missing words. 🎧 Listen and check.

A: What are your plans for the summer, Max?
B: Haven't I told you, Helen? This **1)** .... next week, I'll be working in the Science Museum!
A: Really? How did you find that job?
B: There was an advert online.
A: And what will you be doing there?
B: Mostly I'll be showing visitors around the museum, but I might also work in the gift shop.
A: Wow! How **2)** .... will you work there?
B: Until the end of August. By **3)** ...., I'll have earned enough money to buy the laptop I need! What about you?
A: Well, this time next week I'll be flying **4)** .... New York to see my cousins.
B: Sounds **5)** .... fun!

4 👥 Imagine you have found a summer job as a gardener in a vertical farm. Use the advert to act out a similar dialogue. Use language from the box.

Do you have green fingers?

We're looking for temporary gardeners for our vertical farm.
Time: three-month contract (June - August)
Duties: water plants; change soil; check temperatures

Click here to apply

Asking about future plans	Giving information
• (Do you have) any plans for ...?	• Haven't I told you?
• What are your plans for ...?	• This time next week, I'll ...
• What will your duties be there?	• My duties will include ...
• How long will you work/stay there?	• I'll be there until/from ...

Pronunciation: /uː/, /ʊ/

5 🎧 Listen and tick (✓), then repeat.

	/uː/	/ʊ/		/uː/	/ʊ/
pool			fool		
pull			shoot		
full			should		

Reading & Writing

6 Read the essay and put the paragraphs into the correct order. In which paragraph does the writer give their opinion?

The Future of Health

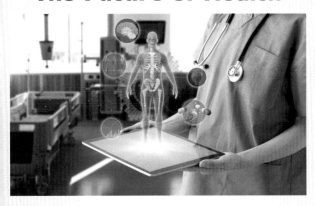

A ☐ On the other hand, future technology might mean we get even less exercise than we do now. For example, with drone deliveries we won't need to leave our homes to do the shopping. This might cause more and more people to gain weight and suffer from obesity and heart disease.

B ☐ Imagine living until the age of 150. In my opinion, this will soon be possible. In the future, we will improve health care so that people can live longer and healthier lives.

C ☐ To sum up, I believe that we should be positive about the future of health. We need to make sure, though, that we get enough exercise and eat healthily. If we do this, we can all live past 100!

D ☐ Already, we have medicines for diseases, and in the future, we will discover more cures that will help us live longer. Also, in 50 years, everyone will be using wearable devices, such as smart watches, to monitor their heart rate and other body functions. By doing this, we'll know immediately if we need medical attention. Also, robots will be performing complicated surgeries, and we'll have invented robots that can look after disabled and elderly people.

Writing Tip

Introduction techniques
We can start an essay by making a statement or with a question to attract the reader's attention. This makes the reader want to read on.

7 How has the writer started the essay? Suggest another introduction using the other type in the Writing Tip.

Word formation
Forming verbs
We can use these suffixes to form verbs from adjectives or nouns: *-ate* *(active – activate)*, *-en* *(dark – darken)*, *-ise* *(real – realise)*.

8 Complete the sentences with verbs formed from the words in brackets.

1 We can .... our lives by exercising. **(LENGTH)**

2 The company .... in electronic cars. **(SPECIAL)**

3 We need to .... the amount of fossil fuels we use. **(LESS)**

4 They plan to .... the solar windows in a local newspaper. **(ADVERT)**

Writing (an essay making predictions)

9 Look at the spidergram. Which do you think are positive/negative predictions? Add your own ideas.

houses
underground

health
longer lives

food
meal pills

relationships
fewer friends

life in
50 years

jobs
better paid

education
robot teachers

the environment
fewer wild animals

10 Your English teacher wants you to write an essay about life in 50 years. Write your essay using ideas from Ex. 9 (120-150 words). Follow the plan.

Plan

Para 1: present topic; state opinion
Para 2: positive predictions (with examples/reasons)
Para 3: negative predictions (with examples/reasons)
Para 4: restate opinion

VALUES
Determination
The best way to predict the future is to create it.
Abraham Lincoln

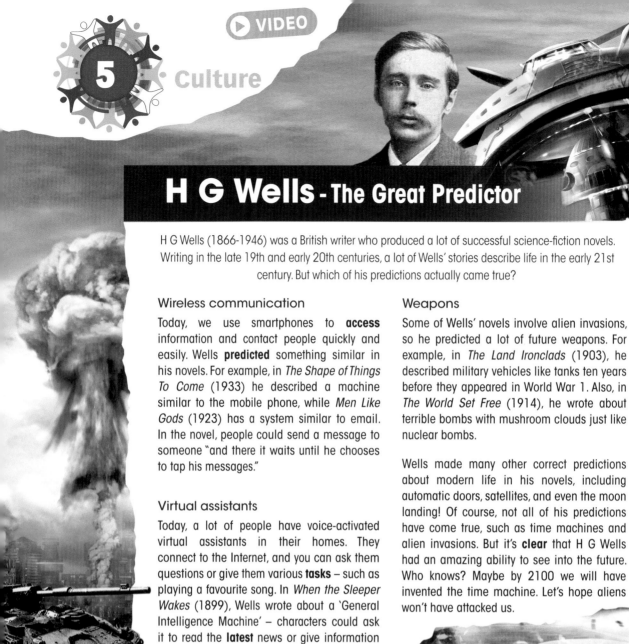

▶ VIDEO

H G Wells - The Great Predictor

H G Wells (1866-1946) was a British writer who produced a lot of successful science-fiction novels. Writing in the late 19th and early 20th centuries, a lot of Wells' stories describe life in the early 21st century. But which of his predictions actually came true?

Wireless communication

Today, we use smartphones to **access** information and contact people quickly and easily. Wells **predicted** something similar in his novels. For example, in *The Shape of Things To Come* (1933) he described a machine similar to the mobile phone, while *Men Like Gods* (1923) has a system similar to email. In the novel, people could send a message to someone "and there it waits until he chooses to tap his messages."

Virtual assistants

Today, a lot of people have voice-activated virtual assistants in their homes. They connect to the Internet, and you can ask them questions or give them various **tasks** – such as playing a favourite song. In *When the Sleeper Wakes* (1899), Wells wrote about a 'General Intelligence Machine' – characters could ask it to read the **latest** news or give information about new products!

Weapons

Some of Wells' novels involve alien invasions, so he predicted a lot of future weapons. For example, in *The Land Ironclads* (1903), he described military vehicles like tanks ten years before they appeared in World War 1. Also, in *The World Set Free* (1914), he wrote about terrible bombs with mushroom clouds just like nuclear bombs.

Wells made many other correct predictions about modern life in his novels, including automatic doors, satellites, and even the moon landing! Of course, not all of his predictions have come true, such as time machines and alien invasions. But it's **clear** that H G Wells had an amazing ability to see into the future. Who knows? Maybe by 2100 we will have invented the time machine. Let's hope aliens won't have attacked us.

Listening & Reading

1 **What do you know about H G Wells? What kind of books did he write? What did he predict in his books about the modern world?**

🎧 **Listen and read to find out.**

2 **Read the text again and complete the sentences. Then explain the words in bold.**

1 Wells wrote in the 19th and ....

2 *Men Like Gods* has a system like ....

3 Wells' virtual assistant can provide ....
....

4 In *The World Set Free*, Wells predicted weapons like
....

5 Two of Wells' predictions that have not come true are alien invasions and ....

✓ Check these words

tap, voice-activated, virtual assistant, alien invasion, weapon, military vehicle, nuclear bomb, automatic doors, satellite, attack

Speaking & Writing

3 **THINK** **Imagine you are a science-fiction writer. You are trying to think of ideas for your next novel set in 2100. What will your novel be about? How will you describe life in 2100 in your novel? Make a short plot outline. Tell the class.**

4 **ICT** **Research a film or TV series about the future from your country or another country. Write a short paragraph about it and the predictions it made.**

Vocabulary

1 Fill in: *affordable, serious, crowded, traffic, floating.*

1 The scientist is trying to find a cure for cancer, which is a(n) .... disease.

2 They are constructing a(n) .... building off the coast.

3 Electric cars won't solve the problem of .... jams.

4 Today, a lot of cities are far too ....

5 Travelling into space isn't .... for most people.

(5 x 3 = 15)

2 Choose the correct word.

1 The company **delivers/transports** its parcels to homes by drone.

2 Jack lives on his own but he isn't **alone/lonely**.

3 **Solar/Sun** power will become our main source of energy.

4 **Vertical/Vacuum** tube trains will allow us to get around quickly.

5 Most cities will have charging **stations/farms** for electric cars.

(5 x 2 = 10)

3 Choose the correct item.

1 He can't deal **for/with** the problem now.

2 How did you come **round/across** this camera?

3 She came **into/across** lots of money when her grandpa died.

4 We need to be hopeful **about/with** the future.

5 Mark fixed the laptop **within/inside** minutes.

(5 x 4 = 20)

Grammar

4 Choose the correct item.

1 We **will be living/will have lived** in underground cities in 2100.

2 I'll watch the film at midnight – I **won't be falling/won't have fallen** asleep by then.

3 Greg **won't be joining/won't have joined** us at the cinema later.

4 At five o'clock tomorrow, they **will be starting/will have started** the tour.

5 We **will be running/will have run** out of fossil fuels by 2100.

(5 x 4 = 20)

5 Put the verbs in brackets into the future continuous or the future perfect.

1 By the time they return from Italy, Bob .... **(learn)** to speak Italian.

2 This time next week, I .... **(give)** a speech at the college lecture hall.

3 .... **(you/finish)** your project by tomorrow morning?

4 .... **(you/work)** in the office at 1 o'clock tomorrow?

5 By 2080, the population of the city .... **(increase)** to 1 million.

(5 x 4 = 20)

Everyday English

6 Match the sentences.

1 ☐ What are your plans for the summer?

2 ☐ What will your duties be there?

3 ☐ How long will you work there?

4 ☐ How did you find that job?

5 ☐ I can't wait.

a I'll be working on a farm.

b Until mid-September.

c Sounds like fun!

d I'll be serving customers.

e There was an advert online.

(5 x 3 = 15)
Total 100

Competences

GOOD ✓	
VERY GOOD ✓✓	
EXCELLENT ✓✓✓	

Lexical Competence

understand words/phrases related to:

• cities of the future

• future predictions

Reading Competence

• understand texts related to predictions (read for gist – match headings to paragraphs; read for specific information – sentence completion)

Listening Competence

• listen to and understand a dialogue related to predictions (listen for specific information – R/W/DS statements)

Speaking Competence

• discuss future plans

Writing Competence

• write an essay making predictions

6

The Big Screen ▶ VIDEO

A long time ago in a galaxy far, far away ... a young **film-maker** had an idea for a sci-fi film called *Star Wars*. George Lucas's space opera about a farm boy who becomes a hero came out in the summer of 1977 and it was a huge hit. It was more than just a blockbuster film, though – *Star Wars* took on a life of its own.

Audiences fell in love with the **adventures** of Luke Skywalker, Leia Organa, Han Solo and the terrible Darth Vader. Fans joined the **queues** outside cinemas to see the film again and again, and the catchphrase "May the **Force** be with you" was everywhere. Audiences couldn't get enough and **demanded** a second film.

That film, *The Empire Strikes Back*, is considered to be one of the best sequels ever. *Return of the Jedi* followed in 1983, but it was not the end. The first film's name was changed to *Star Wars: Episode IV – A New Hope* and more and more films were made.

These days, we have a new *Star Wars* film almost every year, there are cartoons on TV, and live-action TV **series** are being planned.

Star Wars **appeared** on the big screen many years ago, so why is it still popular? One reason might be the easily recognisable music by the composer John Williams. The films also have the latest **special effects**, amazing actors and clever storytelling. Fans love the different planets, droids, the Jedi knights and the different bad guys. Star Wars is so well-liked that even celebrity guests appear in small roles. To prove that Star Wars is a big part of popular culture, there is *Star Wars* day every year on 4th May, when fans play with the films' catchphrase and **proudly** say, "May the Fourth be with you!"

! The hashtag *"May The Fourth Be With You"* is used on Twitter around the world.

> ✓ **Check these words**
>
> galaxy, space opera, blockbuster, catchphrase, audience, sequel, composer, prove

Reading & Listening

1 Look at the pictures. Do you recognise any of the characters? Think of some typical film heroes or heroines. What are the good things they do?

2 Read the sentences and decide if they are *T* (True), *F* (False) or *DS* (Doesn't Say). Read or listen to the text and check your answers.

1 George Lucas grew up on a farm. ....
2 The original Star Wars film had a famous line in it. ....
3 *The Empire Strikes Back* sold more tickets than *Star Wars*. ....
4 None of the Star Wars actors are very famous. ....
5 *Star Wars* was released on May 4th. ....

3 Read the text and complete the sentences. Then explain the words in bold.

1 *Star Wars: Episode IV – A New Hope* was directed by ....

2 *The Empire Strikes Back* appeared before ....

3 The music for *Star Wars* was written by ....

4 Fans celebrate *Star Wars* on ....

Vocabulary

Types of films

4 a) Which type of film does each film title match?

- action-adventure • cartoon • animation
- comedy • drama • sci-fi • crime • documentary
- horror • fantasy • western • thriller • musical

1

5

2

6

Mission Impossible FALLOUT

3

7

b) 🗣 Talk about various types of films, as in the example. Use the adjectives in the list.

- amusing • enjoyable • exciting • boring • funny
- interesting • scary • disgusting

A: *Do you like musicals?*
B: *I love them. I find them enjoyable./I'm not crazy about them. I think they're boring.*

5 COLLOCATIONS Fill in: *blockbuster, special, big, bad, celebrity, live-action.* Use the phrases in sentences of your own.

1 a .... film
2 a .... TV series
3 the .... screen
4 .... effects
5 .... guy
6 .... guest

6 PREPOSITIONS Fill in: *about, on, in, at, to.*

DID YOU KNOW?

- The only characters that appear **1)** .... all the *Star Wars* films are C-3PO and R2-D2.
- The sentence "I have a bad feeling **2)** .... this" is said in every film.
- Luke's name was changed from Luke Starkiller **3)** .... Skywalker.
- R2-D2 stands **4)** .... a height of 96 cm.
- The *Millennium Falcon's* design, which is a spaceship, was partly based **5)** .... a burger George Lucas was eating at the time.

7 WORDS EASILY CONFUSED Choose the correct word. Check in your dictionary. Make sentences using the other words.

1 **Spectators/Audiences** loved the first *Star Wars* film.

2 The special **effects/affects** are out of this world.

3 The film was so popular that we waited in the queue **outside/outdoors** the cinema for an hour.

4 George Lucas **created/did** *Star Wars* over forty years ago.

5 Kurt Russell and Sylvester Stallone were some of the actors who wanted to **act/play** the role of Han Solo.

8 PHRASAL VERBS Fill in the correct particle(s).

> **give sth away:** to ruin a surprise
> **give back:** to return sth
> **give in: 1)** to finally agree to what sb wants; **2)** to stop fighting or competing
> **give up:** to stop doing sth you used to do regularly

1 Sam gave .... trying to become a film actor.

2 Did you give .... Mark's *Star Wars* DVD?

3 Han Solo never gives .... without a fight.

4 I bought Ruby a Darth Vader action figure as a surprise, but Tom gave it ....

Speaking & Writing

9 ICT Think of your favourite film. Collect information and prepare a 'Did you know?' fact sheet with 5 facts. Present it to the class.

Grammar in Use

1 Do the quiz.

🎧 Listen and check your answers.

FILM
Quiz

1 When were the first Oscars awarded?
   A 1929 **B** 1949 **C** 1969

2 What was George Lucas's dog named?
   A Chewie **B** Indiana **C** Luke

3 Which was the first film to be filmed in Iceland?
   A *Land Ho!* **B** *Noah*
   C *Sons of the Soil*

4 How many Oscars were won by the film *Jaws*?
   A 3 **B** 0 **C** 1

5 Which of these films wasn't directed by Steven Spielberg?
   A *Hook* **B** *The Post* **C** *Good Time*

2 Read the theory and find examples in the quiz.

The passive (*to be* + past participle of the main verb) ▶ pp. GR8-9

	Active		Passive
Present simple:	watch	→	is watched
Present continuous:	is making	→	is being made
Past simple:	gave	→	was given
Past continuous:	was playing	→	was being played
Present perfect:	has seen	→	has been seen
Past perfect:	had taken	→	had been taken
Future simple:	will open	→	will be opened
Modals:	can sing	→	can be sung

We use the passive when the action is more important than the agent.
*The film **was shot** in Iceland.*
The agent (*by ...*) is omitted when it is not important or is easily understood.
*The tickets **have been sent** to my phone.* – agent not important (by the cinema)
*The film **will be released** next year.* – agent easily understood (by the company)
Note: When we turn an active sentence, which includes a preposition after the verb, into the passive voice, the preposition remains after the verb.
*They **turned** the lights **off** when the film began.* → *The lights **were turned off** when the film began.*

3 Read sentences A & B. Identify the *subject* (S), the *verb* (V) and the *object* (O) in sentence A. Then, answer the questions.

A George Lucas directed *Star Wars Episode IV: A New Hope*. **(active)**

B *Star Wars Episode IV: A New Hope* was directed by George Lucas. **(passive)**

1 What changes do you notice in sentence B?
2 How do we form the passive?
3 In which sentence is the action more important than the person who does it?
4 In which sentence is the person more important than the action?

4 Choose the correct item.

1 Reviewers were **showed/shown** the film last week.
2 DVDs of the play can **buy/be bought** online.
3 The actors **are being/are** interviewed at the moment.
4 His next film **had/will be** based on a true story.
5 The film **has/was** been awarded seven Oscars.
6 Visitors **will/are** not allowed on the film set.

5 Read the theory, then use *with* or *by* to complete the sentences.

with/by ▶ p. GR9

with + instrument/material/ingredient – *The film was shot **with** special 3D cameras.*
by + person/people – *The space battles were created **by** the special effects team.*

1 The sound of fire was made .... plastic bags.
2 *Hamlet* was written .... William Shakespeare.
3 Film blood is often made .... corn syrup.
4 The song from *Titanic* was sung .... Celine Dion.
5 The award will be presented .... Leonardo DiCaprio.

6 a) Read questions A & B and say how we form passive questions with *who*. Can we omit *by* in this type of passive question?

A Who directed *Mamma Mia! Here We Go Again*? **(active)**

B Who was *Mamma Mia! Here We Go Again* directed by? **(passive)**

b) Rewrite the following questions in the passive. Then, in pairs, ask and answer using the facts in the list.

• Marvel Studios • Steven Spielberg • John Williams • Adele • J. K. Rowling • Sir Arthur Conan Doyle

1 Who directed *Jurassic Park*?
Who was Jurassic Park directed by?
It was directed by Steven Spielberg.

2 Who sang the title song from the film *Skyfall*?

3 Who wrote the Harry Potter books?

4 Who composed the music to *Star Wars*?

5 Who created the character of Sherlock Holmes?

6 Which film studio made *Avengers: Infinity War*?

7 Rewrite the headlines in the passive.

> **FILM PREMIERE CALLED OFF YESTERDAY BECAUSE OF BAD WEATHER**

....

> **NEW CINEMA TO BE OPENED BY MAYOR MONDAY EVENING**

....

> **'DUNKIRK' AWARDED THREE OSCARS LAST NIGHT**

....

> **CINEMA DESTROYED IN FIRE LAST SATURDAY**

....

> **Theatre thieves still not caught**

....

8 Complete the second sentence so that it means the same as the first. Use two to five words, including the word in bold.

1 Steven Spielberg directed the film. **BY**
The film .... Steven Spielberg.

2 They will close the theatre soon. **BE**
The theatre .... soon.

3 He made me pay for the tickets. **WAS**
I .... for the tickets.

4 The secretary has sent the invitations. **HAVE**
The invitations .... by the secretary.

5 The usher showed us to our seats. **WERE**
We . ... by the usher.

6 You can book tickets to the concert online. **BE**
Tickets to the concert .... online.

Reflexive/Emphatic pronouns ▷ p. GR9

We use **reflexive pronouns** when the subject and the object of the verb are the same person. *He introduced himself to the members of the club.*
We use **emphatic pronouns** to emphasise the subject or the object of a sentence. *The Queen herself opened the new cinema.* (It was actually the Queen.)

---

9 Fill in the correct pronoun. Decide when it is reflexive *(R)* or emphatic *(E)*.

1 He cut *himself* while he was putting out the props for the performance.   *R*

2 They .... put up all the posters.   ....

3 Lisa taught .... how to edit her videos.   ....

4 The actor .... signed the autographs.   ....

5 Look at .... in the mirror.   ....

6 The President .... attended the opening night of the play.   ....

7 Don't hurt .... when you climb down from the stage.   ....

8 Ted burnt .... when he was making popcorn for the film.   ....

10 THINK Prepare a quiz like the one on p. 48. Use the passive.

Skills in Action

Vocabulary

Types of TV programmes

1 Discuss the types of TV programmes shown in the TV guide. Use the adjectives in the list and follow the example.

- great • interesting • amusing • funny • silly
- awful • boring • terrible

Friday 3/12	18:00	19:00	19:30	20:00
Prime Channel	News at Six (news)	Victoria Road (soap opera)	Fix it! (DIY programme)	Sleeping on the Streets (documentary)
Star Two	Katy's Kitchen (cookery programme)	Time to Talk with Ruby Kent (chat show)	The Crazy Crew (sitcom)	Ocean's Eight (film)
Three 4 Me	3 – 2 – Win! (game show)	Off the Beaten Track (travel show)	Winter Birds (wildlife programme)	The Model Life! (reality show)

A: *Do you watch game shows?*
B: *To be honest, I'm not a fan. I find them boring. I prefer cookery programmes.*
A: *Oh! I love cookery programmes, too.*

Listening

2 You will hear three short recordings. Read the questions and look at the pictures. Listen and put a tick (✓) in the correct box for each question.

1 What time does the film start?

A ☐   B ☐   C ☐

2 How much does a ticket cost?

A ☐   B ☐   C ☐

3 What will they watch on TV tonight?

A ☐   B ☐   C ☐

Everyday English

Making a recommendation

3 a) Ann and Bob are talking about a TV series. Use sentences A-F to complete their dialogue. Two sentences are extra.

A What's it about, anyway?
B What day is it on?
C Is it any good?
D You can stream it online.
E What did you like so much about it?
F I don't want to spoil it for you.

> **Ann:** Have you seen *Stranger Things* yet?
> **Bob:** No, I haven't. **1)** ....
> **Ann:** Yeah, it's amazing. You really must see it.
> **Bob:** **2)** ....
> **Ann:** Well, the acting is excellent. The cast is so talented.
> **Bob:** I see. **3)** ....
> **Ann:** It's a sci-fi story about strange disappearances and secret experiments.
> **Bob:** Sounds interesting. Tell me more!
> **Ann:** **4)** .... You'll have to see it yourself.

b) Listen and check.

4 Act out similar dialogues about a new film/TV series you have recently seen. Use language from the language box.

Asking about a film/TV series	Recommending
• Was it any good? • What's it about? • Who stars in it? • What did you like most?	• It's a must-see. • You won't regret it! • You mustn't miss it!

Pronunciation /ʌ/, /æ/

5 Listen and tick. Listen again and repeat.

	/ʌ/	/æ/		/ʌ/	/æ/
fan			rang		
fun			rung		
sang			stunned		
sung			stand		

Reading & Writing

Writing Tip

Tenses in reviews
We use present tenses to describe the plot of a film/book.

6 Read the review and fill in the gaps with adjectives formed from the words in brackets. What tenses has the writer used? What is each paragraph about? Has the writer revealed the end of the film? Why/Why not?

FILM Reviews

A If you're a fan of **1)** .... **(excite)** action films, then *Avengers: Infinity War* is just the film for you. It was directed by Anthony and Joe Russo and stars Robert Downey Jr., Chris Hemsworth, Mark Ruffalo and Chris Evans.

B The Avengers including Iron Man, Thor, Hulk, Captain America and their friends come together again to save the universe. They need all the help they can get to try to defeat the **2)** .... **(power)** Thanos who wants to wipe out half of all life everywhere using the Infinity Stones. Can the Avengers stop him?

C All the actors are really **3)** .... **(talent)** and there are some **4)** .... **(amaze)** performances. This film has lots of action and the special effects are extremely **5)** .... **(real)**.

D *Avengers: Infinity War* is a **6)** .... **(wonder)** film for anyone who loves action-adventure blockbusters. Don't miss it!

7 Find the word that does not belong in each sentence. Check in your dictionary.

1 The cast is **amazing/talented/fast**.
2 The special effects are **fantastic/imaginative/slow**.
3 The acting is **excellent/tired/terrible**.
4 The characters are **slow/brilliant/boring**.
5 The plot is **clever/interesting/excited**.
6 The script is **well-written/bored/original**.

Recommending/Criticising

8 a) Which of the expressions below would be used for recommending or criticising a film?

- Don't miss it. I highly recommend it.
- It was disappointing. I wouldn't recommend it.
- It's worth seeing. You should try to see it.
- Don't bother. It's a waste of time.

b) 🗣️ Read the exchange. Does the speaker recommend the film or not? Act out similar exchanges recommending or criticising a film.

A: *Have you seen 'Aquaman'?*
B: *Yes, I have. The special effects are amazing. Don't miss it!*

Writing (a film review)

9 Read the task. Find the key words, then complete the spidergram in your notebook.

Your college English magazine wants reviews about favourite films. Write a review of your favourite film. (120-150 words).

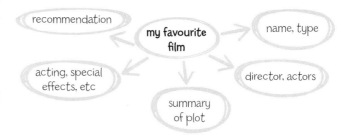

recommendation — my favourite film → name, type
acting, special effects, etc — director, actors
summary of plot

10 Use your notes in Ex. 9 to write your review. Follow the plan.

Plan

Introduction
Para 1: title, type, director, actors
Main body
Para 2: main points of the plot
Para 3: acting, special effects, etc
Conclusion
Para 4: recommendation

VALUES

Openness
Cinema is universal, beyond flags and borders and passports.
Alejandro González Iñárritu

▶ VIDEO

The Royal Albert Hall's Festival of Film
Celebrating movie magic and cinema's best soundtracks

29th Sept – 6th Nov

Celebrating Soundtracks

007 drives off in his sports car to the sound of the James Bond **theme**. The *Star Wars* theme takes the audience to another galaxy, and the music to *Jurassic Park* welcomes us to a world of dinosaurs. All blockbuster films have a soundtrack that adds extra excitement to the film, and sometimes you remember the music more than the film itself.

The Festival of Film is a celebration of film music that **1)** .... every year at the Royal Albert Hall in London, UK. There are **showings** of famous films as well as **2)** .... orchestral performances of film music. There are interviews with composers and also exhibitions and other special events. The festival takes **3)** .... every autumn.

One of the organisers, Lucy Noble, believes that the festival "is introducing people to classical music and orchestras without them **realising**. They come for the title of the film and **4)** .... of those people have never seen an orchestra before. They are having an introduction to classical music **5)** .... watching a film." She adds that, "it's not your **typical** film festival. We are bringing music to the centre stage."

Reading & Listening

1 🎧 **Listen and match the extracts to the types of music.**

a ☐ dance   c ☐ hip hop   e ☐ rock
b ☐ classical   d ☐ jazz   f ☐ Latin

2 Read the poster. What type of music do you think you can hear at the Festival of Film? Read the text to find out.

3 Read the text and fill in the gaps (1-5) with the correct item (A-D). 🎧 Listen and check. Then, explain the words in bold.

	A	B	C	D
1	is held	holds	has held	is holding
2	alive	live	living	lively
3	over	after	place	off
4	lot	many	much	more
5	as	because	then	while

✓ Check these words

soundtrack, excitement, orchestral performance

Speaking & Writing

4 💬 THINK What films would you present at a film music festival? Why? Present your ideas to the class.

5 💬 ICT Collect information about a music or film festival in your country. Prepare a poster advertising it.

Vocabulary

1 **Choose the correct word.**

1 Fans **appeared/demanded** a second film.
2 The new **sitcom/thriller** is very amusing.
3 Do you like action and **crime/adventure** films?
4 Sally can't wait for new **episodes/shows** of her favourite TV series.
5 Did you see any **celebrities/audiences** at the event?
6 *Star Wars* quickly became a **catchphrase/blockbuster**.
7 The **audience/actors** went quiet as the film began.
8 We waited in the **force/queue** in the rain for tickets.

(8 x 2 = 16)

2 **Fill in:** *chat, reality, special effects, documentary, series, soap, role, animated.*

1 There's a wildlife .... on TV tonight.
2 The special .... are out of this world.
3 I hate watching .... operas.
4 Katy has a small .... in the film.
5 The actor talked about her new film on the .... show.
6 The .... show puts celebrities in the jungle.
7 Walt Disney produced .... films kids loved all around the world.
8 *The Force Awakens* is another sequel in the Star Wars ....

(8 x 2 = 16)

3 **Choose the correct item.**

1 He has appeared **to/in** every film of the series.
2 She changed her name **to/at** Margo.
3 Don't give **up/away** the surprise.
4 He gave **in/back** without a fight.
5 A colleague introduced me **on/to** the Star War films.

(5 x 3 = 15)

Grammar

4 **Complete the sentences with the correct passive form of the verb in brackets. Fill in** *by* **or** *with*.

1 A film .... **(shot)** in our area these days .... a famous director.
2 All the walls .... **(already/ cover)** .... film posters.
3 Swords that actors use .... **(not/make)** .... real metal.
4 The band Imagine Dragons .... **(love)** .... millions of fans.
5 The play .... **(review)** .... a theatre critic last week.
6 The festival tickets .... **(book)** online .... Mike tomorrow.

(6 x 3 = 18)

5 **Choose the correct reflexive/emphatic pronoun.**

1 We **ourselves/myself** filmed the movie.
2 They **themselves/ourselves** made the poster.
3 The actor looked at **himself/yourself** in the mirror.
4 Tina fell off the stage and hurt **myself/herself**.
5 Did you write the music and lyrics **himself/yourself**?

(5 x 3 = 15)

Everyday English

6 **Match the sentences.**

1 ☐ Is it any good?
2 ☐ What's it about?
3 ☐ What did you like about it?
4 ☐ When is it on?

a The special effects were amazing.
b It's amazing. Don't miss it.
c Next Monday.
d It's a drama about two sisters.

(4 x 5 = 20)

Total 100

Values: Self-confidence

 ▶ VIDEO

Ask the experts ...

Home   Ask Question   Questions ∨   User ∨   Contact Us

Your first stop online for expert advice   Join Now

Q: How can I make sure I give a good speech?

 I've been asked to give a speech at the opening night of a film festival in my city. It's going to take place in ten days' time and I've written the speech. The problem is – I'm terrified! I've never done it before and I'm sure I'll just **dry up** the minute I go on stage. I'll just be standing there like an idiot in front of 200 people, saying nothing.

[Mark Lewis, student]

A: Lots of people have a fear or even a phobia of speaking in front of an audience. And everyone feels nervous the first time they do it! Here are some **tips** to make sure you won't 'dry up'!

Feel confident

It all begins on the inside. You won't come across as confident if you're not confident about your **material**. You say you have your speech ready, but have you practised it? Stand in front of a mirror and deliver it. Don't forget to time it to see if it's too short or too long. Then try again. This time, film yourself doing it, then watch the video to see what you can **improve**.

Look confident

If you **deliver** your speech with your head down and a sad look on your face, you won't connect with your audience – no matter how good your speech is. Look up at the ceiling just before you go in front of your audience, because this will **lighten** your expression. Stand up straight with your head high – a good trick is to look at a member of the audience towards the back of the room. Look down at your cue cards only when you're moving on to the next point.

Sound confident

A dull voice is not interesting to listeners, and a low voice is just as annoying. Again, record yourself. Can you understand what you're saying? If not, you're going to have to **raise your voice**. Speak loudly and clearly. You don't have to shout – just think about that poor person at the back, trying to hear you. And don't **rush** – you're not trying to win a race!

[Lorraine Principal, public speaking coach]

1 Read the question (Q) at the beginning of the advice column. What advice do you think might be given?

🎧 Listen and read to find out.

2 Read the text again and decide if the sentences are *T* (True), *F* (False) or *DS* (Doesn't Say). Then explain the words in bold.

1 Mark Lewis is making a speech for the first time. ....
2 Lorraine Principal has worked with many first-time public speakers. ....
3 She says Mark should watch himself making the speech. ....
4 She advises Mark to look at the ceiling while speaking. ....
5 She recommends speaking quickly. ....

3 THINK Give three reasons why someone might feel unconfident about a presentation and what he/she could do to feel more confident.

4 ICT Research other tips for feeling confident when giving a speech. Tell the class.

Public Speaking Skills

1 Read the task. What type of speech is it asking for?

> You are in a film club that is putting on a festival in honour of a famous director. You have been asked to give a speech about the director and the film the audience will be watching.

2 🎧 Listen to and read the model. Number the cue cards correctly. Complete the gaps (1-3).

A ☐

- *Ready Player One*: sci-fi, 2018
- set in 2045, the OASIS
- Wade Watts (**1**) ....), Nolan Sorrento (Ben Mendelsohn)
- fast-moving, amazing special effects, familiar characters

B ☐

- "Every time I go to a movie, it's magic, no matter what the movie's about."
- Steven Spielberg
- *Jaws*, the Indiana Jones films, *Jurassic Park*, **2)** ....

C ☐

- born Ohio, USA, **3)** ....
- first film aged 12
- job at Universal Studios
- *Jaws*
- sci-fi films

3 **ICT** Think of a famous director. Research him/her and complete the spidergram. Make sure the information you find is accurate. Use your notes to make cue cards and give a speech introducing him/her and the film the audience will be watching.

- description of film showing
- biggest films
- director
- career
- early life

Good evening, film fans, and welcome to our annual film festival, where every year we celebrate a different director.

"Every time I go to a movie, it's magic, no matter what the movie's about." These are the words of Steven Spielberg, and show his deep love of film-making, which has made him one of the most important directors of all time. We'll be watching some of his classics this week, such as *Jaws*, the Indiana Jones films, *Jurassic Park* and *War of the Worlds*, as well as some of his more recent films.

Spielberg was born in Ohio, USA, in 1946. He made his first film aged 12, and continued writing and directing small films with his friends in his teens. While at university, he was offered a job at Universal Studios, where his work was so impressive that he was made a director. He dropped out of university and never looked back. His first big success was *Jaws*, that famous thriller about a giant shark, and he went on to make one blockbuster after another. He has made nearly every type of film, but one of his great loves has always been sci-fi, and we're going to see one of those today.

Ready Player One is a sci-fi film that was released in 2018. It is set in 2045, when most people spend more and more of their time in a virtual reality world called the OASIS. The main character, Wade Watts, who is played by Tye Sheridan, has to win a special game to take control of the OASIS, and stop it destroying people's lives. But he has to compete against a big company run by businessman Nolan Sorrento, played by Ben Mendelsohn. It's a fast-moving film with amazing special effects and lots of familiar characters from films and video games over the past 40 years.

I'm sure you'll enjoy it just as much as I did. Now I'm going to let the film speak for itself. Thank you for your time and let me present: Steven Spielberg's *Ready Player One*!

Vocabulary: disasters; emergency services
Grammar: reported speech (statements, questions, orders, instructions, commands), *say – tell*, special introductory verbs

Everyday English: calling the emergency services
Writing: a news report

7 Narrow Escapes

Vocabulary

Disasters

1 Choose the correct item. Check in your dictionary.

1 DOZENS TRAPPED IN CARS IN LAST NIGHT'S **FLOOD/EXPLOSION**

2 Hundreds of flights cancelled because of ash from **earthquake/volcanic eruption**

3 **Fire/Thunderstorm** in Dane Forest now under control

4 RESCUERS SEARCH RUBBLE AFTER **EARTHQUAKE/HEAVY SNOWFALL** HITS

5 GAS **EXPLOSION/TYPHOON** IN FACTORY INJURES 70

6 MAN BURIED IN **EARTHQUAKE/AVALANCHE** FOR 5 HOURS SURVIVES

2 Match disasters 1-6 in Ex. 1 to comments (A-F).

A ◯ The whole building was shaking!

B ◯ There was a loud bang and we ran outside.

C ◯ It spread quickly because of the wind.

D ◯ I was waiting patiently on the roof of my house for the rescue boats to come.

E ◯ He ignored the warning signs for skiers.

F ◯ We saw lava running down the mountainside.

Listening & Reading

3 Read the title and look at the map. What do you think the text is about?

🎧 Listen to and read the text to find out.

Rescued
from the Depths

BOYS FOUND

PATTAYA BEACH

On Tuesday, 10th July, a cave in northern Thailand made international news when a difficult rescue was successfully completed there. Twelve boys and their football coach were **trapped** inside the six-mile-long Tham Luang cave near the town of Mae Sai for over two weeks.

The boys – aged 11 to 17 – went to **explore** the cave with their coach, 25-year-old Ekkapol Chantawong, on 23rd June. It was a place they often visited, but this time heavy rains flooded the cave and they couldn't get out. They found a high rock to sit on, four kilometres inside the cave. Their mobile phones didn't work and they had to wait for nine days in the dark before help came.

Outside the cave, a huge search began after the boys' bicycles were found there. Divers searched the dark, narrow, rocky tunnels, which were full of water. Conditions got worse as the heavy rains continued and the water got higher.

4 a) Read the text and for questions 1-4 choose the best answer (A, B, C or D).

1 What is the writer doing in the text?
  A describing his role as part of a rescue team
  B warning people about the dangers of caving
  C explaining how to prepare for a visit to a cave
  D reporting an event of major world interest

2 What does the writer say about the search?
  A Some rescuers got stuck in the tunnels.
  B Lots of people were involved.
  C The search began at night.
  D The equipment was very heavy.

VIDEO

ENTRANCE

NARROW FLOODED PASSAGE

Then, on 2nd July, two British divers finally **discovered** the group. Amazingly, everyone was alive and unhurt. When the boys said they were hungry and asked what day it was, the divers told them it was Monday and they promised to return with food, lights and blankets.

Up above, teams hurried to organise the group's rescue; they were afraid of more rain to come. Meanwhile, divers brought the boys and their coach supplies. It took six days before anyone could leave. Because of the flooded tunnels, the only way out was through the water. Each boy had to put on scuba **gear**. Then he was tied to a diver, who swam out with him on a dangerous five-hour journey. The rescue took three days, with the last four boys and their coach getting out on 10th July.

They were all immediately taken to hospital, where they **recovered** quickly. The young players and their parents all thanked the coach for his **efforts** inside the cave. He found clean water for the boys to drink and helped them to stay **calm**. As an old teammate said about him, "He took care of all the boys in there. He was a real hero."

✓ **Check these words**

rescue, narrow, conditions, alive, unhurt, promise, meanwhile, supplies, tie

3 When the British divers discovered the boys, they were
  A keen to get them out at once.
  B worried more floods would stop the rescue.
  C surprised to find everyone was all right.
  D unsure about when they would return.

4 What does the writer conclude about the coach?
  A He made a big mistake.
  B He was thankful to the rescuers.
  C He tried very hard to escape.
  D He acted in a responsible way.

b) **Explain the words in bold.**

5 **COLLOCATIONS** Fill in: *scuba, football, real, international, flooded, clean, huge, heavy.* **Use the phrases to make sentences based on the text.**

1 .... news
5 .... water
2 .... coach
6 .... tunnels
3 .... rains
7 .... gear
4 .... search
8 .... hero

6 **PREPOSITIONS** Fill in: *on, out, to, with, for, in.*

1 The cave was flooded .... water.
2 They had to sit .... a high rock.
3 They waited five days .... help to come.
4 The boys waited .... the dark.
5 The boys swam .... of the cave to safety.
6 They took them all .... hospital.

7 **WORDS EASILY CONFUSED** **Choose the correct item. Check in your dictionary.**

1 The town was **hit/beaten** by a devastating earthquake.
2 We heard someone **striking/knocking** on the door.
3 The house was **struck/beaten** by lightning.

8 **PHRASAL VERBS** **Fill in the correct particle.**

put out: to stop a fire burning
put up: to let sb stay in your house
put on: to cover part of one's body with clothes, shoes, etc
put off: to postpone

1 They put .... their helmets and entered the cave.
2 He put .... the trip until the rain stopped.
3 Bill put us .... for the night as we couldn't find anywhere else to stay.
4 Don't forget to put .... the fire before you go to bed.

Speaking & Writing

9 **ICT** **Find more information about this rescue. Prepare cards with notes about it. Imagine you are one of the rescue divers. Give the class a presentation.**

Grammar in Use

Tragedy at Sea

*E*va Hart was only seven years old when she and her parents boarded the brand-new ship Titanic in 1912. Everyone said it was impossible for the ship to sink because it was so big. But Eva's mother felt worried and couldn't sleep on the first night. Eva asked her why she wasn't sleeping. She said she had a bad feeling. On the night of 14th April, Mrs Hart felt something. "Will you go and check what's happening?" she asked her husband. When he came back, he said to them, "We've hit an iceberg. We need to go up on deck now!" When they got there, the crew told people not to panic. Mr Hart quickly helped his wife and daughter into a lifeboat. "Hold your mother's hand," he said to Eva as she got on board. He stayed to help the other passengers, but there weren't enough lifeboats. Eva never saw him again.

Reported speech ▷ p. GR10

1 a) Study the examples and answer the questions.

Direct speech: *"We need to go up on deck now!" he said to them.*

Reported speech: *He told them (that) they needed to go up on deck immediately.*

1 How do pronouns change in reported speech?

2 What happens to the tenses in reported speech?

3 What do you notice about the quotation marks?

4 How does the time word *now* change in reported speech?

b) Find examples of direct/reported statements in the newspaper clipping.

2 Fill in the gaps with *said* or *told*.

1 "Bring an umbrella in case it rains," he .... to me.

2 Susan .... the class about her lucky escape.

3 They .... that the weather on their trip was terrible.

4 "Don't light a fire. It's too warm!" she .... to him.

5 Mark .... them they could explore the cave.

6 Peter .... that he would join the rescuers.

7 Grace .... us that she saw the accident.

8 She .... that she couldn't sleep that night.

3 Rewrite the sentences in reported speech.

1 "This is bad news," they said to us.
   They told us (that) that was bad news.

2 "I'm phoning the ambulance now," the man said.
   ....

3 "We won't go out tonight because of the storm," Craig said to his wife.
   ....

4 "They have just cleared the snow from the roads round here," the man said.
   ....

5 "I took a photo of the accident this morning," the man said to the police.
   ....

6 "They have been fighting the fire all afternoon," the reporter said.
   ....

7 "It was raining here yesterday," my friend said to me.
   ....

4 Study the examples. Then answer the questions. Find examples in the newspaper clipping.

Reported speech (questions) ▷ p. GR11

Direct speech: *"Are the boys alone?" a reporter **asked** the locals.*

Reported speech: *A reporter **asked** the locals **if/whether** the boys **were** alone.*

Direct speech: *"Where did these men come from?" they **asked** each other.*

Reported speech: *They **asked** each other **where** those men **had come** from.*

1 Which introductory verb is used in reported questions?

2 When do we use *if/whether* in reported questions?

3 What is the word order in a reported question when the direct question begins with a *wh*-question word?

5 Rewrite the questions Lucy Parker asked a motorist in reported speech, as in the example.

1 "Do you mind answering a few questions, sir?"
She asked him if/whether he minded answering a few questions.

2 "Where were you driving to in the snowstorm?"
....

3 "How long were you trapped in your car?"
....

4 "When did the emergency services arrive?"
....

5 "Have you ever had a similar experience?"
....

6 "Are you planning to buy snow chains for your car?"
....

6 Study the examples. Find examples in the newspaper clipping on p. 58.

Reported speech (orders, instructions, commands) ▷ p. GR11

Direct speech: *"Hold your mother's hand," he said to me.*
Reported speech: *He told me to hold my mother's hand.*
Direct speech: *"Don't play on the rocks, Patrick!" his mother said.*
Reported speech: *Patrick's mother told him not to play on the rocks.*

7 Match the pictures to the orders and report them. Start with: *I told her* ...

1 ☐ Don't let the children play near the pool!
2 ☐ Keep hot irons away from the kids.
3 ☐ Keep medicines out of reach of the children.
4 ☐ Don't leave the candle burning during the night.

Reported speech (reporting verbs) ▷ pp. GR11-12

We can use a variety of **reporting verbs** instead of *said/told* in reported speech (for advice, invitations, offers, suggestions, requests, etc.).
Direct speech: *"Let's go to the shelter," he said.*
Reported speech: *He suggested going to the shelter.*

8 Read the theory. Rewrite the sentences in reported speech using the verbs in brackets, as in the example. Check in the Grammar Reference section.

1 "I think you should call the fire service," she said to them. **(ADVISE)**
She advised them to call the fire service.

2 "Don't go too near the edge of the cliff," the teacher said to the children. **(WARN)**

3 "I'm sorry I didn't check the weather forecast," she said. **(APOLOGISE)**

4 "I'll return very soon with some help," he said. **(PROMISE)**

5 "Can I give you a tour of the volcano?" the guide asked us. **(OFFER)**

6 "Yes, I'll bring my first aid kit along," said Tom. **(AGREE)**

9 Complete the sentences using the words in bold. Use no more than three words, as in the example.

1 "Be careful on the ski slopes," the instructor said to us. **TOLD**
The instructor *told us to* be careful on the ski slopes.

2 "Have you visited the volcano yet?" he asked me. **HAD**
He asked me .... visited the volcano yet.

3 "Don't forget to take a map," Dad said to us. **NOT**
Dad told us .... to take a map.

4 "What were you doing when the earthquake hit?" my friend asked me. **BEEN**
My friend asked me what I .... when the earthquake hit.

5 "The mayor will visit the flood victims tomorrow," said the journalist. **THE**
The journalist said the mayor would visit the flood victims .... day.

10 SPEAKING 💬 Two students act out a short dialogue about a disaster. A third student reports the dialogue to another group.

Skills in Action

Vocabulary

Emergency services

1 Which of the following services do we contact when there is a(n): *fire*? *crime*? *medical emergency*? *boating accident*? *rock-climbing accident*? *emergency underground*?

1 the police
2 the fire service
3 the coastguard
4 the mountain rescue service
5 the ambulance service
6 the cave rescue service

2 Match the services in Ex. 1 to the TV reporter's comments (A-F).

A ☐ A group of ten students were trapped underground for two days.

B ☐ **The man told rescuers he had been lucky to reach the summit with just a broken ankle.**

C ☐ A cloud of dark smoke can be seen from fifty miles away.

D ☐ **An eyewitness said she saw someone behaving suspiciously outside the bank.**

E ☐ Six people were rushed to hospital suffering from severe burns.

F ☐ The man got into difficulties when his boat started letting in water.

Listening

3 🎧 You will hear a news report about a natural disaster. For questions 1-4, choose the best answer (A, B, C or D).

1 Where are the fires?
   A 900 km from Sydney   C close to Sydney
   B in Sydney   D 2,000 km from Sydney

2 What is NOT true about the fires?
   A Some residents lost their homes.
   B Electricity supplies were affected.
   C Some people were killed.
   D They caused damage to farms.

3 What started the fires?
   A the weather   C a campfire
   B a barbecue   D criminal activity

4 What does David Owens say about the fires?
   A They can put them out this weekend.
   B The weather could make them worse.
   C The weather forecast is not always reliable.
   D They have been burning all week.

Everyday English

Calling the emergency services

4 a) Read sentences A-D. What seems to be the problem? Complete the dialogue.

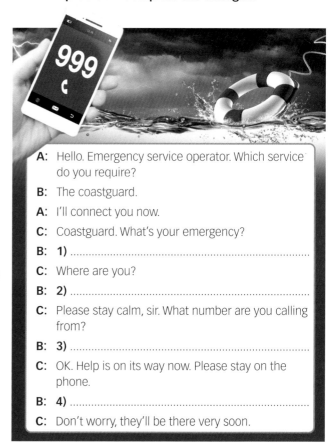

A: Hello. Emergency service operator. Which service do you require?

B: The coastguard.

A: I'll connect you now.

C: Coastguard. What's your emergency?

B: 1) ....

C: Where are you?

B: 2) ....

C: Please stay calm, sir. What number are you calling from?

B: 3) ....

C: OK. Help is on its way now. Please stay on the phone.

B: 4) ....

C: Don't worry, they'll be there very soon.

A I'm not exactly sure, but somewhere in Mount's Bay.

B Please help! There's a terrible storm and the boat's letting in water!

C Will they be long?

D I don't know ... I need help quickly ... I'm sinking!

b) 🎧 Listen and check.

5 💬 There's a fire in your kitchen, which was started by the microwave oven. Act out a dialogue similar to the one in Ex. 4.

Pronunciation: /tʃ/, /dʒ/

6 🎧 Listen and tick. Then listen and repeat.

	/tʃ/	/dʒ/		/tʃ/	/dʒ/
damage			injury		
chicken			coach		
reach			emergency		

Reading & Writing

7 a) Read the news report and put the paragraphs in the correct order. What is each paragraph about?

Typhoon Jebi hits Japan

A ☐ The typhoon struck at 12 noon local time. Ten people have been killed and over 200 injured. Over one million homes are without electricity and hundreds of buildings and vehicles have been destroyed. The storm trapped 3,000 people at Osaka International Airport when floods covered the whole airport runway. The only **1)** .... (suit) means of rescue was by speedboat.

B ☐ The government has said it will do everything it can to get things back to normal as soon as possible, but local people are shocked. "It was **2)** .... (terror)," said a local man. "When you lose your home in a **3)** .... (nature) disaster like this, everything seems so **4)** .... (hope)!"

C ☐ A powerful typhoon reached Japan early on Tuesday morning, with strong 162-kilometre-per-hour winds, heavy rain and giant waves. This is the country's worst **5)** .... **(environment)** disaster for many years. In cities like Kyoto and Osaka, the government advised over one million people to leave their homes.

Word formation (forming adjectives)
- We can form adjectives from **nouns** by adding **-less** *(care – careless)*, **-able/-ible** *(fashion – fashionable / horror – horrible)*, **-al** *(function – functional)*.

b) Read the article again and fill in the gaps with adjectives derived from the words in brackets.

 Writing Tip

News reports

A news report differs from a story. It gives only **facts** whereas a story has a personal, chatty style. A news report always has a **headline** and does not contain the writer's feelings or emotions. It is written in a **formal, impersonal style** using **full verb forms** and the **passive voice**. **Direct speech** can be used to mention people's comments.

8 Read the tip. Find examples in the news report in Ex. 7.

9 Read the extract. Rewrite it in an impersonal style.

Everyone's talking about a shocking gas explosion that ripped through a chemical factory in Birmingham this morning. It injured loads of people when it blew out the windows. One factory worker said that he was very lucky that he hadn't been at work that day. They're now carrying out repairs. Let's hope the factory will reopen in the coming week.

Writing (a news report)

10 a) Look at the picture and the list of words/phrases. What kind of news report do you expect to hear? *people injured, lost their homes, damaged buildings, electrical problems, rubble.*

b) 🎧 Listen and complete the spidergram in your notebook.

11 Using the information from Ex. 10, write your news report (120-150 words). Follow the plan.

Plan

Title
Para 1: summary of the event (what, when, where, who)
Para 2: detailed description; consequences; action taken
Para 3: people's comments & ongoing action

VALUES

Compassion
True compassion means not only feeling another's pain but also being moved to help relieve it. **Daniel Goleman**

PUDDING LANE EC3
CITY OF LONDON

The Great FiRE of London

1 ☐

London in the 17th century had a population of 350,000, making it one of the biggest cities in Europe. The Port of London did trade with places all over the world and some of London's greatest architecture was built then. With its royal court and its high society and fashion, London was the place to be!

2 ☐

Then, around the middle of the century, **disaster** struck! The Great Plague **broke out** in London in 1665 and soon **spread** over the country. It was a terrible disease and more than 60,000 people died as there was no cure. Then, as if that wasn't enough, the very next year in 1666, the Great Fire of London happened.

3 ☐

It all started with a **careless** mistake in a bakery. Thomas Farynor, a baker with a shop in Pudding Lane near London Bridge, had not **put out** the oven fire properly when he went to bed. His family woke up on Sunday, 2nd September to a house filled with smoke. There was no fire service in London back then. People just used buckets of water, so the fire soon spread.

4 ☐

Within minutes, the houses near the bakery were also on fire. It had been a long, hot, dry summer, which made them burn very easily. And when a strong east wind started blowing, that helped the fire even more! People decided to **knock down** some buildings to stop the fire from spreading. But, as they were made of wood, this just made it spread faster!

5 ☐

The guards of the Tower of London **blew up** some buildings with gunpowder. This helped to get the fire under control. On 5th September, it was finally over, but London was a horrible smoking ruin. Only six people were reported dead, but over 13,000 houses were destroyed, leaving 70,000 people without homes.

6 ☐

London took thirty years to rebuild. As well as homes, many important buildings were lost. The great English architect Sir Christopher Wren rebuilt much of the city after the disaster. His Monument to the Great Fire can still be seen in London today.

✓ **Check these words**

trade, royal court, high society, cure, guard, gunpowder, ruin

Listening & Reading

1 Read the title, then look at the pictures. How are they related to the Great Fire of London?

🎧 Listen and read to find out. Then explain the words in bold. Which of them are phrasal verbs?

2 Choose the most suitable heading from the list (A-F) for each paragraph (1-6).

A Worsened by the weather

B Repairing the damage

C Counting the cost

D Important times

E Where the problem began

F One following the other

3 Look at the highlighted words. What does each refer to?

Speaking & Writing

4 THINK Retell the story as though you witnessed the fire.

5 ICT Collect information about a disaster in your country or another country. Write a short text about it. Read it to the class.

Vocabulary

1 **Fill in:** *eruption, avalanche, flood, explosion, earthquake.*

1 The fields were under water during the ....
2 We heard a loud .... like a bomb going off.
3 A(n) .... swept down the ski slope.
4 Another volcanic .... is expected soon.
5 The .... shook the whole building.

(5 x 2 = 10)

2 **Read the definitions and complete the words.**

1 This service takes you to hospital. **a** _ _ _ _ _ _ _ _
2 This service helps climbers. **m** _ _ _ _ _ _ _ **r** _ _ _ _ _
3 This service rescues people at sea. **c** _ _ _ _ _ _ _ _ _
4 Call it when your house is on fire. **f** _ _ _ **s** _ _ _ _ _ _
5 They investigate criminal activity. **p** _ _ _ _ _

(5 x 2 = 10)

3 **Choose the correct item.**

1 They managed to swim **off/out** of the cave.
2 They put **out/off** the event because of the flood.
3 The skiers waited **in/for** help to come.
4 The firefighters managed to put **on/out** the fire.
5 They put us **on/up** for the night.

(5 x 2 = 10)

Grammar

4 **Choose the correct item.**

1 "The weather is too bad to go hiking," he **said/told**.
2 They **said/told** us that the volcano had just erupted.
3 "I wish help would come soon," he **told/said** sadly.
4 "Don't forget to pack a torch," she **said/told** to her team.

(4 x 3 = 12)

5 **Rewrite the sentences in reported speech.**

1 "I'm training to be a firefighter," said Philip.
....
2 "Tomorrow will be stormy," said the forecaster.
....
3 "Don't enter this cave!" he said to us.
....
4 "How long have you been waiting for help?" he asked.
....
5 "We had a horrible experience," said the guide.
....
6 "Have you spoken to the police yet?" she asked me.
....

(6 x 3 = 18)

6 **Rewrite the sentences in reported speech. Use:** *apologised, offered, agreed, advised.*

1 "Can I help?" said Oliver to the rescue team.
....
2 "You should all wear your helmets," he said to us.
....
3 "I'm sorry I didn't take more care of the children," said the guide.
....
4 "You're right! It was a very narrow escape!" said Julia.
....

(4 x 5 = 20)

Everyday English

7 **Match the exchanges.**

1 ☐ Which service do you require?
2 ☐ What's your emergency?
3 ☐ Calm down. Where are you?
4 ☐ The fire service is on its way.

a Somewhere in Fernley Forest.
b Will it be long?
c The fire service, please.
d Please help! There's a terrible fire!

(4 x 5 = 20)

Total 100

Vocabulary:	work & jobs; work & education	Everyday English:	talking about your job
Grammar:	conditionals types 2 & 3; wishes; question tags; clauses of concession	Writing:	a for-and-against article

Learning & Earning ▶ VIDEO

Do You Want My Job?

*This week, Careers Magazine looks at some of the **tricky** outdoor jobs people do. Here's what three of them told us.*

Ⓐ **Kamal Gurung**

In my job, you're on top of the world! I'm a mountain guide in the Nepalese Himalayas. It's an exciting job where you meet lots of interesting people. But you have to be an experienced climber because you're **responsible** for people's safety. I started out in a temporary position for just one year, but now I work every summer from May to September. It's not really that well-paid although you work full-time. Wearing suitable equipment in the freezing conditions is really important, especially footwear and snow goggles. Being a mountain guide is hard work and there is always the risk of accidents. However, when you help people reach the **peak**, it's a moment of **pure** joy!

Ⓑ **Maria Garcia**

If I hadn't studied Biology, I would probably have never become a speleologist, a scientist who studies caves for various kinds of information. In the one where I work in Mexico, I carry out research on tiny life forms that can live in the dark. This could help us learn whether life exists on other planets! My salary is $90,000 a year and it's a full-time position on a two-year contract. I love my job – you see such beauty below the ground. It's not without its risks, though. There's always the **possibility** of flooding or rockslides, so I have to wear boots, overalls and a hard hat at all times.

Vocabulary
Work & Jobs

> **Forming nouns describing people's jobs**
> We can form nouns describing people's jobs from other nouns or from verbs by adding: **-ian** *(music – musician)*, **-ist** *(piano – pianist)*, **-or** *(act – actor)*, **-er** *(paint – painter)*

1 Form nouns describing people's jobs from the words in the list. Check in your dictionary.

- direct • bank • journal • photography • library
- clean • reception • sail • engine • farm
- sing • publish

direct – director

2 **THINK** Which of these people: *work indoors/outdoors?* *work full-time/part-time?* *work shifts?* *work regular hours?* *wear a uniform at work?*

Listening & Reading

3 Look at the title of the article. What are these people's jobs?

🎧 Listen to or read the text quickly to find out.

4 Read the article. For questions 1-6, choose from the texts (A-C). Which job ...

1 ⬜⬜ pays well?
2 ⬜ is not permanent?
3 ⬜ is safer now than it used to be?
4 ⬜ can be fatal if you make a mistake?
5 ⬜ involves looking after others?
6 ⬜ offers employment for part of the year only?

Then explain the words in bold.

LIFESTYLE

© Percy West

How would you feel if you spent five hours of your working day underwater? I'm a pearl diver in western Australia, and that's what I do every day as part of my **12-hour shift**. The wages are great – divers can earn $1,200 a day – but it's also pretty **risky**! In the old days, the divers had to hold their breath underwater – but many divers use breathing equipment now. But as you collect the oysters, you have to **watch out for** dangers such as jellyfish, poisonous fish and even sharks! Divers can also get 'the bends' if they come up to the **surface** too quickly. It's a condition that can kill you!

Don't miss next week's column with some more tricky jobs from around the world!

✓ Check these words

mountain guide, temporary, well-paid, life form, contract, overalls, pearl diver, breathing equipment, oyster, poisonous

5 PREPOSITIONS **Fill in:** *in, at, from, out of, for (x2), on (x2).* **Check in your dictionary.**

1 Mountain guides are responsible .... the safety of the people they lead.

2 There are 200 employees .... the company where Tom works.

3 Liz carries out research .... tiny life forms that live in caves.

4 Jack has been .... work for a year now but he's still looking for a job.

5 What does he do .... a living?

6 Mia is often away .... business in her job.

7 Bob is looking forward to retiring .... his job.

8 He earns .... least £50,000 a year.

6 COLLOCATIONS **Fill in:** *poisonous, pearl, temporary, two-year, 12-hour, mountain, snow, breathing.* **Use the phrases in sentences of your own.**

1 .... guide 5 .... diver
2 .... position 6 .... shift
3 .... goggles 7 .... equipment
4 .... contract 8 .... fish

7 WORDS EASILY CONFUSED **Choose the correct word. Check in your dictionary.**

1 The job comes with **a salary/wages** of £65,000 a year.

2 Bob doesn't **win/earn** much money; he only works part-time.

3 Jane's a novelist whose books have **won/earned** many awards.

4 The company pays workers their **salary/wages** every Friday.

8 PHRASAL VERBS **Fill in the correct particle.**

carry on: to continue doing sth
carry off: to succeed in doing sth difficult
carry out: to perform (a task)

1 There were some difficult moments, but the politician carried .... his speech well.

2 You will be expected to carry .... duties like typing and photocopying.

3 I didn't mean to interrupt. Please carry .... with what you were saying.

Speaking & Writing

9 💬 THINK **If you had to do one of the three jobs mentioned in the article, which would you choose and why? Which would you definitely not choose? Why?**

10 👥 **Interview your partner about his/her job. Ask about:** *what they do, the hours they work (full-time, part-time, shifts, etc), uniforms, salary/wages, what they like/don't like about their job.*
Use their answers to write a short text.

Allison works as a/an ...

Grammar in Use

Jobs | What's new | Advice | Members | Q Search

Careers Forum

Lily, 1 day ago
I work as a waitress in a fast-food restaurant and I just hate it! Although I work long hours, it pays very little. I feel like I'm stuck here. I left school at 18 but I didn't finish my A-level exams. I wish I had studied a bit harder. Advice, please!

Elsie, 8 hours ago
If I were you, I'd look for another job where you can use your waiting skills. You deal with people and handle money. If you did a short training course, you'd be able to apply for a job as a hotel receptionist or something like that. Better hours, better pay!

Frank, 2 hours ago
My advice is to go back to college and take your A-level exams. Then you'll have more job opportunities. Look at me. Sure, I made some bad choices, but if I had given up, I wouldn't have made it this far. Now, I'm a business manager.

1 Read the theory. When do we use conditionals types 2 and 3? Find examples in the forum.

Conditionals ▷ p. GR13

Conditionals Type 2

if-clause   Main clause
If + past simple → would/could/might + infinitive without *to* (imaginary, unreal or highly unlikely situations in the present/future; advice)
If we worked all night, we would meet the deadline.
If I were you, I'd talk to the manager.

Conditionals Type 3

if-clause   Main clause
If + past perfect → would/could/might have + past participle (unreal situations in the past)
If you had taken the Tube, you wouldn't have been late.

2 Choose the correct tense. Give reasons.

1 If we **had/had had** more staff, we could get the job done faster.

2 If you had called my secretary, she would **take/have taken** a message.

3 The company might have employed Mike if he **had arrived/arrived** on time for the interview.

4 I **wouldn't have taken/wouldn't take** that job if I had known the pay was so low.

5 I'd apply for the job if I **were/had been** you.

3 Put the verbs in brackets into the correct tense. Identify the type of conditional. Add commas where necessary.

1 I would have sent the emails if he .... **(ask)** me to.

2 If the canteen .... **(serve)** better food, it might have more customers.

3 If you .... **(write)** down the date of the meeting you wouldn't have forgotten it.

4 If I were you I .... **(hire)** a professional painter for your house.

5 If Karen were a bit more patient she .... **(make)** an ideal teacher.

6 If the government .... **(create)** more jobs fewer people would be unemployed.

7 Max .... **(move)** to another city if he got the chance!

8 We could have won the competition if we .... **(not/miss)** the deadline for entry.

4 **THINK** Complete the sentences with your own ideas. Tell your partner.

1 If I had a week off work, ...
....

2 People might enjoy their jobs more if ....
....

3 Life would have been very different for me if ....
....

4 Housework would be less boring if ....
....

5 If more people worked from home, ...
....

6 If I had grown up on a farm, ...
....

7 If I found a job abroad, ...
....

8 My boss would be very pleased if ....
....

5 Read the theory. Find an example in the forum.

Wishes ▷ p. GR13

- ***I wish/If only* + past simple** to express what we would like to be **different in the present**. *I wish I earned more money.* (but I don't)
- ***I wish/If only* + past perfect** to express regret about something that happened or didn't happen in the **past**. *If only I had applied for the job.* (but I didn't)

6 Put the verbs in brackets into the correct tense.

1 A: If only I .... **(not/forget)** to send the email to Mr O'Neil.

   B: Try not to worry about it.

2 A: Colin's really good at his job!

   B: If only he .... **(not/be)** so bossy!

3 A: I'm really sorry you didn't get that job.

   B: I wish I .... **(arrive)** for the interview on time.

4 A: John won't get a promotion.

   B: If only he .... **(work)** harder.

5 A: If only Sam .... **(not/behave)** so rudely during the meeting.

   B: I know. It was really embarrassing.

7 Make sentences, as in the example. Use the past simple or the past perfect.

1 have a job/pay my bills

I wish *I had a job.*
If *I had a job,*
I could pay my bills.

2 not miss the bus/not be late for work

If only ....
If ....
....

3 not have a headache/be able to work faster

If only ....
If ....
....

4 be more careful/not delete files

I wish ....
If ....
....

8 👤👤 Make wishes with your partner.

• I wish I had • I wish I were • I wish I hadn't • If only I • If only my friends • I wish my teacher hadn't

A: *I wish I had a part-time job.*
B: *I wish I were ...*

9 Read the theory. Fill in the appropriate question tags. 🎧 Listen and tick the correct box.

Question tags ▷ p. GR13

Question tags are short questions at the end of statements used to confirm something or to find out if something is true or not. They are formed with an **auxiliary/modal verb + subject pronoun**. A **positive statement** takes a **negative question tag**. *He's a pianist, isn't he?* A **negative statement** takes a **positive question tag**. *You don't work here, do you?* Some verbs/phrases form question tags differently.

• ***I am → aren't I?*** *I'm on the 9 o'clock flight, **aren't I**?*
• ***Let's → shall we?*** *Let's take a short break, **shall we**?*
• ***You have (got)*** (possession) ***→ haven't you?*** *You've got a new office, **haven't you**?*
• ***I have*** (idiomatically) ***→ don't I?*** *I had a bath, **didn't I**?*
• ***This/That is → isn't it?*** *That's a good website, **isn't it**?*
• ***Don't → will you?*** *Don't use my laptop again, **will you**?*
• ***Someone/Anyone/Everyone → don't/didn't they?*** *Someone took the files from my desk, **didn't they**?*
• ***No one → do/did they?*** *No one phoned, **did they**?*

1	She's sick today, ...?	☐	☐
2	Don't be late, ...?	☐	☐
3	That's good news, ...?	☐	☐
4	You aren't going to leave, ...?	☐	☐
5	I'm back on that project, ...?	☐	☐
6	Let's get started, ...?	☐	☐
7	Someone asked for Jane, ...?	☐	☐
8	No one came, ...?	☐	☐

10 Read the theory. Find an example in the forum on p. 66. Use the words in bold to join the sentences.

Clauses of concession ▷ pp. GR13-14

Clauses of concession are used to express contrast.
***Although/Even though* + clause** *Although/Even though he applied for the job, he didn't get it.*
In spite of/Despite* + noun/gerund/*the fact that *Despite applying for the job, he didn't get it. In spite of the fact that he applied for the job, he didn't get it.*

1 He is hard-working. He didn't get a promotion. **(Even though)**

2 She lives close to work. She drives there. **(Although)**

3 He works from home. He never feels lonely. **(Despite)**

4 Ann knows a lot about computers. She doesn't have a degree. **(In spite of the fact that)**

Skills in Action

Vocabulary
Work & Education

1 Which of these jobs can you see in the pictures? **Which:** *can you become qualified for at a vocational school/university*? *do not require a degree*?

- captain • travel agent • lawyer • lecturer
- personal trainer • marine biologist • librarian
- reporter • taxi driver • security guard • porter

2 **Fill in:** *certificate, marks, training, qualifications, advanced, course.*

1 Bernard always got top .... at school.

2 All our gym instructors have a(n) .... in personal training.

3 Our six-month online .... will help you upgrade your IT skills.

4 What .... does this job require apart from a university degree?

5 There are beginner, intermediate and .... acting classes to join.

6 Most doctors need to do at least seven years of .... before they qualify.

Study Skills

Multiple matching

Read the sentences and underline the key words. Try to think of words related to them. This will help you do the task.

Listening

3 🎧 You will hear four people talking about their jobs. Listen and match the statements (A-E) to the speakers (1-4). One statement does not fit. Can you guess what each person's job is?

A This speaker takes care of their appearance.

B This speaker enjoys working for themselves.

C This speaker would like to be paid more.

D This speaker wishes they had more opportunities.

E This speaker works both indoors and outdoors.

Speaker 1 ☐ Speaker 2 ☐ Speaker 3 ☐ Speaker 4 ☐

Everyday English
Talking about your job

4 What does Paul like about his new job?
🎧 Listen and read to find out.

Linda:	Hi, Paul. Congratulations on the new job! You work as a cameraman now, don't you?
Paul:	Thanks, Linda. Yes, that's right. I'm a TV camera operator.
Linda:	Wow, that's exciting! What do you do in your new job?
Paul:	I have to set up all the equipment before we start filming, plan shots, solve technical problems and study scripts.
Linda:	What's the best part about the job?
Paul:	The pay is pretty good! I earn around £350 a day. It's also very creative. You work closely with the director deciding on how to get the best shots.
Linda:	So I guess you're very happy in your new job, aren't you?
Paul:	Yes, I love it, even though the working hours can be long and antisocial, and it's demanding and stressful at times.
Linda:	I see. It sounds really interesting, though! What qualifications did you need?
Paul:	I had to have technical skills and experience, but I didn't need a degree.
Linda:	Great!

5 👥 Act out a similar dialogue about a security guard job. Use sentences from the language box.

Asking about a job	Responding
• I hear you're working as ... • What do you have to do there? • What do you like best about it? • I guess you like it, don't you? • What qualifications did they ask for?	• You heard right. I'm ... • I'm responsible for ... . I also need to ensure (that) ... • I really love the (hours/people I work with etc). I also like (the fact that) ... • One of the main problems is (that) ... . You also have to be (very) ... . It can also be ... • I needed to have ... but it wasn't necessary to have ...

Pronunciation: /uː/, /juː/

6 🎧 Listen and repeat.

/uː/ shoot, true, proof, cool
/juː/ cute, music, new, few

Reading & Writing

7 **Read the task and answer the questions.**

A magazine called *Careers* has asked its readers to send in articles about their jobs. This month, they want articles on the advantages and disadvantages of working as a surgeon. Write your article for the magazine (120-150 words).

1 What are you going to write? Who for?
2 What should you write about?
3 How many words should you write?

8 **a)** **Read the article and choose the correct linkers.**

Being a surgeon
THE GOOD & THE BAD

Working as a surgeon may seem like an attractive job and one that is much admired. What exactly are its advantages and disadvantages, though?

A career as a surgeon has clear advantages. **1) To begin with/ What is more**, it is well paid. Surgeons do an extremely difficult job and, **2) for instance/as a result**, their salaries are high. **3) Besides/Despite** this, much personal pleasure can be gained from helping others. **4) This is because/For this reason** surgeons help save people's lives.

5) However/Although, being a surgeon has its disadvantages. **6) Secondly/Firstly**, it is stressful. **7) For example/Furthermore**, there is the risk of making a mistake or, even worse, losing a patient. **8) Nevertheless/In addition**, it takes years to qualify **9) also/since** training takes a long time.

10) For this reason/In conclusion, although there are good and bad points to this job, I believe it is well worth doing. As Hippocrates said, "Wherever the art of medicine is loved, there is also a love of humanity."

 Writing Tip

Formal style
Articles discussing advantages and disadvantages are normally formal in style. Characteristics of formal style include:

- full verb forms: *It is necessary ...*
- the passive: *Formal qualifications are required.*
- complex sentences & formal linkers: *Being a doctor means working long hours and, **therefore**, the job can be very tiring.*

b) **Find examples of formal style in the article.**

 Writing Tip

Topic sentences
Introduce each main body paragraph with a topic sentence that summarises the content of the paragraph.

9 **Find the topic sentences in the article. Which of these sentences could replace them?**

1 On the other hand, there are disadvantages to being a surgeon.
2 Working as a surgeon has many positive points.
3 The disadvantages of being a surgeon outweigh the advantages.

Writing (a for-and-against article)

10 **a)** Listen to someone talking about being a journalist and complete the table.

Pros	Justifications
• improve your knowledge • exciting	learn lots of **1)** .... **2)** .... interesting people

Cons	Justifications
• **3)** .... • long unsociable **4)**	have to meet deadlines have to work weekends & public **5)** ....

b) **Use the information in Ex. 10a to write an article discussing the advantages and disadvantages of working as a journalist. Follow the plan and give your article a title.**

Plan

Introduction
Para 1: present the topic
Main Body
Para 2: points for & reasons/examples
Para 3: points against & reasons/examples
Conclusion
Para 4: your opinion

VALUES

Responsibility
A bad workman always blames his tools.
saying

8 Culture

▶ VIDEO

The Bird Man

Being Her Majesty's Swan Marker is a special job with a long history!

It all goes back to the 12th century, when swans on the River Thames were royal property, as they still are today. Roast swan was a very popular dish at royal meals in those days, so keepers were **employed** to count and mark the swans each year. **1** ☐ Anyone doing so went to prison for a year!

Swan is not on the menu at Buckingham Palace today, but the Swan Marker still **looks after** the swans. He's kept busy all year but the most enjoyable part of his job is the five-day Swan Upping ceremony which takes place every July. It's a great **occasion**! The Swan Marker and his team of 18 Uppers make the 79-mile journey along the River Thames from London to Oxfordshire to count the royal swans. The six wooden rowing boats are decorated with royal flags and the men wear special uniforms. **2** ☐

But apart from keeping tradition alive, the job they do is very important for the environment. The Uppers get their name from the fact that they go up the river and lift the swans up onto the **riverbank** to be weighed, measured and checked for injury or disease. **3** ☐ If you asked the Swan Marker, he would soon tell you why: "Pollution and loss of habitat have **affected** the birds, so the job we do is necessary to check on how they're doing." Other dangers for swans on the Thames include being **attacked** by dogs and getting caught up in fishing lines.

4 ☐ From protecting the Royal table, it's now about protecting these beautiful birds and educating people about them. As the Swan Marker says: "We want to **preserve** the swan population for the future."

Reading & Listening

1 Look at the picture and read the introduction. What sort of job do these men do? Read through to find out.

2 Read the text again and complete gaps 1-4 with sentences A-F. Two sentences are extra.

🎧 Listen and check. Then explain the words in bold.

A It's surprising how few people know about this event.

B The Swan Marker's job has come a long way.

C Things were very different back then.

D Uppers are dressed in red and white, and the Swan Marker wears a red and gold jacket and a feather in his cap.

E This kept a check on their numbers and made sure no one else ate them.

F Before they are sent back into the water, the Marker puts a ring on their leg to keep track of them.

✓ Check these words

swan, prison, ceremony, rowing boat, lift, weigh, measure, injury, disease, keep track of

Speaking & Writing

3 👥 THINK Do you agree that it is important to keep traditional jobs alive? Why/Why not? Share your ideas with your partner.

4 ICT Collect information about a traditional job in your country or another country. Make notes under the headings: *title of job – origins – what the job involves – why important today*. **Present the job to the class.**

Vocabulary

1 Choose the correct word.

1 Max **earns/wins** a lot of money as a diver.

2 Jack is working the evening **job/shift** this week.

3 Ted works **part-time/regular** just three hours a day.

4 I got a **temporary/permanent** job for just six weeks.

5 Mountain guides need to wear snow **goggles/hats**.

6 He likes his job although it isn't **well-paid/advanced**.

(6 x 2 = 12)

2 Fill in: *training, top, certificate, course, degree, qualifications.*

1 Jane has got a .... in Psychology.

2 He always got .... marks at school.

3 He did a month of .... when he started the job.

4 She attended a .... on graphic design.

5 You can't get a good job without any ....

6 Do I need a .... to be a personal trainer?

(6 x 2 = 12)

3 Choose the correct item.

1 Who is responsible **for/at** closing the shop?

2 After lunch, we all carried **out/on** with our work.

3 What do you do **in/for** a living?

4 He retired **out of/from** his job in 2017.

5 She always carries **out/off** her duties cheerfully.

(5 x 2 = 10)

Grammar

4 Choose the correct item.

1 I wish I **had/had had** more patience, but I don't.

2 If only I **hadn't failed/didn't fail** my exam.

3 I wish you **applied/had applied** for that job you read about!

4 **Although/Despite** he was tired, he kept on working.

(4 x 4 = 16)

5 Put the verbs in brackets into the correct tense.

1 He wouldn't have been late for work if he .... **(go)** to bed early last night.

2 The office .... **(run)** better if we employed a secretary.

3 If the weather .... **(not-be)** so bad yesterday, the schools wouldn't have closed.

4 John .... **(get)** higher marks if he had studied more.

5 If public transport was cheaper, more people .... **(use)** it.

6 If they .... **(offer)** you the job, would you have taken it?

(6 x 3 = 18)

6 Complete the question tags.

1 Everyone likes weekends, ...?

2 I'm late again, ...?

3 Don't miss the meeting, ...?

4 You have lunch in the canteen, ...?

5 That's your old Maths teacher, ...?

6 No one saw my car keys, ...?

(6 x 2 = 12)

Everyday English

7 Match the exchanges.

1 ☐ I hear you're working as a hotel receptionist.

2 ☐ What do you do there?

3 ☐ What's the best part of the job?

4 ☐ So I guess you're happy in your job.

5 ☐ What qualifications did you need?

a Yes, even though I have to work shifts.

b I had to have a degree in French.

c Yes, that's right.

d I love the people I work with.

e I'm responsible for the bookings.

(5 x 4 = 20)

Total 100

Competences

GOOD ✓

VERY GOOD ✓ ✓

EXCELLENT ✓ ✓ ✓

Lexical Competence

understand words/phrases related to:

• work & jobs

• work & education

Reading Competence

• understand texts related to work, jobs & education (read for specific information – multiple matching; read for cohesion & coherence – missing sentences)

Listening Competence

• listen to and understand monologues related to jobs (listen for specific information – multiple matching)

Speaking Competence

• interview someone about their job

• talk about your job

Writing Competence

• write a short text about a job

• write a for-and-against article about a job

71

Vocabulary: sports & equipment; sports & places
Grammar: (*to*-)infinitive/-*ing* form, forms of infinitive/-*ing* form; singular/plural nouns
Everyday English: asking for information
Writing: a blog entry about ways to get fit

Want to play?

▶ **VIDEO**

Vocabulary

Sports & Equipment

1 a) **Look at the pictures. Which of these sports are:** *extreme sports*? *team sports*? *water sports*? *indoor sports*?

1 swimming **2** boxing **3** hockey **4** rugby

5 motor racing **6** climbing **7** squash **8** cricket

b) **Match the equipment to the sports.**
You need ... to play/do/go ...

trainers • swimsuit • rope • helmet • racket • ball • bat • boxing gloves • stick

Reading & Listening

2 👤👤 **Tick the statements (1-7) you think are true about people who do extreme sports.**

1 They are usually terrified. ☐
2 They enjoy excitement. ☐
3 They can be any age. ☐
4 They forget their everyday problems. ☐
5 They are careful. ☐
6 They enjoy winning prizes. ☐
7 They are very fit. ☐

🎧 **Listen to and read the article to check your answers.**

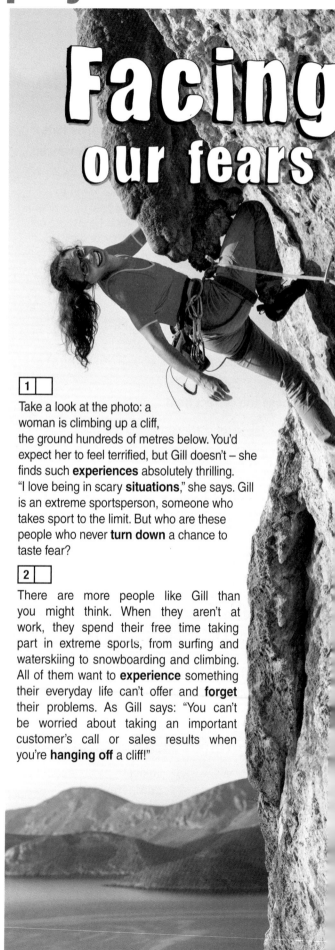

Facing our fears

1 ☐

Take a look at the photo: a woman is climbing up a cliff, the ground hundreds of metres below. You'd expect her to feel terrified, but Gill doesn't – she finds such **experiences** absolutely thrilling. "I love being in scary **situations**," she says. Gill is an extreme sportsperson, someone who takes sport to the limit. But who are these people who never **turn down** a chance to taste fear?

2 ☐

There are more people like Gill than you might think. When they aren't at work, they spend their free time taking part in extreme sports, from surfing and waterskiing to snowboarding and climbing. All of them want to **experience** something their everyday life can't offer and **forget** their problems. As Gill says: "You can't be worried about taking an important customer's call or sales results when you're **hanging off** a cliff!"

3

Some of them even think everyone should be doing extreme sports. Bob is a snowboarding **instructor**. He teaches people to whizz down mountains at speeds of up to 70 km/h. "I don't believe that people take enough chances these days," he says, "but once they do, they're always happier. There's a love of danger inside each one of us – it's just **hidden away** somewhere."

4

Extreme sports, in Bob's opinion, offer us something that is missing in modern life. Life today is **fairly** safe – we are not usually scared that a bear will **attack** us as we walk down the street! But fear is our body's way of dealing with danger, which makes the heart beat faster and fills us with **energy**. For fans of extreme sports, their activity lets them experience that again, but under safer conditions.

5

There is an **element** of risk in all extreme sports. "If you don't do things right, you are asking for trouble," says Bob. But training and proper equipment help to make these sports safer. The difference between extreme sports and 'normal' sports is that, although there are organised **competitions** for extreme sports, extreme sports fans are usually more interested in testing their abilities than in winning prizes. In fact, most of them would agree with mountaineer Sir Edmund Hillary's **reply** when asked why he wanted to climb Everest: "Because it's there."

 Check these words

face, to the limit, sales results, whizz, deal with, beat, risk, ask for trouble, proper, win, prize

Study Skills

Read each paragraph carefully to see how information is paraphrased in the headings, e.g. with synonyms. Match the easy headings first and then move on to the more difficult ones..

3 Read the article again. Choose the most suitable heading (A-F) for each paragraph (1-5). One heading is extra. Then explain the words in bold.

A Frightening Fun

B The Biology of Fear

C Facing the Challenge

D The Extreme is for Everybody

E Scared of the Everyday

F Fear Takes the Mind off Work

4 PREPOSITIONS Fill in: *for, about, with (x2), of, under, in (x2), to, at*. **Make sentences using the phrases**.

1 take .... the limit
2 worried ....
3 .... speeds of
4 love .... danger
5 .... modern life
6 deal ....
7 .... control
8 ask .... trouble
9 interested ....
10 agree .... sb

5 COLLOCATIONS Fill in: *call, chance, look, mind*.

1 Surfing takes my .... off my problems.

2 I can't take this .... right now – get their name and number and I'll call them back.

3 You should take a .... and try waterskiing.

4 Jo's hurt her ankle. Can you take a ....?

6 WORDS EASILY CONFUSED Fill in: *win, earn, beat* or *gain* **in the correct form**.

1 They were good, but we .... in the end.

2 Uruguay .... Argentina 4-2 in the first World Cup Final in 1930.

3 We .... an advantage by putting our tallest player up front.

4 How much money does a top footballer ....?

7 PHRASAL VERBS **Fill in the correct particle**.

turn down: 1) to refuse to accept; **2)** to decrease volume, power, etc
turn into: to change into
turn on/off: to switch on/off
turn up: to increase volume, power, etc (≠ turn down)

1 I turned .... the radio and turned the sound .... to full.

2 The coach turned the team .... cup winners.

3 The bank turned him .... for a loan.

4 Turn .... that music or at least turn it .... – I'm trying to read.

Speaking & Writing

8 THINK **Do you know any other extreme sports? Why do people do them?**

9 **Write a blog entry describing an extreme sport you would like to try. Write about:** *name – equipment – why you would like to try it.*

Grammar in Use

Imagine going to a gym where you don't have to wait to use the equipment. Where you can decide to come at a certain time and know the gym won't be full. Where the staff know your name, and what you like drinking after you finish your session, and are always available with some helpful advice.

If that's what you're after, then join Fit Spot. We're a small neighbourhood gym that believes working out should be as private and personal as possible. We want you to be relaxed, to feel like coming and to think of the place as your home. That's why the maximum number in the gym at one time is ten, and every member has their own personal trainer.

If you love exercising, but would like to enjoy quieter work-out sessions, let us help you to stay fit! We look forward to seeing you!

(And don't forget to bring the coupon with you!)

COUPON 50%
off the cost of annual membership!

Infinitive/-ing form ▶ pp. GR14-15

1 Read the advert. What do we use after the following: *to*-infinitive, infinitive without *to* or *-ing* form?

1 like/love/enjoy/hate/don't mind + *-ing form*

2 suggest/avoid/miss/fancy/imagine + ...

3 would like/would love/would prefer + ...

4 can/should/ought to/have to + ...

5 make/let/had better/would rather + ...

6 want/need/ask/used + ...

7 look forward to/can't stand/be used to + ...

2 Choose the correct form.

1 I love **play/playing** tennis.

2 We'd like **to join/joining** the gym.

3 You should **practise/practising** more if you want to win the tournament.

4 Imagine **to compete/competing** in the Olympic Games!

5 You have to **being/be** brave if you want **try/to try** rock climbing.

6 Tom suggested **meeting/to meet** us at the pool.

7 I'm used to **run/running** five miles a day now.

8 She doesn't mind **to get/getting** up early.

9 I'd prefer **to play/playing** darts rather than tennis.

10 She made me **leave/to leave** the team.

3 Put the verbs in brackets into the correct form: (*to-*) infinitive or *-ing* form.

I have always enjoyed **1)** .... **(take part)** in team sports, so when my PE teacher asked me if I wanted **2)** .... **(learn)** how **3)** .... **(play)** rugby, I decided **4)** .... **(try)** it. It sounded ideal for me as I don't mind **5)** .... **(be)** outside in cold weather, and I like **6)** .... **(exercise)**. I expected **7)** .... **(find)** it easy, but it wasn't. I kept **8)** .... **(practise)**, though, and now I'm quite good. My coach thinks I may **9)** .... **(become)** a professional rugby player one day.

Forms of the infinitive/-ing form ▶ pp. GR14-15

Active voice	Passive voice
Present (to) write/writing	(to) be written/being written
Present continuous (to) be writing/—	—
Perfect (to) have written/having written	(to) have been written/having been written
Perfect continuous (to) have been writing/—	—

Forms of the infinitive/-ing form corresponding to verb tenses:
- present simple/*will* → present infinitive/-*ing* form
- present continuous/future continuous → present continuous infinitive
- past simple/present perfect/past perfect/future perfect → perfect infinitive/-*ing* form
- past continuous/present perfect continuous/past perfect continuous/future perfect continuous → perfect continuous infinitive

4 Read the theory. Choose the correct item.

1 The team are out on the pitch **practising/being practised**.

2 The baseball player ran to **catch/have caught** the ball.

3 You must **practise/have been practising** a lot recently – you play so much better!

4 Gillian would love to **be climbing/have been climbing** in the mountains right now.

5 Imagine **having chosen/having been chosen** to play in the World Cup!

6 He seems to **hurt/have hurt** his arm playing squash earlier.

5 Put the verbs in brackets into the *to*-infinitive or the *-ing* form. Check in the Grammar Reference section.

1 Jenny stopped .... **(go)** to the gym after three months.

2 Getting fit means .... **(change)** your diet and exercising regularly.

3 I've never forgotten .... **(drive)** a racing car when I was fifteen.

4 Sorry! I didn't mean .... **(drop)** my racket on your toe!

5 We regret .... **(tell)** you all that the match has been cancelled due to rain.

6 Did you remember .... **(book)** the squash court for Sunday?

7 Peter tried .... **(lift)** the heavy weights, but he couldn't.

6 SPEAKING Use these verbs/phrases to continue the story: *want*, *look forward to*, *stop*, *remember*, *try*, *should*, *spend*, *need*, *suggest*.

Sally and Jessie **wanted** *to go surfing.*
They were **looking forward to** *doing tricks on the waves.*

7 Read the theory. Find examples in the advert on p. 74.

Singular/Plural nouns ▶p. GR15

We use **singular verb forms** with:

- **uncountable nouns:** *air, bread, butter, cheese, gold, juice, wood,* etc. *There is some juice left in the fridge.*
- **school/college subjects:** *Geography, Maths, Physics,* etc. *Maths was my best subject at school.*
- **an amount of money** *(£12),* **distance** *(10 kilometres),* **weight** *(51 kg),* etc. *£60 for this racket is cheap.*
- **games and sports:** *athletics, gymnastics,* etc. *Gymnastics is my favourite event in the Olympics.*
- **diseases:** *flu, measles, mumps,* etc. *Mumps is a childhood disease.*
- **some other nouns:** *advice, equipment, furniture, hair, homework, information, jewellery, luggage, money, news, rubbish,* etc. *The news isn't good.*

We use **plural verb forms** with:

- **objects consisting of two parts:** *items of clothing (pyjamas, shorts, trousers,* etc), **tools and instruments** *(binoculars, scissors,* etc). *These scissors are sharp.*
- **group nouns:** *crew, family, team, staff,* etc, when we mean the individuals that make up the group. *The team are wearing red jerseys and white shorts.* **BUT** *The team is in first place.* (as a unit)
- nouns such as: ***clothes, people, police*** etc. *Where are my clothes?*

8 Fill in *is* or *are*.

1 Eight kilometres .... a long way to go for your first run.

2 .... my tennis shorts in the laundry?

3 Sugar .... the first thing you need to reduce.

4 At college, Chemistry .... my favourite subject.

5 Athletics .... not just one sport – it includes the high jump, the long jump and many others.

6 The equipment a golfer needs .... expensive.

7 The news at 8 pm .... showing an interview with my favourite volleyball player.

8 Your binoculars .... perfect for watching the match from up here!

9 The measles .... easy to catch.

10 These scissors .... for cutting hair with.

9 Complete the second sentence so that it means the same as the first sentence.

1 I can't find my tracksuit trousers.
I don't know where ....

2 There are five members in my family.
My family ....

3 I love playing darts most.
Darts ....

4 Someone needs your advice.
Your advice ....

5 They will give me £150 for the job.
£150 ....

10 Complete the second sentence so that it has the same meaning as the first, using the word given. Use between two and five words.

1 It's too cold to play tennis. **ENOUGH**
It's .... tennis.

2 I hope they choose me for the team. **CHOSEN**
I want .... for the team.

3 I don't like it when others tell me what to do. **TOLD**
I don't like .... what to do.

4 He likes Physics more than any other subject. **FAVOURITE**
Physics .... subject.

Skills in Action

Vocabulary

Sports & Places

1 **a)** Copy the Venn diagram into your notebook and fill it in. Use: *badminton, baseball, basketball, cycling, diving, football, ice skating, jogging, golf, sailing, windsurfing, tennis, volleyball, water skiing.*

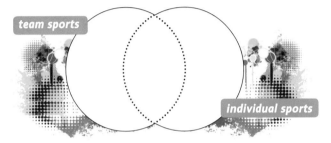

team sports

individual sports

b) Which of the sports in Ex. 1a can you play/go/ **do** *on a court/pitch/rink/track/field/course – in the sea/a sports centre/a swimming pool*?

2 Complete the sentences with sports from Ex. 1a.

1 .... can be lonely, but it helps you burn calories fast and you can do it almost everywhere at no cost.

2 Playing .... teaches you teamwork, but tall players have a big advantage.

3 .... can be very relaxing; as the boat moves on the water you feel free, but it can be expensive.

4 .... is exciting because you can ride at high speeds, but it can get lonely.

5 .... can be dangerous, and injuries are common if you fall on the ice, but it's a great way to exercise.

Listening

3 Listen to a podcast where three fitness experts discuss the advantages and disadvantages of team and individual sports. Complete the gaps in the table.

team sports	individual sports
• **1)** .... • team helps you to keep going	• feel independent • you are responsible for your own **3)** .... or failure
• difficult to **2)**	• **4)** ....

Everyday English

Asking for information

4 What exercise class is Bob interested in? Which days are the classes on? How much do classes cost? Listen and read to find out.

Joe:	Hello, how can I help you?
Bob:	Hi! I have some questions about the sports centre.
Joe:	What would you like to know?
Bob:	First of all, how much is the special offer for membership?
Joe:	It's £260 and that gives you full annual membership.
Bob:	That's great. And what does membership include?
Joe:	It allows you to use the swimming pool and gym. And you get 25% off any exercise classes you take.
Bob:	Oh, good. Are there TRX® classes?
Joe:	Yes. There's a beginners' and an advanced class.
Bob:	How much do they cost?
Joe:	That's ... £45 a month after your discount.
Bob:	How often are they?
Joe:	Twice a week, on Tuesdays and Thursdays.
Bob:	What time are they at?
Joe:	Beginners from 7 to 8 pm, advanced 8 to 9.
Bob:	Can I join today?
Joe:	Of course. Let me get you a form to fill in.

5 You want to join Valley Sports Centre and take an exercise class there. Use the information in the advert and the language from the box to act out a dialogue similar to the one in Ex. 4.

Asking for information	
• How much ...?	• How often ...?
• What does ... include?	• What time ...?

Valley Sports Centre

• 2 swimming pools • gym
• aerobics • Zumba
Special offer: £180 for full annual membership & 20% off all classes

Pronunciation: /ei/, /ai/

6 Listen and tick (✓). Then listen and repeat.

	/ei/	/ai/		/ei/	/ai/
skate			mind		
weight			sail		
height			fight		

Reading & Writing

Word formation (forming abstract nouns)

We can form abstract nouns from verbs by adding: **-ing** (surf – surf**ing**), **-ion** (act – act**ion**), **-ment** (encourage – encourage**ment**) and **-ance/-ence** (appear – appear**ance**, refer – refer**ence**).

We can form abstract nouns from adjectives by adding: **-ity** (able – abil**ity**) and **-ness** (ill – ill**ness**).

We can form abstract nouns from nouns by adding: **-ship** (friend – friend**ship**) and **-hood** (child – child**hood**).

7 Read the Word formation box, then read the blog entry and fill in the gaps with nouns derived from the words in brackets.

Team or individual?

Today, I want to have a **1)** .... (discuss) about the advantages of both team and individual sports for everyday **2)** .... (fit).

► Team sports

- They're sociable, and can lead to new **3)** .... (friend), so for lots of people they're a lot of fun. And if you enjoy yourself, you're more likely to keep going.

- Being part of a team encourages you to try your best. This is because you don't want to let your teammates down.

► Individual sports

- With many individual sports you are completely flexible. For example, when you want to go **4)** .... **(jog)**, you can head straight out into your **5)** .... (neighbour).

- You are responsible for how fit you become, and can be proud of your **6)** .... (achieve), because you managed it alone.

Remember, no matter how old you are, you should be doing some kind of exercise. It will make all the **7)** .... (differ) to the way you feel! Whether you choose a team sport or an individual one depends on what suits your **8)** .... (person) and lifestyle.

Leave a comment

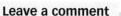

Writing Tip

Justify your arguments with reasons. This makes your arguments stronger.

8 Read the blog entry in Ex. 7 again. How does the writer justify each argument?

Writing (a blog entry about ways to get fit)

9 Read the task and answer the questions.

You write a blog about fitness and you want to write a post about the benefits of getting fit with a personal trainer and with an exercise class. Write your blog entry in 120-150 words.

1 What are you going to write? Who for?

2 What are you going to write about?

3 How long should it be?

10 🎧 Listen to a podcast where three fitness experts discuss the advantages of having a personal trainer and joining an exercise class. Complete the gaps in the table.

personal trainer	individual attention	everyone is **1)** ....
	2)	trainer doesn't let you give up
exercise class	team spirit	you try **3)** ....
	4)	you want to attend the class

11 Use the ideas in Ex. 10 to write your blog entry (120-150 words). Follow the plan.

Plan

Para 1: introduce the topic

Para 2: personal trainer (arguments for with reasons)

Para 3: exercise class (arguments for with reasons)

Para 4: conclusion

VALUES

Team spirit

Talent wins games, but teamwork wins championships.

Michael Jordan

VIDEO

The FASTEST game on grass

Reading & Listening

1 You are going to read about an Irish sport called hurling. Look at the pictures. How do you think the sport is played? Is it a team sport?
🎧 Listen and read to find out.

2 Read the text again and answer the questions. Then explain the words in bold.

1 How old is hurling? ....
....

2 What is a hurley? ....
....

3 How long does a hurling match last?
....

4 How many points is one goal worth?
....

5 How fast can a *sliotar* travel? ....
....

Speaking & Writing

3 👤👤 THINK Invent your own team sport. Think about: name, players, equipment, place, rules. Present it to the class.

4 ICT Think of a sport that started in your country or in another country and is still played today. Collect information about it under the headings: *name – players – equipment – place – rules*. **Write a text about it for an e-magazine.**

✓ **Check these words**

record, except, swing, fast and furious

They've been playing hurling for well over 3,000 years in Ireland, which makes it one of the oldest sports in the world. The **earliest** record of it is in a myth dating back to 1200 BC, where the legendary hero Cú Chulainn wins a fight using a *sliotar* (a hurling ball)! Today, hurling is still played mainly in Ireland, but you can find matches being played across the world, and there is also a women's version called camogie.

A hurling pitch is about the same width as a football pitch but much longer, with goals that are the **shape** of an H. Each of the 15 players in a team carries a hurley, a stick made of a very hard wood called ash. It's **shaped** a little like a hockey stick, except that it's flat and has a wider end.

Players are allowed to swing their hurleys over their heads and hit the ball into the air to send it across the pitch, which is why all players have to wear helmets.

Each match has two halves lasting 35 minutes each. There are two ways to **score** points. The first is to hit the ball into the goal (the bottom half of the H), which is protected by a goalkeeper. This is called a goal and is worth three points. The other way is to hit the ball through the top half of the H, which scores one point. Whichever team has the most points **in total** at the end of 70 minutes wins.

If it is hit well enough, a hurling ball can travel at 150 km/h and 110 m in distance. This means the ball can travel from one end of the pitch to the other in seconds, so games are fast and furious. That's why hurling has the nickname "the fastest game on grass".

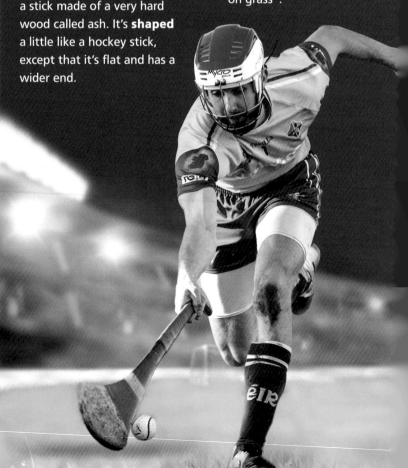

Vocabulary

1 **Fill in:** *boxing, cricket, cycling, ice skating, motor racing, squash.*

1 In ...., both fighters must wear gloves.
2 Carl was carrying a bat and ball; he was going to play ....
3 .... drivers have to be brave to drive at such high speeds.
4 I love .... at this rink – it's so big!
5 In some .... races, the riders go around a track.
6 Jimmy won the .... match with a great shot that his opponent couldn't reach.

(6 x 2 = 12)

2 **Choose the correct word.**

1 Did Sarah **win/beat** the race yesterday?
2 I went **jogging/sailing** in John's boat yesterday.
3 There is an **element/energy** of risk in all sports.
4 It's difficult for him to **attack/face** his fear of water.
5 You play basketball on a **pitch/court**.
6 Snowboarding is an **indoor/extreme** sport.
7 She has practice in the swimming **ring/pool** today.
8 Lots of people prefer **team/individual** sports because they're more social.
9 Your team always **wins/beats** mine when we play!
10 Take a **look/chance** and join a gym. You'll love it.

(10 x 1 = 10)

3 **Choose the correct item.**

1 He is worried **for/about** losing the cup final.
2 I turned **up/on** the TV so I could watch the match.
3 He has to deal **about/with** the situation.
4 My coach turned me **into/on** a great player.
5 They have everything **in/under** control.

(6 x 2 = 12)

Grammar

4 **Choose the correct item.**

1 We enjoy **to go/going** to the gym.
2 Did you remember **to record/recording** the match?
3 Sam would prefer not **to train/training** today.
4 He avoids **working/to work** out in front of others.
5 I made Paul **go/to go** for a jog.
6 The runners stopped **to drink/drinking** some water.

(6 x 2 = 12)

5 **Put the verbs in brackets into the correct infinitive or -ing form.**

1 Tom's eyes are red. He appears .... **(cry)**.
2 Do you remember .... **(hit)** by the ball?
3 I hope .... **(go)** surfing one day.
4 You should .... **(stop)** years ago.

(4 x 6 = 24)

6 **Choose the correct item.**

1 Your trousers **is/are** on the bed.
2 Gymnastics **is/are** my favourite sports event.
3 The scissors **is/are** in the drawer.
4 **Is/Are** twenty kilometres too far to run?
5 Come quickly! The news **is/are** showing your team!

(5 x 2 = 10)

Everyday English

7 **Match the exchanges.**

1 ☐ How often is it?
2 ☐ What time?
3 ☐ How much does it cost?
4 ☐ What does it include?
5 ☐ I have a question.

a Use of the gym.
b 10 pm.
c Twice a week.
d Go ahead.
e £350.

(5 x 4 = 20)
Total 100

Competences

GOOD ✓
VERY GOOD ✓✓
EXCELLENT ✓✓✓

Lexical Competence
understand words/ phrases related to:
• sports & equipment
• sports & places

Reading Competence
• understand texts related to sports (read for gist – match headings to paragraphs; read for detail – answer questions)

Listening Competence
• listen to and understand dialogues related to sports & ways of getting fit (listen for specific information – gap-fill)

Speaking Competence
• ask for information

Writing Competence
• write a blog entry about ways to get fit

Values: Appreciation

Thanks a million!
You're the best!
Appreciate it! You shouldn't have!
Cheers!
Much obliged!
You rock! Ta!
That's very kind! I owe you one!
Good of you!

THX
THNQ
TY

▶ VIDEO

Layouts Typography Contact Forum Shop

Home ˅ Layouts ˅ Posts ˅ Food ˅ Fashion ˅ Archives ˅ Features ˅ Contact

Four ways to ... show your appreciation
by Phyllis Brown

I'm sure you're **grateful** to your family, your friends, your fellow students or colleagues for what they do for you, but do *they* know you're grateful? As businesswoman Mary Kay Ash once said, "If you **appreciate** someone, don't keep it a secret!" So here are four ways you can show it!

1

Have people forgotten this **facial expression**? I held a door open for someone just the other day and they just walked straight through, with a big **frown** on their face! I don't expect a 'thank you', but can't you 'turn that frown upside down' for a moment?

2

It sounds simple, but does anyone do it anymore? It used to be the first thing parents taught their children (or the second, after 'Say please.') Nowadays, some people avoid it – almost as if there were something wrong with the phrase!

3

A text or an email is a common way to thank someone and it's all very nice, but something you write by hand means so much more! Not many messages are handwritten these days, but it is so much more **personal** than a printed one even if it seems a bit **old-fashioned**.

4

It doesn't have to be big or expensive, but if you choose it with care and have the person you want to show appreciation to **in mind**, it will be a true symbol of how grateful you are for that person's help. A pen, for example, will remind the person of your appreciation every time they **pick** it **up** to write something.

1 What do you do to show you are grateful to someone for something they've done for you? Do you think it is mentioned in the article? Read through quickly to find out.

2 Read the article again and match headings A-F to paragraphs 1-4. Two headings are extra.
🎧 Listen and check. Then, explain the words in bold.

A A thank-you note
B Give and take
C A thoughtful gift
D Smile
E A bouquet of flowers
F Say 'thank you'

3 THINK What is the author's purpose? How successful has she been?

4 👥 Read the three situations. How would you show your appreciation? Discuss with your partner. – *you spent your summer holidays at a friend's house – your friend helped you with your homework – a person you work with helped you move into your new flat.*

Public Speaking Skills

Using emotional language

Farewell speeches are given to say goodbye and express appreciation to a person. Just like any other form of public speaking, they need to have a clear introduction, main body and conclusion, but they need language that is expressive and emotional rather than informative or persuasive.

1 **a)** **Read the task. What is it asking you to do?**

A colleague is leaving the company where you work and you have been asked to give a farewell speech on his/her last day.

b)  **Listen to and read the model. How does the speaker sound? Underline phrases that communicate emotion.**

2 **Tick what the speaker does in his speech.**

1 gives personal details about the person   ....
2 describes the place where the person works   ....
3 makes jokes   ....
4 explains how the person has been valuable   ....

3 **Imagine you have been chosen to give the farewell speech for a friend who is leaving. Make notes under the headings:** *name – where going – first meeting – relationship with friend.* **Use the headings to prepare and give your speech. Use emotional language.**

So, the day has come for us to say goodbye to our great colleague and dear friend, Jane. Unfortunately for us, Jane will be leaving us all behind as she heads out to Canada to start a new chapter in her life and become much better at building snowmen! I wish I could go with you, Jane, but you know I can't stand the cold.

Over the past six years, Jane has lit up the office with her friendly face, positive attitude and very loud laughter. I can't believe that from tomorrow, we will get some peace and quiet and Jane's desk by the window will finally be empty so I can come in early and get my hands on it first.

Right from the start, Jane has been a team player who was always keen to help out. Whether that meant staying late or being the first to get up and make everyone coffee. To be honest it wasn't the best coffee in the world, but I admit, it did get better eventually. Jane has always made work more enjoyable for us all and I can't imagine what it will be like without her here each day.

Jane, we will all miss you very much, but we wish you every bit of luck for the future. Before you go, here's a little gift from us all – it's that T-shirt you said you liked, which you can now wear on those rare occasions when the Canadian weather reaches a tropical ten degrees Celsius.

Jane, thank you for everything and good luck!

Tech world

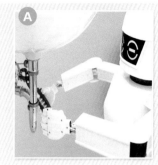 **A**
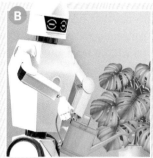 **B**
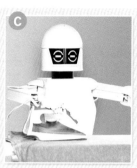 **C**
 **D**
 **E**

Vocabulary

Chores

1 **a)** Which of the chores in the list can you see in the pictures (A-G)?

- do the laundry • feed the pet • mop the floor
- do DIY • water the plants • make the bed
- do the ironing • serve meals • lay the table
- cook dinner • do the vacuuming

b) Which of these do you *sometimes, usually, often, never* do in your home?

Reading

2 How do you think robots can help in our everyday life? Listen and read to find out.

 **VIDEO**

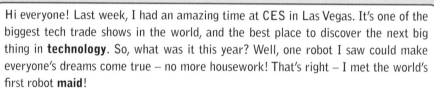

Home | **About** | **Photos** | **Contact**

Ted's TechBlog

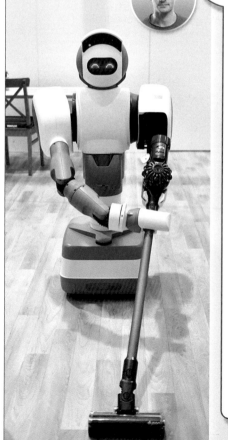

Hi everyone! Last week, I had an amazing time at CES in Las Vegas. It's one of the biggest tech trade shows in the world, and the best place to discover the next big thing in **technology**. So, what was it this year? Well, one robot I saw could make everyone's dreams come true – no more housework! That's right – I met the world's first robot **maid**!

We already have a lot of devices that have been in our homes and do household chores for years such as washing machines and dishwashers. Now there are robotic vacuum cleaners and laundry folders, but these are still very slow. The Aeolus Robot, which was designed by a Californian company, is the first robot that can do a wide variety of housework.

This robot moves around on two wheels, has two high-definition cameras on its head, and two hands that can hold onto things. At the trade show, the robot vacuumed and mopped a floor (using a normal vacuum cleaner and mop), while it also picked up items and quickly put them in their correct places – all without the help of its **designers**. And, best of all, the robot **served** someone a can of cola from a fridge!

The robot **connects** to a smartphone **app**, which you speak into to give it instructions. The amazing thing about the Aeolus Robot, though, is that it can learn on its own. Over time, it can tell the difference between human faces, and it can learn which family member owns which items, and where they usually keep them. In fact, it can remember where more than 1,000 household items should be! Also, each robot can **share** information with other Aeolus Robots. So, if one robot learns how to open a cola can, then it will send this information to other Aeolus Robots around the world!

Sounds **awesome**, doesn't it? Would you like to make this robot the newest member of your family? Write a comment below!

✓ **Check these words**

trade show, device, high-definition, household item

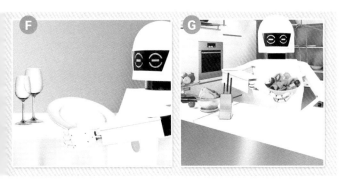

3 **Read again and for questions 1-5 choose the correct item. Then, explain the words in bold.**

1 What is the writer doing in the text?
  A giving information about a new robot
  B encouraging people to buy a new robot
  C describing a trip he took to Las Vegas
  D explaining why he worries about future technology

2 How is the Aeolus Robot different from other devices that help with housework?
  A It was designed in California.
  B It can keep working for longer.
  C It is able to do more than one job.
  D It can do housework quicker than humans can.

3 The robot that the writer saw at the trade show
  A worked very slowly.
  B poured a drink into a glass.
  C needed some help to do a job.
  D used ordinary equipment to do housework.

4 To ask the robot to do a chore, you must
  A speak to it directly.
  B show your face to it.
  C connect it to your smartphone.
  D be someone the robot has met before.

5 Which could be a title for the blog entry?
  A *In shops now – your robot maid*
  B At last – a cheap housework robot
  C **The best from CES:** My review of the trade show
  D Introducing the Aeolus Robot

4 COLLOCATIONS **Fill in:** *smartphone, household, washing, trade, vacuum, family, robot, high-definition.* **Use the phrases in sentences of your own.**

1 .... show
2 .... maid
3 .... chores
4 .... machine
5 .... cameras
6 .... cleaner
7 .... app
8 .... member

5 PREPOSITIONS **Choose the correct item.**

1 The robotics experts always share their research **for/with** each other.
2 The robot doesn't walk – it moves **in/on** wheels.
3 This app can connect your smartphone **at/to** a TV.
4 He tried to learn how to use the app **on/in** his own.
5 Can you tell the difference **from/between** the two models?

6 WORDS EASILY CONFUSED **Fill in the correct word:** *take* or *bring*.

1 Brian told the robot to .... him his slippers.
2 Before you leave, remember to .... a leaflet about our new robot.
3 Please, ... this book to James.
4 Steve, could you please .... me a glass of water?

7 PHRASAL VERBS **Fill in the correct particle(s).**

> **get across:** to communicate
> **get along/on with:** to have a friendly relationship with sb
> **get on/off:** to enter/exit a train, bus, etc
> **get over:** to recover from an illness, shocking event, etc
> **get by:** to have enough (money, food, etc) to survive

1 It was difficult for Henry to get .... when he lost his job.
2 The teacher had difficulty getting .... the meaning of the poem.
3 Helen gets .... well with the other members of the robotics club.
4 Max felt a little nervous when he got .... the driverless bus.
5 It took Mary a long time to get .... the death of her dog.

Speaking & Writing

8 THINK **What would the drawbacks of the robot assistant described in the blog entry be?**

9 **Write a comment to post on the blog expressing your opinion on having a robot like this.**

Grammar in Use

Kate: Hello. I'm interested in joining the college robotics club. **May** I ask you some questions first?

Paul: Yes, of course. What would you like to know?

Kate: Well, do members **have to** pay a membership fee?

Paul: It's £25 per term, but you **needn't** pay straightaway. I think you **should** come to a few meetings to see if you like the club first.

Kate: That's a good idea. And does the club have any rules about borrowing robotics equipment?

Paul: Well, you **mustn't** take any of the equipment home with you. It's very expensive, you see.

Kate: OK, I understand. So, **shall** I fill out this form here?

Paul: Yes, please! You just **need to** write your name, student ID number and an email address.

Kate: OK, got it. And when is the first meeting?

Paul: On Wednesday at 8 pm in Gilford Hall. A lot of people **might** come for the first meeting, so arrive early to get a seat!

Kate: Hmm, Gilford Hall? **Would** you give me directions there, please?

Paul: There's a map of the college on the wall over there. I **can** show you on that.

Kate: OK, thanks a lot!

1 Read the dialogue. Which modal verb in bold in the dialogue is used to express: *necessity*? *obligation*? *a lack of necessity*? *permission*? *possibility*? *prohibition*? *ability*? *an offer*? *a request*? *advice*?

Modals ▶ pp. GR15-16

Ability/Inability (*can/be able to – could/was able to*)
He *can/is able to* type very fast. (He has the ability.)
He *could* use a computer at the age of six. (He had the ability. – general ability)
He *was able to* finish the video game. (He managed to. – specific ability)
She *couldn't/wasn't able to* install the new printer. (She didn't manage to. – specific negative ability)

Advice/Recommendation (*must/mustn't – should/shouldn't/ought to/ought not to*)
You *must* turn off your computer now. (It's very important that you do it. – strong advice)
You *should/ought to* update your antivirus software regularly. (I advise you to.)

Necessity/Lack of necessity (*have to/need to – don't have to/don't need to/needn't*)
You *have to/need to* enter your password to access your emails. (It's necessary.)
You *don't have to/don't need to/needn't* delete emails from your account. (It's not necessary.)

Obligation (*must/have to/had to*)
You *have to* put away your smartphones during the test. (People are obliged to. It's a rule/the law. – external obligation)
We *must* change our passwords. (It's our obligation. We say so. – obligation coming from the speaker)

Offers (*shall/can*)
Shall/Can I help you connect to the Internet? (Do you want me to …?)

Permission (*can/could/may/be allowed to*)
Can I borrow your tablet to check my emails? (Is it OK? – informal)
Could/May we have the Wi-Fi password, please? (Would you mind if …? – formal/polite)
You *can/may* use the computer lab during school hours. (You have permission.)
Are we *allowed to* write our lecture notes on our laptops? (What's the rule?)

Possibility (*could/may/might*)
Emma *could/may/might* buy a new smartphone. (There's a possibility. It's possible.)

Prohibition (*mustn't/can't*)
You *mustn't/can't* play games on the library computers. (It's prohibited. You're not allowed. It's forbidden.)

Requests (*can/could/would you …?*)
Can/Could/Would you help me open a social media account? (Are you willing to …?)

2 Read the theory. Choose the correct item. Give reasons.

1 **Shall/Can't** I show you how to install the program or can you do it yourself?

2 In case your computer has a problem, you **ought to/shall** put your files on a hard drive.

3 You **couldn't/needn't** turn on your laptop – we can find the address on my smartphone.

4 Paula **might/can** buy a new laptop – she's seriously thinking about it.

5 **Can/Would** I make a short call on your mobile phone, Lisa?

6 **Would/May** you show me how to change my password? I've tried, but I can't do it.

7 **Could/Should** you tell me your email address, please?

8 All passengers **have to/need** turn off electronic devices when the plane is taking off and landing.

3 Fill in: *should*, *needn't*, *couldn't*, *might*, *would*, *may*, *shall* or *can't*.

1 You .... pay your bills at the bank. Now, you can use online banking.

2 .... you show me how to scan a document?

3 I .... connect to the Internet yesterday.

4 .... I connect the speakers to the PC for you?

5 You .... talk on your phone in the library. It's against the rules.

6 You .... get a new phone, Alice. That one doesn't have enough memory.

7 .... I see the manager, please?

8 I .... come to the computer games competition tomorrow. I'm not completely sure yet.

4 Use the modals in the list to explain the sentences in the notice, as in the example.

- mustn't • needn't • have to • might
- can • should

Home   Blog   Team   Info

Hereford Public Library

Computer Lab Rules

- It's not necessary to pay to use library computers.
- It's forbidden to access social media on library computers.
- It's the rule to wear earphones when you use sound on a computer.
- We advise you to log out of your email account after using a computer.
- You have permission to use a computer for up to two hours.
- There's a possibility our IT department will check users' Internet activity.

You needn't pay to use library computers.

5 Rewrite the sentences. Use the modals in the list.

- would • need to • mustn't • wasn't able to
- might • can

1 She didn't manage to find a Wi-Fi signal.

2 It's prohibited to download films without paying for them.

3 There's a possibility that my older brother will give me his old tablet.

4 Are you willing to help me create a presentation?

5 You have permission to use the Internet to research for your project.

6 It's necessary for you to have an email address to shop online.

Modals of deduction ⟩ pp. GR16-17

- **I'm sure** he **is** at work.
  *He **must be** at work.*
- **I'm sure** he **isn't** at home.
  *He **can't/couldn't be** at home.*
- **Maybe** he **is** on the phone to his friend.
  *He **may/might/could be** on the phone to his friend.*
- **I'm sure** he **has received** some good news.
  *He **must have received** some good news.*
- **I'm sure** he **didn't miss** a deadline at work.
  *He **can't/couldn't have missed** a deadline at work.*
- **I think** he **was** at the trade show yesterday evening.
  *He **may/might/could have been** at the trade show yesterday evening.*

NOTE: *Can* can be used in questions to express possibility. *Where **can** they be? Where **can** he have put the flash drive?*

6 Read the examples. Fill in: *must*, *can*, *can't/couldn't* or *may/might/could*.

1 Steve .... be online now. He has football practice at this time.

2 Where .... he be?

3 Lisa .... have been at the video games tournament. I can't remember.

4 She .... be working on the new project, but I'm not sure.

5 She .... know how to set up a social media account. After all, she's online all day.

7 Complete the second sentence so that it means the same as the first. Use two to five words, including the word in bold.

1 There's a possibility that I'll be online later this evening.
MAY I .... later this evening.

2 I'm sure they haven't downloaded the app.
HAVE They .... the app.

3 I think Kate hasn't found her phone charger.
MAY Kate .... her phone charger.

4 I'm sure he sent the documents.
HAVE He .... the documents.

5 I'm sure Tony isn't using the IT room now.
BE Tony .... the IT room now.

Skills in Action

Vocabulary
Digital communication

1 Look at the graph. Use the phrases to talk about teens' communication habits.

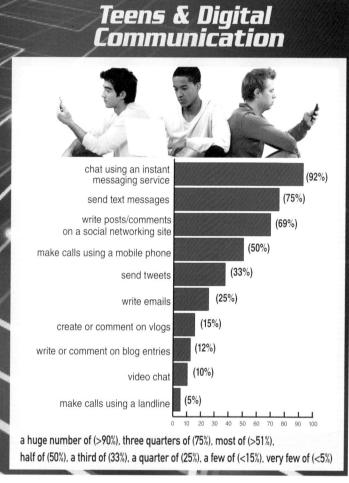

Teens & Digital Communication

chat using an instant messaging service	(92%)
send text messages	(75%)
write posts/comments on a social networking site	(69%)
make calls using a mobile phone	(50%)
send tweets	(33%)
write emails	(25%)
create or comment on vlogs	(15%)
write or comment on blog entries	(12%)
video chat	(10%)
make calls using a landline	(5%)

0 10 20 30 40 50 60 70 80 90 100

a huge number of (>90%), three quarters of (75%), most of (>51%), half of (50%), a third of (33%), a quarter of (25%), a few of (<15%), very few of (<5%)

A huge number of teens in the survey chat using an instant messaging service.

2 What about your communication habits? Tell your partner.

I prefer using instant messaging services to writing emails.

Listening

3 🎧 You will hear four people talking about social media. Match the speakers (1-4) to the sentences (A-E). One sentence is extra.

A ☐ Using social media can be dangerous for children.

B ☐ Social media has had a negative effect on my studies.

C ☐ I don't see the point of social media.

D ☐ Social media helps me in my career.

E ☐ I reconnect with old friends through social media.

Everyday English
Giving instructions

4 🎧 Listen to and read the dialogue. Put the steps in the correct order.

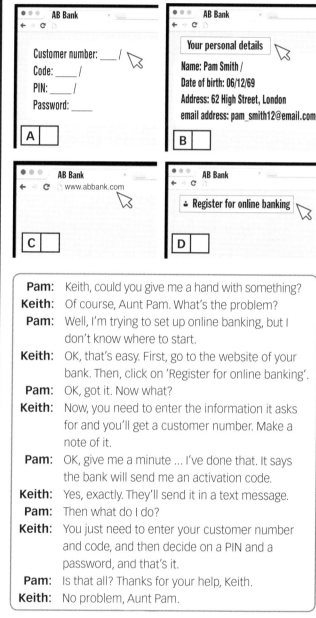

A ☐ Customer number: ___ / Code: ___ / PIN: ___ / Password: ___

B ☐ Your personal details — Name: Pam Smith / Date of birth: 06/12/69 Address: 62 High Street, London email address: pam_smith12@email.com

C ☐ www.abbank.com

D ☐ Register for online banking

Pam:	Keith, could you give me a hand with something?
Keith:	Of course, Aunt Pam. What's the problem?
Pam:	Well, I'm trying to set up online banking, but I don't know where to start.
Keith:	OK, that's easy. First, go to the website of your bank. Then, click on 'Register for online banking'.
Pam:	OK, got it. Now what?
Keith:	Now, you need to enter the information it asks for and you'll get a customer number. Make a note of it.
Pam:	OK, give me a minute … I've done that. It says the bank will send me an activation code.
Keith:	Yes, exactly. They'll send it in a text message.
Pam:	Then what do I do?
Keith:	You just need to enter your customer number and code, and then decide on a PIN and a password, and that's it.
Pam:	Is that all? Thanks for your help, Keith.
Keith:	No problem, Aunt Pam.

5 👥 Use the ideas from the dialogue to explain to your partner how to set up online banking.

Pronunciation: /əʊ/, /ɔː/

6 🎧 Listen and repeat. Can you think of more words with these sounds?

/əʊ/ chose, boat, show, code
/ɔː/ chores, bought, all, law

Reading & Writing

Word formation (forming adverbs)
- We form adverbs from adjectives by adding *-ly* (sad – sad**ly**, private – private**ly**).
- When the adjective ends in *-y*, we drop it and add *-ily* (happy – happ**ily**). When it ends in *-ic*, we add *-ally* (logic – logic**ally**). When it ends in *-le*, we drop the *-e* and add *-y* (possible – possib**ly**)

7 Read the article and complete the gaps with the correct adverbs formed from the words in bold.

From social media to instant messaging services, these days we communicate **1)** .... **(easy)** with our friends in a wide variety of ways. To my mind, though, texting is **2)** .... **(definite)** the best way to keep in touch.

Firstly, texting is **3)** .... **(extreme)** fast. Unlike other communication over the Internet, you don't have to log in or connect to the Internet. Instead, you can read and reply to a text very **4)** .... **(quick)**.

Secondly, texting is private. Your message goes **5)** .... **(direct)** from your phone to another phone. It's not easy for anyone else to see, just the person you **6)** .... **(specific)** send it to.

All in all, I **7)** .... **(strong)** believe that texting is the best way for people to communicate with friends, and it **8)** .... **(probable)** always will be. After all, do you think you could live without texting?

8 **a)** Copy and complete the table in your notebook.

Viewpoints	Reasons/Examples

b) Find two phrases the writer uses to express their opinion.

Expressing an opinion
- I think/feel (that) ... • I (strongly) believe ... • As far as I'm concerned, ... • In my opinion/view, ... • To my mind, ...

Writing Tip

You can start/end an article with:
- **a general statement:** *A lot of people these days have a smartphone.*
- **a rhetorical question** (a question that doesn't need an answer): *Would teenagers today be able to live without their smartphones?*
- **addressing the reader directly:** *What thoughts go through your mind when you can't find your smartphone?*

9 What techniques does the writer of the article in Ex. 7 use to start/end their article?

Writing (an article giving an opinion)

10 **a)** **BRAINSTORMING** Read the task and underline the key words. Then match the viewpoints (1-3) to the reasons/examples (a-c).

You see this notice in an English-language magazine.
SEND US YOUR ARTICLES ON SOCIAL MEDIA
Does social media improve communication?
Write an article answering this question (120-150 words). The most interesting article will appear in next month's issue.

1 ☐ search for old friends
2 ☐ user-friendly way to communicate
3 ☐ opportunity to meet new people

a can chat and post pictures and videos very easily
b can reconnect with old schoolmates
c can make friends with people with similar interests

b) Use the ideas in Ex. 10a or your own ideas to write your article. Follow the plan.

Plan

Para 1: present the topic & give your opinion
Para 2: first viewpoint & reasons/examples
Para 3: second viewpoint & reasons/examples
Para 4: restate opinion

VALUES

Rationality
The real problem is not whether machines think but whether men do.
B.F. Skinner

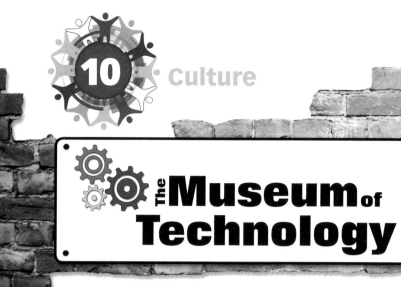

▶ VIDEO

The Museum of Technology

Technology has changed a lot in the last 250 years. **1** ☐ Then, though, people began to **invent** machines for factories – and this 'technological revolution' continued **throughout** the 19th and 20th centuries – right up to the electronic devices we use today. A great place to learn about this story is the Museum of Technology in Lincolnshire, England.

2 ☐ There are different sections in the museum that display **various** kinds of devices. For example, the audio section includes some of the **earliest** gramophones and radios, while the photography section has old cameras which look like big metal boxes! Most of the devices on display are behind glass. **3** ☐ And, in fact, many of them still work!

This museum is a wonderful place to visit for people of all ages. Firstly, younger people, who have grown up with modern technology, can see the big, heavy devices people used years ago. **4** ☐ At the same time, the museum gives older people the **chance** to step back in time and remember the devices they used decades ago.

The Museum of Technology shows how technology has changed the way people live in a very short amount of time. It's an experience you won't forget!

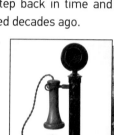

Reading & Listening

1 **What can you see in the pictures? In what ways are these devices different from the modern versions we have today? Read through to find out.**

2 **Read the text and complete the gaps (1-4) with the sentences (A-E). There is one extra sentence. Then, explain the words in bold.**

A Technology museums are becoming increasingly popular.

B A lot of children are amazed to see huge computers, and love trying out a rotary phone with a dial.

C This museum opened in 2012, and takes visitors through the history of technology from 1850 to 1980.

D Up until around 1760, when the Industrial Revolution began, the technology we had was very simple.

E However, visitors can handle lots of items, too.

Check these words

display, gramophone, handle, grow up, decade

3 THINK 🎧 **Listen to and read the text. How can a visit to this museum be interesting to 10-year-old children?**

Speaking & Writing

4 **ICT Collect information about a museum of technology in your country or in another country. Write a short article about it. Include:** *name, location, opening times, history* **and** *what visitors can see there.* **Present it to the class.**

Vocabulary

1 **Choose the correct word.**

1 Kate usually **does/makes** the laundry on Saturdays.
2 Can you **take/bring** this camera to John?
3 The floor's wet because I've just **mopped/vacuumed** it.
4 I always **make/do** the ironing after I dry the clothes.
5 Have you **served/fed** the cat yet today?

(5 x 3 = 15)

2 **Fill in:** *instant, high-definition, text, trade, landline, video, app, social, blog.*

1 There is a(n) .... camera on this tablet.
2 Jane chats to her friends on .... messaging services.
3 Susan doesn't have an account on this .... networking site.
4 Kate posted a comment to Brian's .... entry.
5 These days, I hardly ever use my .... to call people; I use my smartphone, instead.
6 Kate mostly sends .... messages to her friends.
7 Steve has downloaded the new .... on his smartphone.
8 We attended a(n) .... show that displayed new robots.
9 He often .... chats with his friends abroad.

(9 x 2 = 18)

3 **Fill in:** *over, between, on (x2), to, across.*

1 The robot moves around .... four wheels.
2 He didn't manage to get the message ....
3 They get .... well with their new IT tutor.
4 It was hard for Emily to get .... the bad news.
5 I can't connect my laptop .... the TV.
6 What is the difference .... the two cameras?

(6 x 2 = 12)

Grammar

4 **Choose the correct item.**

1 Kate **must/could/ought** be at the tech festival – I'm not certain.
2 Steve is very late – where **shall/can/may** he be?
3 Tim **needn't/mustn't/wasn't able to** sleep – his phone was ringing all the time.
4 Jane **might/can/would** like this app, but I'm not sure.
5 Helen **can't/should/must** be at work – she doesn't work on Saturdays.

(5 x 3 = 15)

5 **Rewrite the sentences using the correct modal verbs from the list.**

• couldn't • may • would • don't have to • mustn't

1 He didn't have the ability to open the file.
He ....
2 It's not necessary for you to download this program.
You ....
3 You have permission to use my tablet.
You ....
4 It's forbidden for us to eat or drink in the computer lab.
We ....
5 Are you willing to help me print the document?
.... ?

(5 x 4 = 20)

Everyday English

6 **Match the exchanges.**

1 ☐ I don't know how to make a video call.
2 ☐ Thanks for your help!
3 ☐ Now, you add your friends to your list.
4 ☐ OK, got it. Now what?
5 ☐ Could you give me a hand with something?

a Of course, Uncle Dan.
b Now, you need to enter your password.
c No problem!
d OK, that's easy.
e How do I do that?

(5 x 4 = 20)
Total 100

Competences

Lexical Competence	Reading Competence	Speaking Competence
understand words/phrases related to: • chores • digital communication	• understand texts related to technology (read for specific information – multiple choice; read for cohesion – missing sentences) **Listening Competence** • listen to and understand monologues related to digital communication (listen for specific information – multiple matching)	• express preference • give instructions **Writing Competence** • write a comment for a blog entry • write an article giving an opinion

Vocabulary: ways of cooking; tastes; customer complaints
Grammar: comparisons; countable/uncountable nouns – quantifiers & partitives; *some/any/no/every* & compounds

Everyday English: making a complaint
Writing: an online complaint form

11 Food for Thought

 VIDEO

Travel diaries

HOME   BLOG   ABOUT   CONTACT

Around the World in Four Bites

As a travel writer, I've been to lots of countries and eaten in a lot of restaurants, but to really get to know a place, I think you have to try the street food. So, here are some of my favourite street snacks from around the world. Feeling hungry? Then let's get started!

See article ▶

A Greece – gyros

Whenever I visit Greece, I just can't keep away from the places that sell gyros. It is made from grilled meat, cooked by turning slowly next to an upright grill. The meat is served in a pitta with onions, tomato, chips and tzatziki, a sauce made with garlic, cucumber and yoghurt. It's so **filling** – I can only eat one!

B Canada – poutine

It might not be the most attractive dish in the world but **ignore** the appearance and **trust** the taste, because poutine is a real treat! This Canadian dish is a mix of double-fried chips, pieces of soft cheese and gravy. You can find this dish in fancy restaurants with a range of toppings, but I recommend getting it from a food truck. You'll definitely want to go back for **seconds**!

C South Korea - beondegi

South Korea has some amazing street food, but for something completely different, get some beondegi. This traditional snack is made from boiled silkworms! Yes, I was pretty **disgusted** at first, too – but you'll get used to it! Street vendors sell them in paper cups, and you eat them with a toothpick. They're cheap, nutritious and, best of all, really tasty! Just close your eyes, and try to forget what you're eating!

D Argentina – empanada

You can find empanadas all over South America, but I think they're far tastier in Argentina! This street food is a small pastry with a huge **choice** of fillings – from chicken and onion to boiled egg and olives! Often, vendors burn a letter into the dough, so they know which fillings they have! Sometimes empanadas are fried but usually they're baked. Either way, they're really delicious!

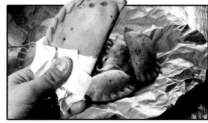

Reading & Listening

1 Look at the pictures in the article. Which of these dishes are: *fried*, *roasted*, *grilled*, *baked*, *boiled*? What are they made from?

🎧 Listen to and read the blog to find out.

✓ **Check these words**

upright grill, pitta, tzatziki, gravy, topping, silkworm, vendor, toothpick, nutritious, pastry, filling, dough

2 a) **Read the blog and decide if the sentences (1-8) are** *T* **(True),** *F* **(False) or** *DS* **(Doesn't Say). Correct the false statements.**

1 People usually eat two servings of gyros. ....
2 Gyros is always eaten with tzatziki. ....
3 Traditionally, poutine has three main ingredients. ....
4 You can only buy poutine in the street. ....
5 People use their hands to eat beondegi. ....
6 Beondegi are good for your health. ....
7 The empanada is the national food of Argentina. ....
8 Customers never know what filling their empanada will have. ....

b) **Then explain the words in bold.**

Vocabulary

Tastes

3 **Use the words in the box to complete the gaps.**

> **spicy** (= having a flavour of spice; hot), **sweet** (= tasting like sugar), **salty** (= tasting of salt), **sour** (= having a sharp taste like lemon or vinegar)

1 I try to avoid .... foods like chips and crisps for health reasons.
2 The Mexican dish was really .... – it felt like my mouth was on fire!
3 Did you forget to put sugar in the lemonade? It's very ....
4 How much sugar did you put in the cake? It's far too .... for me.

4 PREPOSITIONS **Fill in:** *of*, *with (x2)*, *at*, *for (x2)*.

1 .... first, Kate disliked Italian food, but she soon got used to it.
2 .... something different, try poutine; it's delicious.
3 People usually eat spaghetti .... a fork.
4 They served the fish .... chips and a salad.
5 This supermarket has a wide range .... products.
6 The soup was so nice that Greg went back .... seconds.

5 COLLOCATIONS **Fill in:** *fancy, grilled, travel, boiled, soft, paper, street, food.* **Use the phrases in sentences of your own.**

1 .... food   5 .... cheese
2 .... writer   6 .... truck
3 .... meat   7 .... cup
4 .... restaurants   8 .... eggs

6 WORDS EASILY CONFUSED **Choose the correct word. Check in your dictionary.**

1 I think I'll have some apple pie for **dessert/desert**.
2 Steven had the chicken for his main **course/plate**.
3 Could you give me the **receipt/recipe** for your lasagne?
4 Irish stew is the national **dish/meal** of Ireland.

7 PHRASAL VERBS **Fill in the correct particle(s).**

> **keep away from:** to stop sb/yourself going near sb/sth
> **keep up with:** to move at the same speed as sb/sth
> **keep off:** to not walk on sth
> **keep on:** to continue doing sth
> **keep out:** to not allow sb to enter

1 Please keep .... the grass. It hasn't grown yet.
2 Keep the children .... of the kitchen or they'll see the cake!
3 Dan's a really fast eater – I just can't keep .... him.
4 Some people say you should keep .... microwaves when they're working.
5 Jane kept .... asking questions about the food festival.

Speaking & Writing

8 THINK **Which is the best street food you have tried? Where did you try it? What did you like about it?**

9 ICT **What street food is popular in your country? Collect information and write a paragraph about it. Write:** *name of food – country – how it's made and ingredients – how it's eaten – why it's popular.*

Grammar in Use

More than a Market

No visit to Dubai in the United Arab Emirates is complete without a walk through *Souk Madinat Jumeirah*. This modern market has everything from herbs and spices to more luxurious items like pieces of jewellery and designer scarves.

Souk Madinat Jumeirah is more relaxed than the other markets in the city. It's not as crowded as the traditional Arabic markets, plus, it's much easier to get around, with wide paths and lifts to different levels!

In the evening, the market transforms into one of the most exciting nightspots in Dubai, with plenty of fantastic restaurants and cafés. So, head for *Souk Madinat Jumeirah* for the shopping experience of a lifetime!

1 Read the theory. Find examples in the advert.

Comparisons ▷ pp. GR17-18

- ***as* + adjective/adverb + *as***: for two people, things, etc that are the same. *Jane cooks* ***as well as*** *her dad.*
- ***not as/so* + adjective/adverb + *as***: for two people, things, etc that aren't the same. *This coffee shop* **isn't as expensive as** *the one in Kent Street.*
- ***less* + adjective/adverb + *than***: to express the difference between two people, things, etc. *Chicken is* ***less fattening than*** *lamb.*
- ***the least* + adjective/adverb + *of/in***: to compare one person, thing, etc, with two or more people, things, etc of the same group. *It's* ***the least busy*** *restaurant in the area.*
- ***much/a lot/a little/a bit* + comparative**: to express the degree of difference between two people, things, etc. *The restaurant's new menu is* ***a lot better*** *than their old one.*

2 Choose the correct item.

1 A: Jason made a great meal for us last night.
   B: Yes, he cooks a **lot/much** better than I thought.

2 A: I'll never be able to cook an omelette like you do.
   B: Why not? It's the **least/less** difficult recipe I know!

3 A: Why do you want to move to another table?
   B: Because it's **as/much** quieter over there.

4 A: What do you think of the apple pie I made?
   B: It's **so/as** tasty as the ones from the bakery!

5 A: That new Indian restaurant is really expensive.
   B: Yeah, but it's still less expensive **as/than** the Italian restaurant we go to.

3 a) Put the adjectives/adverbs in brackets into the correct form. Give reasons.

1 That was .... **(rude)** shop assistant I've ever met.

2 Tom's home-made curry is a lot .... **(spicy)** than mine.

3 Clare's Café serves .... **(good)** breakfast in town.

4 The cheesecake is .... **(sweet)** of all the desserts on the menu.

5 London's Oxford Street is one of .... **(crowded)** shopping streets in the world.

6 This soup is a little .... **(salty)** than the one you made last week.

b) Compare restaurants in your area. Use: *elegant, large, cheap, busy, quiet, popular, noisy, modern*.

4 Read the theory. Find examples in the advert.

Countable/Uncountable nouns – Quantifiers & Partitives ▷ pp. GR18-19

Countable nouns are those that can be counted. They have singular and plural forms. *a strawberry, two strawberries*
Uncountable nouns are those that cannot be counted. They have no plural forms and we do not use **a/an** before them. *bread, water*
- We use ***how many, a lot of/lots of, (too/not) many, some, a few/few, no/not any, a couple of, hundreds of, both, several, all, enough, plenty of*** with **countable nouns**.
- We use ***how much, (too/not) much, a lot of/lots of, a bit of, some, a little/little, no/not any, all, enough, plenty of*** with **uncountable nouns**.
- We can use both **countable** and **uncountable** nouns after **partitives**: a ***piece, bowl, jar, jug, cup, slice, loaf, glass, carton, bottle,*** etc of ... *a glass of water*

5 Mark the words as (*C*) countable or (*U*) uncountable. Write the plural forms for the countable nouns.

1	bean	*C – beans*	9	cabbage	....
2	steak	....	10	garlic	....
3	milk	....	11	lamb	....
4	onion	....	12	pasta	....
5	cheese	....	13	butter	....
6	carrot	....	14	cucumber	....
7	turkey	....	15	spinach	....
8	yoghurt	....	16	lemon	....

6 Fill in the gaps with the partitives in the list.

• packet • loaf • cup • slice • bar • bunch
• can • bag • carton • tin

1 a .... of cake
2 a .... of bread
3 a .... of chocolate
4 a .... of crisps/biscuits
5 a .... of cola
6 a .... of tea/coffee
7 a .... of flowers
8 a .... of sugar/flour
9 a .... of soup/peas
10 a .... of milk/juice

7 Choose the correct item. Match the exchanges to the shops.

• baker's • newsagent's • bookshop • clothes shop

1 A: Hi, have you got **any/much** Spanish dictionaries?
   B: Yes, we've got **a bit/several** of them in the languages section.
2 A: I'm looking for magazines about football.
   B: We've got a **plenty/few** on the middle shelf over there.
3 A: I'd like **some/few** white bread rolls, please. Could I have ten?
   B: Sorry ... we don't have **any/many** left. Just four.
4 A: I want to buy three shirts like the one in the window. Have you got **many/any** more?
   B: I think we've got a **couple/little** of them in the back. Let me check.

8 SPEAKING Look at the pictures. Act out short exchanges like the ones in Ex. 7. Use quantifiers.

9 Read the table. Then complete the exchanges with *some*, *any*, *no*, *every* and their compounds.

some/any/no/every & compounds ▶ p. GR19				
	Determiner	**Person**	**Thing**	**Place**
Affirmative	some	someone/ somebody	something	somewhere
Interrogative	any	anyone/ anybody	anything	anywhere
Negative	no	no one/ nobody	nothing	nowhere
	every	everyone/ everybody	everything	everything

NOTE: We can use *some* and its compounds in interrogative sentences to make an offer or a request.
*Shall I make you **something** to eat?*

1 A: Do you need .... from the market?
   B: Yes, could you get me .... tomatoes?
2 A: Do you know .... close by that serves Italian food?
   B: Yes. .... time we eat out, we go to Luigi's!
3 A: There's .... at the front door.
   B: Really? I wasn't expecting .... to visit.
4 A: I've looked .... but I can't find my glasses.
   B: Don't worry. I'm sure .... has taken them.
5 A: We need to go shopping. There's .... to eat in the fridge.
   B: OK. Let's get .... we need from the supermarket.
6 A: What an enjoyable meal! .... we ordered was delicious!
   B: Yes, there's .... else in this town I prefer eating than here.

10 Complete the second sentence so that it means the same as the first. Use between two and five words.

1 There weren't many people in the restaurant.
   There were only .... in the restaurant.
2 Ben's Bistro isn't as cheap as Toni's Café.
   Toni's Café is .... Ben's Bistro.
3 My dad is the best cook in my family.
   No one in my family .... my dad.
4 My favourite meal is shepherd's pie.
   There .... I like more than shepherd's pie.
5 Jake wanted his apple pie without ice cream.
   Jake didn't .... ice cream on his apple pie.

Skills in Action

Vocabulary
Customer complaints

1 **Complete the sentences with**: *order*, *bill*, *manager*, *change*, *sell-by date*, *credit card*, *refund*, *receipt*, *note*, *tables*. **Check in your dictionary.**

1 I don't understand why I can't pay for the meal with my .... Can I speak to the ...., please?

2 I'm afraid you've given me the wrong .... I gave you a twenty-pound ...., not a ten.

3 Could we change ...., please? We don't feel comfortable here next to the door.

4 Excuse me. This is not my .... I wanted the curry, not the spaghetti.

5 I'm sorry, but I've just checked the .... and there are some items on it that we didn't have. Could you check it, please?

6 I bought this frozen pizza from your shop yesterday, but it's past its .... I'd like a full ...., please. It costs £5.99. I have the .... with me.

2 **Read the prompts and use the words/ phrases in Ex. 1 to make complaints.**

- You bought a carton of milk at a supermarket but it's past its sell-by date.
- You want to pay a restaurant bill but it includes drinks you hadn't ordered.
- A waiter has just served you a steak but you ordered grilled chicken.

Listening

3 **You will hear a telephone conversation between a customer and an employee in a restaurant. Listen and fill in the gaps (1-5).**

The Orchard
Customer Complaint Form

Day of meal:	*Tuesday 03/04*
Customer name:	*Sally* 1) ....
Address:	2) .... *Victoria Road, Barton*
Contact number:	*0763 232551*
Complaint:	*bill included* 3) .... *not ordered*
Meal Starter:	*vegetable soup*
Main course:	*salmon with roasted* 4) ....; *steak with rice*
Action taken:	*offered customer a* 5) .... *meal*

Everyday English
Making a complaint

4 **Read the first two exchanges. What do you think the customer's complaint is? What action will the manager take? Listen and read to find out.**

Customer:	Hello. I'd like to speak to the manager, please.
Manager:	Actually, I'm the manager – Tim White. How can I help you?
Customer:	I'm afraid I have a complaint to make.
Manager:	Oh, dear. What seems to be the problem?
Customer:	I bought a carton of milk yesterday, but when I got home, I noticed it was past its sell-by date.
Manager:	I'm sorry to hear that. We usually check them carefully.
Customer:	Yes, well, I certainly don't usually check the sell-by dates since I'm a regular customer and this has never happened before.
Manager:	Of course not. May I see your receipt?
Customer:	Here you are. I'd like a replacement, please.
Manager:	Certainly. Let me get you another carton of milk and here's a money-off coupon for next time.
Customer:	That's very kind of you. Thanks.

5 **Use the prompts below and the language in the box to act out a dialogue similar to the one in Ex. 4.**

Customer: Complain about an out-of-date product.
Manager: Offer to give customer a full refund/ replacement.

Making a complaint	Responding to a complaint
• I'd like to speak to the manager/person in charge, please. • I'm afraid I have a complaint to make. • I was upset to find that ...	• I'm the manager/in charge. • How can/may I help you? • What seems to be the problem? • I'm sorry to hear that. • Could/May I see your receipt? • Let me/What I'm going to do is ...

Pronunciation: /ð/, /z/

6 **Listen and tick. Listen again and repeat.**

	/ð/	/z/		/ð/	/z/
clothe			breathe		
close			with		
breeze			whizz		

Reading & Writing

7
a) Look at the heading and subheadings in the form. Where could you see a form like this? What is it used for?

b) Now, read the complaints form and complete the gaps with the words derived from the words in brackets.

New Tab ☒   New Tab ☒ │ +   – ☐ ✕

← → ⟳ ⌂   c Q   ☆ 🗎 ⬇ 🏠 ≡

The Golden Goose

Please complete the form below with your complaint.

| Customer's full name: Emily Conlon |
| Town/City of residence: Derby |
| Email address: e.conlon_83@mail.com |
| Date of visit to restaurant: 25/10/20... |

Complaint in detail:

I am writing to complain about a meal I had in your restaurant on Thursday, 25th October.

To begin with, our table was very **1)** .... **(comfortable)**. It was too small, even for two people, and because it was next to the kitchen, waiters were **2)** .... **(constant)** walking past us. What is more, the **3)** .... **(serve)** was extremely slow. After we gave our order, we had to wait over 40 minutes for our meals. Then, when they finally arrived, they were cold. To make matters worse, when we complained about this to our waiter, he refused to **4)** .... **(apology)**. Instead, he **5)** .... **(rude)** told us that he was too busy to talk to us.

All in all, I was very **6)** .... **(disappoint)** with your restaurant and believe that I am entitled to a refund and an apology. I look forward to your prompt reply.

[Send]

 Writing Tip

When we fill in a complaint form, we should use formal language. We usually use:
- **full verb forms:** *I am writing ...*
- **formal linking words/phrases:** *to begin with, firstly, what is more, to make matters worse,* etc

Unlike emails/letters of complaint, we shouldn't include a greeting/ending (*Dear Sir/Madam,* etc) when we fill in a complaint form.

8
Underline the linking words/phrases that the writer uses to: *list their complaints; introduce the conclusion.* In which paragraph does the writer state the actions they expect the restaurant to take?

9
Fill in the gaps with the words in the list. Which sentences refer to: *complaints; actions expected to be taken*?

- new • order • waiter • parking • behaviour • apology

1 In the first place, I was very disappointed by the .... of your staff.

2 I expect you to send a(n) .... product as soon as possible.

3 I demand a full refund as well as a written ....

4 I sincerely hope that you will speak to the .... involved.

5 To make matters worse, we were served the wrong ....

6 I also found it very frustrating that your restaurant has no customer ....

Writing (a complaint form)

10
a) 🎧 Listen to a phone conversation between a worker for a catering company and a customer, and complete the table.

Complaint	Details
• **1)** .... wasn't delivered on time	• **2)** .... was served one hour late
• **3)** .... of food was poor	• chips were cold and **4)** .... was dry
• wasn't enough to **5)**	• only food for around **6)** .... people

b) Use the information in Ex. 10a to fill in an online complaint form, similar to the one in the model in Ex. 7. Write 120-150 words. Follow the plan.

Plan

Personal details
Para 1: reason for writing, opening remarks
Para 2: complaints with details
Para 3: expected action(s), closing remarks

VALUES

Patience
Patience and time do more than strength or passion.
Jean de La Fontaine

11 Culture

VIDEO

FOOD Festivals IN THE UK

FRENCH FRIES

CHICKEN & WAFFLE SANDWICH

Listening & Reading

1 Read the title, the introduction and the headings. What do you think is special about these events? Read to find out.

2 Read the text and choose the correct word (A, B, C or D) for each gap (1-5).

1	A	puts	B	takes	C	makes	D	does
2	A	several	B	many	C	lots	D	couple
3	A	on	B	by	C	in	D	with
4	A	why	B	when	C	how	D	where
5	A	living	B	live	C	life	D	alive

🎧 Listen and check.

3 Match the words in bold to their synonyms below.

• collect • enjoyable • tasty • yearly • flavours • try • outside

Speaking & Writing

4 👥 **THINK** Imagine organising a food festival for your village/town/city. Think about: *name – where/when – reason – activities – why it's special*. **Present your idea to the class.**

5 **ICT** Find information about a food festival in your country and present it to the class. Use the same headings as in Ex. 4.

The word 'festival' comes from the word 'feast' – a huge meal to celebrate a special day or event. So, it **1)** .... sense for some festivals to be just about food! Here are three British food festivals that you can really sink your teeth into!

Carnaby Street Eat

Carnaby Street isn't just one of the main shopping areas in the centre of London. All year round, you can enjoy **delicious** food in its many cafés and restaurants. The best time to visit is during the Carnaby Street Eat! It takes place every August on a single Saturday afternoon – and includes **2)** .... of food stalls with **tastes** from all over the world!

Ludlow Food Festival

Surrounded **3)** .... beautiful green countryside, Ludlow Castle in Shropshire is a very popular tourist attraction that comes alive for the **annual** Ludlow Food Festival! This festival takes place over three days in September, and many events are held in the grounds of the castle. You'll get a chance to **sample** local dishes, and meet famous British chefs and food critics. Also, there are workshops where you can pick up some cooking tips yourself!

Fork to Fork Food Festival

There's a good reason **4)** .... the Fork to Fork Food Festival in London is an **outdoor** event. Its main purpose is to **raise** money for a project that tries to get kids out in the open air! It's called Ark Franklin's Open Air Classroom, and it promotes outdoor learning and healthy eating. The festival is held every year in a school playground on a Saturday afternoon in June. There are food stalls run by famous chefs, **5)** .... music and entertainment for younger children. It's a **fun** day out for all the family!

✓ **Check these words**

sink your teeth into, stall, grounds, food critic, workshop, promote

Vocabulary

1 Choose the correct word.

1 He demanded a **refund/receipt** for the bad meal.

2 Fish and chips is her favourite **street/pastry** food.

3 We went to a(n) **fancy/attractive** restaurant for my 21st birthday.

4 Can I pay for the meal by **credit/note** card?

5 Steve bought a sandwich from a street **truck/vendor**.

6 At the festival I tried lots of traditional Mexican **meals/dishes**.

7 This is the wrong **change/order** – you owe me £5.

8 Kate chose the pasta for her main **course/plate**.

(8 x 2 = 16)

2 Fill in: *refund, date, note, bill, order*.

1 We didn't order all of these items on the ....

2 That's a ten-pound ...., not a twenty.

3 My .... was for the chicken – not the pasta.

4 This carton of juice is past its sell-by ....

5 I'd like a new carton of milk or a(n) ....

(5 x 2 = 10)

3 Choose the correct item.

1 **For/At** something different, try gyros.

2 There is a huge range **of/about** dishes to choose from.

3 You should keep **onto/off** the floors until they are dry.

4 Keep **about/away** from me! I've got a cold!

5 Italians eat pizza **by/with** their hands.

(5 x 2 = 10)

Grammar

4 Choose the correct item.

1 Do we have **many/a few/any** flour to make a cake?

2 Gavin ate a **little/couple/few** of slices of toast.

3 There were a **lot/bit/little** of dishes to choose from.

4 There's **plenty/lot/enough** of cheese to eat.

5 The soup needs a **little/few/several** more salt.

(5 x 2 = 10)

5 Complete the sentences with the correct comparative or superlative form.

1 The Grill is definitely .... (**bad**) restaurant in town.

2 Can you walk .... (**fast**)? We'll be late for our reservation!

3 That was .... (**rude**) waiter I've ever met!

4 Laura cooks .... (**good**) of all my friends.

5 This pasta cooks .... (**slowly**) than the one we usually buy.

6 Tim prepared the .... (**tasty**) soup I've ever eaten!

(6 x 4 = 24)

6 Fill in: *every, anyone, everyone, somewhere, nothing*.

1 Has .... read this review of Pizza Palace?

2 Can we go .... nice to eat tonight?

3 Let's wait until .... has arrived before we order.

4 .... time we eat here, we enjoy it.

5 There's .... for vegetarians to eat here.

(5 x 3 = 15)

Everyday English

7 Match the exchanges.

1 ☐ I'd like to speak to the person in charge.

2 ☐ How may I help you?

3 ☐ I noticed it was out of date.

4 ☐ Could I see your receipt?

5 ☐ Let me give you a full refund.

a That's very kind of you.

b Here you are.

c Actually, I'm the manager.

d I have a complaint to make.

e I'm sorry to hear that.

(5 x 3 = 15)

Total 100

Earth, our Home

Vocabulary: environmental problems; eco-activities
Grammar: the causative; clauses of purpose, reason & result; determiners
Everyday English: persuading
Writing: an article providing solutions to a problem

Vocabulary

Environmental problems

1 🎧 Read or listen to the poem. What is it trying to tell us?

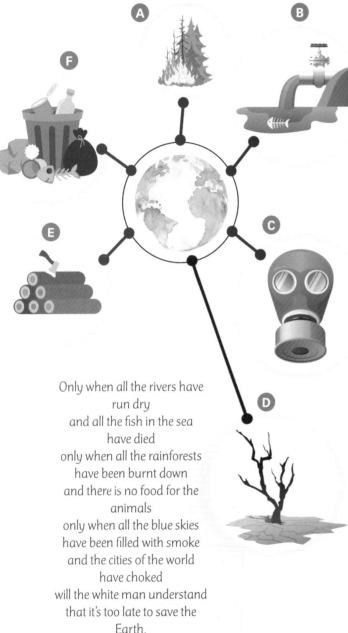

Only when all the rivers have
run dry
and all the fish in the sea
have died
only when all the rainforests
have been burnt down
and there is no food for the
animals
only when all the blue skies
have been filled with smoke
and the cities of the world
have choked
will the white man understand
that it's too late to save the
Earth.
(Native American poem)

2 Look at the list of problems and match them to the pictures.

• water pollution • rubbish • cutting down trees
• air pollution • lack of rain • forest fires

Listening & Reading

3 Read the introduction in the text. Which of the environmental problems in Ex. 2 are mentioned?

4 🎧 Can you think of a solution to the problem that might be in the text? Listen to and read the text to find out.

5 Read the text and for questions 1-4, choose the best answer (A, B, C or D). Then, explain the words in bold.

1 What is the purpose of the text?
   A to persuade people to recycle
   B to describe a difficult situation
   C to give advice on running a business
   D to show how some people have improved their lives

Being fantastic with plastic!

*Pollution from plastic waste and the effects that it has on wildlife is one of the planet's most serious environmental issues. Plastic pollution kills animals, damages oceans, and even **spoils** drinking water and the food we eat. In Kenya, however, one group has started to fight the problem.*

Dadaab in northeast Kenya is one of the world's biggest refugee camps, covering an area of 30 square kilometres. It was set up in 1991 when people from **nearby** Somalia needed to escape from war and has been used ever since. Today, it's home to around a quarter of a million people. Life there is difficult; there's often not enough food and there is **little** fresh water. People live in tents and rely on food from charities such as milk powder and rice, sent in plastic packaging. They cannot leave the camp and look for work. So how can they go on living there?

98

2 Why did the refugees move to the camp?

   A They went there to find work.

   B There was more food there.

   C There was fighting in their country.

   D There were better homes there.

3 People laughed at Adow because he

   A had a strange hobby.

   B did something unusual.

   C couldn't take care of his family.

   D was very poor.

4 Why does the writer think the factory has a future?

   A It can offer a lot of jobs.

   B Recycling is easy to do.

   C The business is cheap to run.

   D There is so much plastic around.

The answer is quite surprising. People support themselves by recycling plastic! This unusual eco-friendly solution was started when refugee Adow Sheikh Aden began collecting old plastic waste from around the camp. People laughed at him at first since **picking up** bottles and broken buckets wasn't a normal thing to do. But Adow explained he was doing it so that the camp would be cleaner and he could earn some money to help him **look after** his family. Finally, others started to **join in**.

Today, there is a recycling factory with eight **staff** and the project is continuing to grow. The workers use a special machine to break up the plastic in order to pack it easily. They then have it delivered to Kenya's capital city, Nairobi, and **receive** money for it. A camp the size of Dadaab has lots of rubbish, so there's plenty of work! The factory recycled six tonnes of plastic in the first year, making around 160,000 Kenyan shillings (equal to 1,600 US dollars) and that was just the start.

One of the workers, Abtidon Ali Mahat, earned enough **wages** to get married, build a home of his own at the camp and buy goats – something none of the refugees ever imagined before the recycling factory opened! Dadaab's war on plastic waste **proves** that everybody can help Mother Earth and make a big difference to our world.

✔ **Check these words**

refugee camp, war, packaging, support myself, bucket, earn, break up, goat

6 COLLOCATIONS **Look at the text and fill in:** *eco-friendly*, *plastic*, *recycling*, *environmental*, *capital*, *drinking*.

1 .... waste   **4** .... solution

2 .... issues   **5** .... city

3 .... water   **6** .... factory

7 PREPOSITIONS **Choose the correct preposition.**

DID YOU KNOW THAT ...

1 two thirds of all polar bears are **in/on** danger of disappearing in the next thirty years?

2 a lack **to/of** green spaces can create more stress?

3 thousands of Indian volunteers joined **in/up** an effort to plant 66 million trees in 12 hours?

4 global temperatures have increased **in/by** 0.9ºC since the 1880s?

8 WORDS EASILY CONFUSED **Fill in with** *clean* **or** *clear*. **Check in your dictionary.**

1 It's .... to me that the planet needs saving.

2 There's a .... sky tonight with lots of stars.

3 It is important to keep the environment ....

4 If we want .... air, we must stop using cars!

9 PHRASAL VERBS **Fill in the correct particle.**

go off: 1) to leave the place where you were; **2)** (of electrical devices) to stop operating
go on: 1) to continue; **2)** to happen
go out: (of a fire or light) to stop burning/shining

1 The fire will go .... if you don't put some more wood on it.

2 How can people go .... using so much plastic?

3 Jules went .... to Brazil to help save the rainforests.

4 What's going .... over there in the park?

5 The washing machine suddenly went .... in the middle of a wash.

Speaking & Writing

10 ICT **Collect information on different ways to reuse empty plastic bottles. Make a poster and present it to the class.**

Grammar in Use

Stef: Hi Lucy. Did you see that programme on TV last night about how pollution is changing the world's climate?

Lucy: Yes, it's shocking what we are doing to the Earth! Our cities are so polluted by car fumes that I've decided to walk from now on. I'll use the car for emergencies only and I'll have it serviced regularly so that it'll use less petrol.

Stef: Good for you. The programme got me thinking, too. I didn't know that we should be eating less meat because producing it is bad for the environment.

Lucy: Yes, apparently we should be eating more vegetables in order to reduce our carbon footprint.

Stef: So, from now on, I plan to have meat just once a week. That'll improve my health, too.

Lucy: That's fantastic, Stef! If every person does something, it will make a big difference!

1 Read the theory. Find an example in the dialogue.

Causative form (*have* + object + past participle of the main verb) ▷ **p. GR20**

	Active	Causative
Present simple:	She **takes** her photo.	→ She **has** her photo **taken**.
Present continuous:	She **is taking** her photo.	→ She **is having** her photo **taken**.
Past simple:	She **took** her photo.	→ She **had** her photo **taken**.
Past continuous:	She **was taking** her photo.	→ She **was having** her photo **taken**.
Future simple:	She **will take** her photo.	→ She **will have** her photo **taken**.
Present perfect:	She **has taken** her photo.	→ She **has had** her photo **taken**.
Modals:	She **can take** her photo.	→ She **can have** her photo **taken**.

We use the **causative** to say that we have **arranged for someone to do something for us**. *Tom had the tickets booked by Jane.* (Tom didn't book the tickets himself. Jane did it for him.)

2 Use the words in brackets to complete the sentences. Use the causative form.

1 John ....
(the leaky tap/fix) last week.

2 The school ....
(a greenhouse/build) at the moment.

3 You ....
(should/your air conditioner/service).

4 They ....
(a herb garden/plant) when it started raining.

5 Sally ....
(her groceries/deliver) tomorrow by the supermarket.

3 Complete the sentences using the causative.

1 We hired a professional to design our roof garden.
We *had our roof garden designed by a professional.*

2 They will ask a mechanic to check their car.
They.. .

3 The electrician has replaced all my old light bulbs with LED ones.
I ....

4 A local company is installing solar panels on our roof.
We ....

5 A gardener was cutting the grass in her garden at 10 am this morning.
She ....

6 You should ask someone to take the newspapers to the recycling centre.
You ....

4 Read the theory. How do we introduce clauses of purpose? Find examples in the dialogue.

Clauses of purpose ▷ **pp. GR20-21**

Clauses of purpose explain **why** someone does something. They are introduced with:

- **to-inf**: *Karen drove to the bottle bank **to recycle** the bottles.*
- **in order (not) to/so as (not) to + inf**: *Mario bought a bicycle **in order to get** around the city more easily.*
- **so that + can/will/could/would + inf**: *They should improve the bus service **so that** more people **can use** public transport.*
- **in case + present tense** (present/future reference) / **past tense** (past reference): *Wear something warm for the tree-planting day **in case** it **gets** cold.* NOT: *in case it will get cold.*

5 **Join the sentences using the words in brackets. Write in your notebook.**

1 Mark turned on the TV. He wanted to watch a wildlife programme. **(in order to)**

2 Please switch off the lights when you leave. Don't waste electricity. **(so as not to)**

3 They're going to close the factory. It won't cause any more pollution. **(so that)**

4 Take gloves. You might plant some trees. **(in case)**

5 Jake went to the bottle bank. He wanted to recycle some bottles. **(to)**

6 **Read the theory. How do we introduce clauses of result? Find an example in the dialogue on p. 100.**

Clauses of result ▷ p. GR21

Clauses of result express **result**. They are introduced with:
- **so**: *It's World Environment Day on 5th June so our school is organising a special event.*
- **such a/an** (+ adj) + **singular countable noun** + **that**: *It's such a polluted city that people have to wear masks.*
- **such** (+ adj) + **uncountable noun/plural noun** + **that**: *Matt takes such great wildlife photos that they have appeared in magazines.*
- **so** + **adj/adverb** + **that**: *Our planet is warming up so quickly that we have to act now!*

7 **Choose the correct item. Give reasons.**

1 The traffic jam was **so/such** bad that it took us three hours to get home.

2 It was **such/such a** dirty beach that we left.

3 We're having **so/such** dry weather that the lake has dried up.

4 The park doesn't have many litter bins **so/such** it's always full of rubbish.

5 It was **such a/so** busy at the festival that we left early.

8 **Read the theory. How do we introduce clauses of reason? Find an example in the dialogue on p. 100.**

Clauses of reason ▷ p. GR21

Clauses of reason explain the **reason why** something happens. They are introduced with:
because; **since/as** (= because); **the/a reason for** + **noun/-ing** form + **is/was** + **noun/-ing** form; **the/a reason why** ... **is/was** + **noun/-ing** form/**that**-clause:
We recycle because we care about the environment.
(OR: *Because we care about the environment, we recycle.*)

9 **Join the sentences using the words in brackets. Write in your notebook.**

1 I buy organic food. It's better for the environment. **(why)**

2 Don't swim in the river. It's polluted. **(because)**

3 Jean will join the park clean-up. She's free on Saturday. **(since)**

4 Cars cause air pollution. **(a reason for)**

5 There weren't any buses to the city centre. We shared a taxi. **(as)**

10 **Read the theory. Find an example in the dialogue on p. 100.**

Determiners ▷ pp. GR21-22

Both ... and ... is followed by a plural verb. *Both Laura and Jenny are taking part in the clean-up day.*
Every and **each** are used with singular countable nouns. *Every volunteer needs to bring their own equipment.*
Neither ... nor/Either ... or take either a singular or plural verb, depending on the subject which follows *nor* or *or*. *Neither Steve nor Alan is coming. Either trousers or shorts are suitable to wear.*
None of refers to more than two people, things or groups. It is followed by either a singular or plural verb. *None of us has/have ever taken part in a clean-up day before.*
All is followed by a plural verb. *All the volunteers are friends of mine.*
Whole is used with singular countable nouns. *The whole day will be spent outdoors.*

11 **Choose the correct item.**

1 Neither Jack **or/nor** Jill owns a car.

2 The **whole/all** planet will be better off if we recycle more.

3 You can choose **neither/either** the bus or the underground to get to the stadium.

4 **Both/Every** Susan and Sally joined the environmental club.

5 **Each/All** house has got its own recycling bin.

6 **None/All** of my friends are vegetarian – I'm the only one.

7 **Whole/Every** child needs to learn how to care for the environment.

8 **Every/All** events at the eco-festival are suitable for children.

12c

Skills in Action

Vocabulary

Eco-activities

1 **a)** **Fill in**: *use, turn, buy, print, plant, leave, send, wrap, take (x2)*.

🎧 **Listen and check.**

DOs & DON'Ts

✔️   ❌

1 .... turns driving each other to work, the shops, etc	**1** .... fruit and vegetables that are out of season
2 .... part in clean-up days	**2** .... 'single-use' products (e.g. paper plates, plastic knives)
3 .... off the tap when brushing teeth or shaving	**3** .... on just one side of the paper
4 .... greetings using email not paper cards	**4** .... food in plastic
5 .... trees that attract birds	**5** .... computers, etc plugged in when not in use

b) **Which of these do/don't you do?**

Listening

2 🎧 **You will hear people talking in four different situations. For questions 1-4, choose the best answer (A, B or C).**

1 Listen to the conversation. Where does it take place?

   A at home   **B** in a car   **C** in a café

2 Listen to a woman talking about factories. What does she suggest?

   A reducing what factories produce
   B ordering some factories to close down
   C building factories outside cities

3 Listen to the conversation. What are the people annoyed about?

   A how the news was reported
   B the dry weather   **C** a careless action

4 You hear this conversation. What are the speakers going to do?

   A use less electricity   **B** save water
   C change shopping habits

Everyday English

Persuading

3 **a)** **Read the dialogue and fill in the missing phrases**.

- could manage
- see you
- come along
- need more
- pick you up

Val:	We've organised a clean-up day at the local park. Do you want to **1)** ....?
Rob:	Sure. When is it?
Val:	Next weekend. It would be great if you could help. We **2)** .... volunteers.
Rob:	Oh, I've got to study for my exams next weekend, but maybe I could spare a couple of hours.
Val:	Every little helps! Whatever you **3)** .... would be really great.
Rob:	Well, I'll be there, then. What time are you meeting?
Val:	At 10 o'clock on Saturday morning. I'll come and **4)** .... if you want.
Rob:	OK, thanks. **5)** .... on Saturday.

b) 🎧 **Listen and check.**

4 👥 **Act out similar dialogues using the prompts below. Use phrases from the language box.**

- clean up a beach/river/lake   • have a recycling day

Inviting	Asking for help/Persuading
• Would you like to join us? • We'd love to see you there.	• Your help would mean a lot. • We're hoping you could help out. • Anything you can manage would be (really) helpful. • Any help is welcome.
Offering transport	
• I'd be glad to give you a lift there. • Why don't I pick you up?	

Pronunciation: /d/, /dʒ/

5 🎧 **Listen and tick. Listen and repeat.**

	/d/	/dʒ/		/d/	/dʒ/
paid			hard		
page			large		
jeep			jog		
deep			dog		

Reading & Writing

6 **a)** Read the article and fill in the gaps with words derived from the words in brackets.

People today buy more products than ever before. This creates **1)** .... **(terror)** amounts of rubbish and is a **2)** .... **(globe)** problem. So how can we reduce waste so that the Earth doesn't turn into a giant rubbish tip?

One useful suggestion is to recycle. **In other words**, used items made of plastic, glass, paper and metal can **3)** .... **(easy)** be taken to the nearest recycling bin. **That way**, we will help protect the environment.

Another way around the problem is to 4) .... **(use)** items instead of throwing them away. **For instance**, empty jars, tins and bottles can be used to keep things in. **This means that** they do not end up in our rubbish bin.

In conclusion, recycling rubbish and using items a second time are both important ways of reducing waste. By taking **5)** .... **(act)**, I believe we will see a great **6)** .... **(improve)** in the environment. 'Good riddance to bad rubbish', as the saying goes.

Linking ideas

Link your points with appropriate linking words/phrases. This helps the reader follow your article.

b) Look at the linkers in bold. Which: *give explanations/examples*? *make suggestions*? *present expected results*?

7 Read the article again and complete the table in your notebook.

Suggestions	Explanations/Examples	Expected results
recycle	**1)**	**2)** ....
3)	keep things in empty jars, tins, bottles	**4)** ....

Writing (an article providing solutions to a problem)

8 Read the task and answer the questions.

An environmental magazine has asked its readers to send in articles about the overuse of plastic in modern society. They will publish the best ones. Write an article for the magazine (120-150 words) suggesting ways of solving the problem.

1 What are you going to write? Who for?

2 What should you write about?

3 How many words should your piece of writing be?

9 **a)** 🎧 Listen to a radio programme about reducing plastic in our everyday lives and complete the table in your notebook.

Suggestions	Explanations/Examples	Expected results
1)	use it again – avoid plastic bags	cleaner environment
Don't buy things sold in plastic	**2)**	**3)** ....

b) Use your notes in Ex. 9a to write your article. Give your article a title. Follow the plan.

Plan

Introduction

Para 1: state problem & cause

Main body

Para 2: first suggestion – explanation/example – expected result

Para 3: second suggestion – explanation/example – expected result

Conclusion

Para 4: summarise points; state your opinion

VALUES

Respect

Try to leave the Earth a better place than when you arrived.

Sidney Sheldon

Listening & Reading

1 Look at the picture and read the title. What do you think Washed Ashore is?

🎧 Listen and read to find out.

▶ VIDEO

Washed Ashore
Art to save the sea

by Alistair White

The sea is full of plastic! People throw their rubbish into it where it stays for a very long time – a plastic bottle can take up to 450 years to break down. 80% of all the sea's rubbish is plastic and it's harming sea animals which eat it, sometimes even killing them. In fact, around 100,000 sea turtles and mammals die every year because of plastic as well as 1,000,000 sea birds. Meanwhile, the plastic goes on **increasing**, with around 8 million metric tons a year ending up in our oceans.

After a while, lots of this rubbish washes up on the beach. And that's the reason Washed Ashore got started. Washed Ashore is an environmental organisation that makes fantastic **giant** sculptures out of plastic sea rubbish. It was **set up** in 2010 in Oregon, USA by artist Angela Pozzi. In just five years, she created over 70 sea creatures using 20 tons of ocean rubbish. She does her sculptures in order to get people to think more seriously about pollution.

Today, the organisation has its plastic collected from beaches in southern Oregon, USA by 10,000 volunteers. After that, it's taken to Angela's workshop, where her team divide the pieces into piles according to size, shape and colour. Then they're ready to start creating. The results are amazing works of art including sharks, jellyfish, octopuses, puffins, parrot fish and other exotic creatures. They are displayed at exhibitions all over the US and **remind** people of the need to keep our environment **clean**. As Angela says, she will **go on** making sculptures until there is no more plastic on the beach!

If you're **curious** to find out if any Washed Ashore exhibitions are happening near you at the moment, visit the organisation's website: www.washedashore.org. There, you can also learn more about the problem of plastic at sea and how you can help.

> ✓ **Check these words**
>
> ashore, mammal, sculpture, divide, pile, jellyfish, octopus, puffin, exhibition

2 Read the text again and complete the summary. Use ONE word in each gap.

The oceans are full of **1)** .... in the form of plastic. This costs the lives of thousands of **2)** .... each year. Washed Ashore is an organisation that creates giant **3)** .... from the plastic that **4)** .... up on the beaches of Oregon in the **5)** .... By doing this, the head of Washed Ashore, Angela Pozzi, hopes to get more people interested in the **6)** .... problem. The sculptures show a range of sea creatures, which you can see at different **7)** .... around the US. More information is available on the organisation's **8)** ....

3 👤👤 Ask and answer questions based on the text. Then, explain the words in bold.

Speaking & Writing

4 👤👤 **THINK** Imagine you are a volunteer for Washed Ashore. What kind of plastic items do you think you would find on the beach? Make a list and compare with your partner.

5 💬 **ICT** Collect information about an environmental organisation in your country or another country. Make notes under the headings: *Name – Details of organisation – What it does – How to get involved*. **Write a short article about it for a magazine.**

Vocabulary

1 **Match the words to form phrases.**

1 ☐ lack of		**a**	fire
2 ☐ clear		**b**	air
3 ☐ forest		**c**	pollution
4 ☐ water		**d**	rain
5 ☐ clean		**e**	sky

(5 x 3 = 15)

2 **Fill in:** *wraps, takes, buys, plants, leaves.*

Amy believes in taking care of the environment. At home, she never **1)** .... her TV or laptop plugged in when not in use. Also, she only **2)** .... fruit and vegetables that are in season and she's in an environmental group which regularly **3)** .... trees in a local forest. When she goes to work, she **4)** .... turns with a friend to drive there, and she never **5)** .... her sandwiches in plastic – she uses a lunchbox. Amy is a great example of how to be eco-friendly!

(5 x 3 = 15)

3 **Choose the correct item.**

1 Is the Earth **in/at** danger of getting too hot?

2 While we were watching the documentary, the TV went **out/off**.

3 Jake went **on/off** to Africa to volunteer there.

4 When I told Tim about the clean-up day, he immediately agreed to join **for/in**.

5 Can you tell me what is going **off/on** here?

(5 x 1 = 5)

Grammar

4 **Choose the correct item.**

1 One reason **why/for** pollution is smoke from factories.

2 We should recycle **in order to/so that** save the planet!

3 It was **so/such** a big fire that it burned for three days.

4 Take a raincoat **as/in** case it rains.

5 **So/Because** she lives nearby, Nellie walks to work.

6 **Every/None** of my classmates speak French.

7 **Each/Either** tree you plant helps the environment.

8 **Neither/Both** Jess nor Sam eats meat.

9 We spent the **whole/all** afternoon cleaning the beach.

10 **All/Both** Kevin and his wife Kathy are keen cyclists.

(10 x 3 = 30)

5 **Rewrite the sentences in the causative.**

1 A mechanic services our car every six months.
We ....

2 Paul should ask someone to fix his water pipes.
Paul ....

3 We will ask them to print our posters on recycled paper.
We ....

4 Gemma has asked her mum to repair her old clothes.
Gemma ....

5 They asked Marta to take their picture.
They ....

(5 x 3 = 15)

Everyday English

6 **Match the exchanges.**

1 ☐ Do you want to join us on the beach clean-up?	**a**	Thanks. See you then.
2 ☐ It would be great if you could help.	**b**	At 10:30 in the morning.
3 ☐ What time are you meeting up?	**c**	OK. When is it?
4 ☐ Why don't I pick you up?	**d**	Sorry. I've got lots to do this weekend.

(4 x 5 = 20)

Total 100

Competences

GOOD ✓

VERY GOOD ✓✓

EXCELLENT ✓✓✓

Lexical Competence
understand words/phrases related to:
- environmental problems
- eco-activities

Reading Competence
- understand texts related to the environment (read for specific information – multiple choice/complete gaps)

Listening Competence
- listen to and understand dialogues/monologues related to the environment (listen for specific information – multiple choice)

Speaking Competence
- persuade someone to participate in an event

Writing Competence
- write an article providing solutions to a problem
- write an article about an environmental organisation

Values: Caution

Home ⌄   Photo Gallery ⌄   Archives ⌄   Features ⌄   Contact

Virtual villains  ▶ VIDEO

NEWS / **TECHNOLOGY**

13 MARCH / **By Philippa Warr**

As well as being citizens of our country and citizens of the world, we are also digital citizens. So, we have to be just as careful when we meet people in cyberspace as we are in the real world. Here's a list of ten **nasty** online personalities to watch out for …

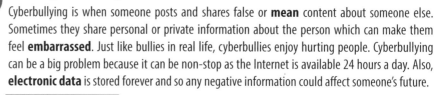

1 The cyberbully

Cyberbullying is when someone posts and shares false or **mean** content about someone else. Sometimes they share personal or private information about the person which can make them feel **embarrassed**. Just like bullies in real life, cyberbullies enjoy hurting people. Cyberbullying can be a big problem because it can be non-stop as the Internet is available 24 hours a day. Also, **electronic data** is stored forever and so any negative information could affect someone's future.

| How to spot a cyberbully |

A cyberbully isn't hard to spot because they don't hide, but cyberbullying can be hard to **deal with**. If it happens to you, report it straight away to the police.

2 The catfish

A catfish is someone who pretends to be someone else online to trick another person. They do this to get attention. They post a picture that isn't theirs and they use a **fake** name. It can be very **upsetting** when the 'friend' you thought you had turns out to be someone completely different.

| How to spot a catfish |

If your online friend won't meet in person or even video chat, then it could be a sign that they are not who they say they are. Also, if they ask you for money or gifts, then you should be **suspicious**.

3 The troll

In Scandinavian fairy tales, a troll is an ugly, mean creature that hides under bridges and waits to attack people. An Internet troll is similar because they are **bitter** and they hide behind their computer screens. They try to cause trouble and post ugly comments in forums and chat rooms to start an argument and upset people.

| How to spot a troll |

It's quite easy because their comments are very **offensive**. There's no point trying to argue with them because that only encourages them. It is always best to ignore them.

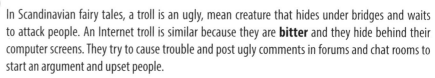

RELATED ARTICLES   VIEW MORE ARTICLES

Next page

---

1 Read the title and the introductory paragraph of the article. What is a 'virtual villain'? Look at the pictures. What examples of virtual villains do you think you are going to read about? 🎧 Listen and read to find out.

2 Read the article again. For questions 1-5, write *CB* for cyberbully, *CF* for catfish or *T* for troll. Who…

1 might cause you trouble years later? ....
2 avoids appearing on camera? ....
3 wants to annoy people? ....
4 should not be answered? ....
5 may be doing something illegal? ....

3 Explain the words/phrases in bold.

4 👥 THINK Have you ever experienced bad behaviour online? Tell your partner.

5 ICT Research hackers online and write a short text like the ones above to add to the list of virtual villains. Give it the title 'The hacker'. Read it to the class.

Public Speaking Skills

1 **Read the task and answer the questions.**

Give a talk to a group of students on the right way to use smartphones.

1 Who are you going to speak to?
2 What is the talk going to be about?
3 What is the purpose of the talk: to entertain, to narrate, to inform or to persuade?

Study Skills

Persuasive approaches
- Appeal to the audience's morals: *Trolling is wrong.*
- Appeal to the audience's emotions: *Cyberbullying makes people feel terrible.*
- Appeal to the audience's logic: *True friendship can't be based on lies, can it?*

---

2 🎧 **Listen to and read the model. Match the persuasive approaches 1-3 with the underlined parts of the talk.**

1 appeal to the audience's morals
2 appeal to the audience's emotions
3 appeal to the audience's logic

3 **What opening/closing techniques are used?**

4 **Read the task and brainstorm for ideas. Then, prepare and give a presentation on the topic.**

Give a talk to a group of students about the right way to use social media.

Hello, everyone. Today, I want to talk to you about healthy, safe and responsible smartphone use.

Who's got a smartphone? Hands up! About 78% of adults in the UK own a smartphone, and why not? It's probably the most powerful communication tool ever. However, it's important to use your smartphone smartly. So, ask yourself three questions.

First of all, are you using your smartphone in a healthy way? Some people use theirs for as much as four hours a day, and answer messages they receive in the middle of the night. I think you'll all agree that's too much. Experts now say screen time late at night can make it difficult for you to fall asleep, so avoid picking your smartphone up for an hour before you go to bed. Also, don't keep your smartphone next to you at night, so it can't wake you up.

Secondly, are you using your smartphone in a safe way? We often have to unlock our smartphones in public, but make sure nobody can see you do it. Smartphones are stolen every day, but nobody can do you much harm unless they gain access. As long as you report the theft quickly, there won't be enough time to hack your phone. That means that, although you may not get the phone back, at least your personal information is safe. Imagine how awful you would feel if it wasn't!

Finally, are you using your smartphone in a responsible way? In other words, do you consider the people around you? For example, you shouldn't talk in a loud voice on the phone in public, such as on a bus or in a lift. And don't you just hate it when a phone starts ringing or constantly beeping with message notifications in the middle of a great film? Well, if you don't like it happening to you, don't do it to others. Put it on silent whenever you are at the cinema or theatre.

There's no doubt that smartphones are useful devices. You can call people, send text messages, take pictures, go on social media, play games and use the Internet. So, of course we all want to own one – but we don't want it to own us, do we?

Many smartphones have an app that shows us our total screen time per week. So, let's try to keep it under control.

A

CLIL: Literature

Listening & Reading

1 Do you know the story of 'The Old Man and the Sea'? If not, can you guess what happens from the picture? Tell the class.

2 🎧 Listen to and read the extract and decide if the sentences (1-5) are *T* (**True**) or *F* (**False**). Then, explain the words in bold.

1 The old man wasn't able to see the moon. ....

2 It was easy for the old man to row the boat. ....

3 When the lines were in the water, the old man kept the boat still. ....

4 The old man was more careful than the other fishermen. ....

5 The old man was sure he wouldn't catch any fish. ....

Study Skills

Figurative language
Authors use figurative language to engage their readers. They often use personification, that is they give an object or animal human qualities or abilities.
The sun smiled in the sky.

---

3 Read the Study Skills box. Find examples of personification in the text.

Speaking & Writing

4 👥 THINK In pairs, discuss what you think happens next in the story. Present your ideas to the class.

5 ICT Collect information about Ernest Hemingway and his works and make notes. Present him and his works in class.

The OLD MAN and the SEA

He began to row out of the harbour in the dark. There were other boats from the other beaches going out to sea, though he could not see them now the moon was below the hills. Sometimes, someone would speak in a boat. But most of the boats were silent. Each fisherman **headed for** the part of the ocean where he hoped to find fish.

In the dark the old man could feel the morning coming. As he rowed, he heard a sound as flying fish jumped out of the water. He was very **fond of** flying fish – they were his friends on the ocean. He was sorry for the birds that were always flying and looking but almost never finding anything.

He was rowing steadily and it was no effort for him since the surface of the ocean was **flat**. As it started to get lighter, he saw he was already further out than he had hoped to be at this hour.

Before it was really light, he had four baits* out. Now, the man watched the sticks over the side of the boat and rowed **gently** to keep the lines straight up and down and at their proper depths. Slowly the sun rose from the sea. The old man could see the other boats in the distance closer to the shore. He kept his lines straighter than anyone else did, so that at each level there would be a bait waiting exactly where he **wished** it to be for any fish that swam there. Other fishermen let their lines move with the current, so they didn't know how far down they were.

"I may have no luck anymore," he thought. "But who knows? Maybe today. It is better to be lucky. But I would rather be exact. Then, when luck comes, you are ready."

Ernest Hemingway (1952)

---
* food which is put on a hook at the end of a fishing line

 Check these words

row, harbour, hill, steadily, depth, shore, current

How 3D Film Technology Works

Watching a film in 3D at the cinema is an amazing experience. Seeing things pop out of the screen and **float** in front of our eyes really brings the film to life. But how is it possible to see a 3D image on a flat cinema screen?

3D **stands for** three-dimensional. Dimensions are the different ways we can describe space. For example, a 2D image has two dimensions — length and width. So, if we draw a box on a piece of paper we can see how tall and how wide it is, but we can't see how far back it goes. This third dimension is called 'depth' — and this is the difference between 'normal' 2D films and 3D films. Most objects we see in our everyday lives have depth — and seeing depth is only **possible** using both of our eyes.

Whenever we look at something, the image we see is actually a **mixture** of two images — one from our left eye and one from our right eye. Hold out one arm with your thumb pointing up. Close one eye, open it again, and then close the other eye. You'll see that your thumb moves **slightly** right or left. When both of our eyes are looking at something, our eyes' images mix, and this lets our brains understand depth — to see things in 3D.

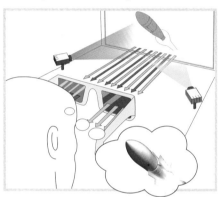

In the same way, 3D films give us two versions of the same image, and this tricks our brains into thinking it has depth. Today, filmmakers shoot each scene of a 3D film using two side-by-side camera lenses — exactly as two human eyes would see the scene. Then, a special cinema projector **displays** both of these versions on the cinema screen — but not at the same time. Instead, they show the two versions in turn — one after the other — but so fast that we don't notice it. Modern 3D glasses are able to separate these two images — so one of our eyes sees one version of the image, and the other eye sees the other version. Then, our brains do the rest — giving us amazing 3D images that we want to reach out and touch — just like we are part of the action.

✓ Check these words

flat, dimensions, length, width, depth, brain, version, trick into, lens

Listening & Reading

1 What's the difference between a 3D film and a normal film? What equipment do you need to be able to watch a 3D film?

🎧 Listen and read to find out.

2 Read the text again and complete the sentences (1-5) with words from the text. Then, explain the words in bold.

1 3D technology lets us see 3D images on .... cinema screens.

2 Unlike 2D films, 3D films allow us to see .... as well as length and width.

3 3D films are filmed using two camera .... beside each other.

4 Cinemas use a special cinema .... to display 3D films.

5 You need to wear 3D .... to experience a 3D film.

Speaking & Writing

3 👥 THINK How do you think cinemas will change in the future? Discuss with your partner.

4 ICT Collect information about a film that was made in 4D. Write a short review of it. Write: *name – director – cast – general comments – recommendation*.

CLIL: Science

Listening & Reading

1 How do earthquakes happen?
🎧 Listen, read and check.

2 Read the text and label the diagram. Use the highlighted words/phrases.

3 Read the text again and decide if the sentences (1-4) are *T* (True) or *F* (False). Then, explain the words in bold.

1 Scientists are able to measure how fast tectonic plates travel. ....

2 When two tectonic plates move towards each other, a mountain can form. ....

3 When two plates get stuck at the edges, they move away from each other. ....

4 An earthquake always involves some shaking in the epicentre. ....

Speaking & Writing

4 Use the diagram to explain how earthquakes happen.

5 💬 ICT Collect information about safely measures in the event of an earthquake. Prepare a presentation.

All the Earth's land and water sits on huge flat pieces of rock called tectonic plates. These plates sit on other **layers** of softer rock closer to the Earth's centre, and are always moving over them, at speeds of around two to five centimetres a year. The places where two plates meet is called a fault line, and different things can happen there. For example, when two plates 'crash' into each other, the two edges can **rise up** and make a mountain.

Plates can also move alongside each other, but, because they don't have perfectly **smooth** edges, they often get stuck at the edges, and have to slow down. The plates keep trying to move in the same direction, though, so they put more and more **pressure** on the point which has stopped them. After maybe hundreds or thousands

of years, the stuck edges finally manage to get unstuck. When this happens, the plates move past each other very quickly. This causes an earthquake.

The place where tectonic plates get unstuck is called the focus of the earthquake, and the epicentre is the place on the surface directly above it. When an earthquake happens, all the energy that has **built up** at the focus is suddenly released. This energy becomes seismic waves – and they cause shaking around the focus. If a lot of energy is released, seismic waves can move up to the surface, and cause **shaking** in and around the epicentre – sometimes resulting in a lot of damage. Around the world, there are around 55 earthquakes every day – but most of them are so small that we don't feel them on the ground.

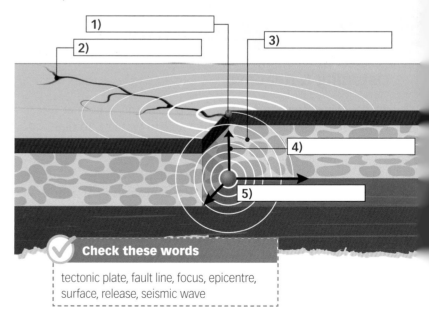

1)
2)
3)
4)
5)

✓ **Check these words**

tectonic plate, fault line, focus, epicentre, surface, release, seismic wave

CAVES

A cave is a large hole in the earth which has been formed by nature. There are caves around the world, on the sides of hills, cliffs and mountains, and, of course, underground. You can even find caves under the sea, or in the ice of a glacier.

Caves form over long periods of time. In fact, some caves are hundreds of thousands of years old. Usually, a cave is formed when water **breaks down** soft rock like limestone, gypsum and dolomite. This is called erosion. Over time, the movement of water against this soft rock can create holes in it, which eventually become a cave. This happens, for example, when waves **hit** against the side of a sea cliff over and over again.

Caves can also form when rainwater or melted snow or ice moves into the earth. When this happens, the water mixes with carbon dioxide in the soil, and this **creates** carbonic acid. This acid can make small holes in the soft rock underground, which slowly get wider and wider and connect. Eventually, a cave is formed. Caves like this are called karst caves.

Many karst caves are filled with what look like giant stone columns — stalactites which hang down from the ceiling, and stalagmites which stick up from the floor. These are made by water coming through small holes in the ceiling of a cave. This water has **tiny** pieces of a mineral called calcite, which is either left on the ceiling of a cave, or falls with **drops** of water to the floor. With each drop of water, the little piles of calcite grow, and stalactites and stalagmites get longer and longer.

Today, people **explore** cave systems as a hobby. This activity is called caving or potholing. Caves can be dangerous places, though, so it's important not to **enter** a cave system without a caving instructor and the correct equipment.

✔ **Check these words**

form, glacier, erosion, carbon dioxide, carbonic acid, karst cave, calcite

Listening & Reading

1 **How are caves formed?**
🎧 **Listen and read to find out.**

2 **Read the text again and complete the sentences (1-5) with words from the text. Then, explain the words in bold.**

1 Caves are usually formed from .... that has been broken down.

2 Carbonic acid is a mixture of water and ....

3 .... are underground caves formed by carbonic acid.

4 .... are columns in caves which rise from the ground.

5 You shouldn't go potholing without the proper .... and an instructor.

Speaking & Writing

3 ICT **Collect information about a cave in your country and make a leaflet advertising it to tourists. Write about:** *name – where it is – how big it is – special features – history*. **Decorate your leaflet with photographs and/or drawings.**

Grammar Reference

Unit 1

Present simple

Form: main verb (+ **-s** in the third person singular)

Affirmative	I/You/We/They **walk.** He/She/It **walks.**
Negative	I/You/We/They **do not/don't walk.** He/She/It **does not/doesn't walk.**
Interrogative	**Do** I/you/we/they **walk?** **Does** he/she/it **walk?**
Short answers	**Yes,** I/you/we/they **do.** **Yes,** he/she/it **does.**
	No, I/you/we/they **don't.** **No,** he/she/it **doesn't.**

Spelling 3rd-person singular affirmative
- Most verbs take **-s** in the third-person singular.
  I cook – he cooks
- Verbs ending in **-ss, -sh, -ch, -x** or **-o** take **-es**.
  I pass – he passes, I push – he pushes, I watch – he watches, I fix – he fixes, I do – he does
- Verbs ending in consonant + **y** drop the **-y** and take **-ies**. *I study – he studies*
- Verbs ending in vowel + **y** take **-s**. *I play – he plays*

Use
We use the **present simple** for:
- **daily routines/repeated actions** (especially with adverbs of frequency: **often, usually, always,** etc).
  She starts work at 8.00.
- **habits.** *She plays tennis twice a week.*
- **permanent states.** *He works as a doctor.*
- **timetables/schedules** (future meaning).
  The bus arrives at 11.00.
- **general truths and laws of nature.**
  The sun sets in the west.
- **reviews/sports commentaries/narrations.**
  Rogers catches the ball with an amazing dive!

> **Time words/phrases used with the *present simple*:** every day/month/hour/summer/morning/evening, etc, usually, often, sometimes, always, etc, on Sundays/Tuesdays, etc

Adverbs of frequency

- **Adverbs of frequency** tell us how often sth happens. These are: always (100%), usually (90%), often (70%), sometimes (50%), occasionally (30%), rarely/seldom (10%), never (0%).
- **Adverbs of frequency** go **before** the **main verb** but **after** the main verb **be** and auxiliary verbs **be, have, do** and modals such as **will, may,** etc.
  She often goes to school on foot. She is rarely late.

Present continuous

Form: subject + verb ***to be*** *(am/is/are)* + main verb **-ing**

Affirmative	Negative
I**'m talking.** You**'re talking.** He/She/It**'s talking.** We/You/They**'re talking.**	I**'m not talking.** You **aren't talking.** He/She/It **isn't talking.** We/You/They **aren't talking**
Interrogative	**Short answers**
Am I **talking?** **Are** you **talking?** **Is** he/she/it **talking?** **Are** we/you/they **talking?**	**Yes,** I am./**No,** I'm **not.** **Yes,** you are./**No,** you **aren't.** **Yes,** he/she/it **is.**/ **No,** he/she/it **isn't.** **Yes,** we/you/they **are.**/ **No,** we/you/they **aren't.**

Spelling of the present participle
- Most verbs take **-ing** after the base form of the main verb. *walk – walking, read – reading*
- Verbs ending in **-e** drop the **-e** and take **-ing**.
  dance – dancing, arrive – arriving
- Verbs ending in **one vowel + consonant** and which are stressed on the last syllable, **double the consonant** and take **-ing**. *run – running, admit – admitting* **BUT** *cover – covering* (stress on 1st syllable)
- Verbs ending in **-ie** change the **-ie** to **-y** and add **-ing**.
  tie – tying

Use
We use the **present continuous** for:
- actions happening **now**, at the moment of speaking.
  He is swimming now.
- actions happening **around the time of speaking**.
  She is studying hard for her exams these days.
- **fixed arrangements** in the **near future**, especially when we know the time and the place.
  We're flying to Paris.
- **temporary situations**.
  He is spending the week with his father.
- **changing or developing situations.**
  Sue is getting more and more impatient.
- frequently repeated actions, with **always, constantly** and **continually**, to express annoyance or criticism.
  You are always interrupting me!

Note: The following verbs do not usually have a continuous form: *have* (= possess), *like, love, hate, want, know, remember, forget, understand, think, believe, cost*, etc. *I don't know where Mary lives.*

> **Time words/phrases used with the *present continuous*:** now, at the moment, at present, nowadays, these days, today, tomorrow, next month, etc

Present simple vs Present continuous

Present simple	Present continuous
permanent states & facts *He **works** in a bank.*	**temporary situations** *They**'re staying** with their grandparents this week.*
habits/routines *Max usually **takes** the bus to work.*	**actions happening now/ around the time of speaking** *He's **talking** on the phone.*
timetables (future) *The ferry **departs** at 18:00.*	**future arrangements** *He's **meeting** his friends later.*

Stative verbs

Stative verbs are verbs which describe a state rather than an action, and do not usually have a continuous form. These are:

- verbs of the **senses** (*appear*, *feel*, *hear*, *look*, *see*, *smell*, *sound*, *taste*, etc). *He **looks** excited.*
- verbs of **perception** (*believe*, *forget*, *know*, *understand*, etc). *I don't **understand** what he is saying.*
- verbs which express **feelings** and **emotions** (*desire*, *enjoy*, *hate*, *like*, *love*, *prefer*, *want*, etc). *He **loves** rock music.*
- other verbs: *agree*, *be*, *belong*, *contain*, *cost*, *fit*, *have*, *include*, *keep*, *need*, *owe*, *own*, etc. *His house **costs** a lot of money.*

Some of these verbs can be used in continuous tenses, but with a difference in meaning.

Present simple	Present continuous
*I **think** he's telling the truth.* (= believe)	*He **is thinking** of going to Rome in the summer.* (= is considering)
*They **have** a very old car.* (= own, possess)	*Nick **is having** lunch.* (= is eating) *Mary **is having** some guests tonight.* (= is hosting)
*We can **see** the river from our hotel room.* (= the river is visible) *I **see** what you mean.* (= understand)	*He **is seeing** the dentist later.* (= is meeting)
*This food **tastes** good.* (= the flavour of the food is)	*She **is tasting** the chicken to check if it needs more salt.* (= is trying)
*The candle **smells** like roses.* (= has the aroma of)	*Ann **is smelling** the flowers.* (= is sniffing)
*He **appears** to be tired.* (= seems)	*She **is appearing** in the new Bond film.* (= is performing)
*The cat's fur **feels** very soft.* (= has the texture of)	*The doctor's **feeling** her forehead to see if she has a fever.* (= is touching)

*Sue **is** very sensitive.* (character – permanent state)	*You **are being** very impolite.* (behaviour – temporary state)
*This top **fits** you well.* (= is the right size)	*They **are fitting** new cupboards in the kitchen.* (= are putting)
*He **looks** sad.* (= appears)	*He **is looking** at the statue.* (= is taking a look at)

Note: The verb *enjoy* can be used in continuous tenses to express a **specific preference**. *She **enjoys** travelling.* (general preference) **BUT** *They **are enjoying** themselves at the cinema.* (specific preference)
The verbs *look* (when we refer to somebody's appearance), *feel* (when we experience a particular emotion), *hurt* and *ache* can be used in simple or continuous tenses with no difference in meaning. *I **feel** exhausted. = I'm **feeling** exhausted.*

Relatives

We use relative pronouns (who, whose, which, that) and relative adverbs (where, when, why) to introduce relative clauses. We use relative clauses to identify/describe the person/place/thing in the main clause.

Relative clause
*The man **who** directed the film is my uncle.*

Relative pronouns

people	**who/ that**	*Mr Smith is the person **who** owns the new restaurant.*
objects/ animals	**which/ that**	*The suit **which** you're wearing looks expensive.*
people	**whose**	*My friend bought a house **whose** garden is very big.*

Notes:
- *Who*, *which* and *that* can be omitted when they are the object of the relative clause, that is when there is a noun or a subject pronoun between the relative pronoun and the verb. *The film **(which/that)** I am watching is about ancient Greeks.*
- *Who*, *which* and *that* are not omitted when they are the subject of the relative clause. *The couple **who** bought the flat are from London.*
- *Whose* is never omitted. *Lisa is the girl **whose** short story won first prize.*
- *That* can be used instead of *who*, *whom* or *which*, but it is never used after commas or prepositions. *Sue is the one **who/that** suggested travelling to Spain. Paul, **who's** never been abroad, is flying to Vienna next summer.*

Grammar Reference

Relative adverbs

- We use **where** to refer to places. *The hotel where we stayed was near the beach.*
- We use **why** to give a reason. *Nobody knows the reason why she left work early.*
- We use **when** to refer to time. *I will never forget the day when I first met my best friend.*

Note: When using **where** or **when**, we do not need a preposition. *The restaurant where we usually eat is by the sea.* (NOT: ~~The restaurant where we usually eat at is by the sea.~~)

Defining & Non-defining relative clauses

- A **defining relative clause** gives necessary information, essential to the meaning of the main sentence. It is not put in commas and is introduced with **who, which, that, whose, where, when** or **the reason (why)**. The relative pronoun can be omitted when it is the object of the relative clause. *The market where I buy fruit is close to my house. The taxi (which) we took broke down and we had to walk back home.*
- A **non-defining relative clause** gives extra information and is not essential to the meaning of the main sentence. It is put in commas and is introduced with **who, which, whose, where** or **when**. The relative pronoun cannot be omitted. *Mark, who lives next door, has got three cats.*

Note: We usually avoid using prepositions before relative pronouns. When we do, we use **whom**, not **who**. *The waitress to whom we gave our order was very polite.* (formal)
The waitress who/that we gave our order to was very polite. (less usual)
The waitress we gave our order to was very polite. (everyday English)

Unit 2

Past simple

Form: regular verb + **-ed**
The **past simple** affirmative of regular verbs is formed by adding **-ed** to the verb. Some verbs have an irregular past form (See Irregular Verbs list at the back of the book).

Affirmative	Negative
I/You/He/She/It/We/They **looked/ran.**	I/You/He/She/It/We/They **did not/ didn't look/run.**
Interrogative	**Short answers**
Did I/you/he/she/it/we/they **look/run?**	**Yes,** I/you/he/she/it/we/they **did. No,** I/you/he/she/it/we/they **didn't.**

Spelling
- We add **-d** to verbs ending in **-e**. *I save – I saved*
- For verbs ending in consonant + **-y**, we drop the **-y** and add **-ied**. *I try – I tried*
- For verbs ending in vowel + **-y**, we add **-ed**. *I stay – I stayed*
- For verbs ending in one stressed vowel between two consonants, we double the last consonant and add **-ed**. *I drop – I dropped*

Use
We use the **past simple** for:
- actions which happened at **a specific time** (stated, implied or already known) **in the past**.
  He visited New York last year. (When? Last year.)
  Jill went with him. (When? The time is implied/already known, last year.)
- **past habits**. *He went swimming when he was little.*
- past actions which happened **one immediately after the other**. *He put on his jacket, got his schoolbag and left for school.*
- past actions which **won't take place again**. *William Shakespeare wrote many plays.*

> **Time words/phrases used with the *past simple*:** yesterday, yesterday morning/evening etc, last night/ week etc, two weeks/a month ago, in 2010, etc

Past continuous

Form: *was/were* + main verb + **-ing**

Affirmative	Negative
I/He/She/It **was sleeping.** We/You/They **were sleeping.**	I/He/She/It **was not/ wasn't sleeping.** We/You/They **were not/ weren't sleeping.**
Interrogative	**Short answers**
Was I/he/she/it **sleeping?** **Were** we/you/they **sleeping?**	**Yes,** I/he/she/it **was./ No,** I/he/she it **wasn't.** **Yes,** we/you/they **were./ No,** we/you/they **weren't.**

We use the **past continuous** for:
- an action which was **in progress** at a stated time in the past. We do not know when the action started or finished. *Jenny was surfing the Net at 9:00.*
- a past action which was **in progress** when another action **interrupted** it. We use the past continuous for the action in progress (longer action) and the past simple for the action which interrupted it (shorter action). *She was running when she slipped and fell down.*
- two or more actions which were happening at the same time in the past (**simultaneous actions**). *I was doing my homework while my brother was playing computer games.*

- to give **background information** in a story. *It was a beautiful spring day. The sun was shining and the birds were singing.*

> **Time words/phrases used with the *past continuous*:** while, when, as, at 11:00 yesterday, etc

Past simple vs Past continuous

Past simple	Past continuous
actions which happened at a **stated time** in the past. *Bob travelled to Australia last August.*	actions **in progress** at a stated time in the past. *The children were playing outside yesterday morning.*
actions which happened **one after the other** in the past. *First Sue had a shower and then she prepared dinner.*	two or more actions which were happening **at the same time** in the past. *She was talking on the phone while she was typing.*

used to – would – Past simple

- We use *used to*/**past simple** to talk about past habits or actions that happened regularly in the past, but no longer happen. *She used to go/went skiing twice a year.* (She doesn't do that anymore.)
- We use *would/used to* for repeated actions or routines in the past. We don't use *would* with **stative verbs**. *Paul used to play/would play the drums when he was at school.* **BUT** *We used to have two cats at home.* (NOT: ~~We would have two cats at home.~~)
- We use the **past simple** for an action that happened at a definite time in the past. *Jenny moved to Athens two years ago.* (NOT: ~~Jenny used to/would move to Athens two years ago.~~)

Prepositions of movement

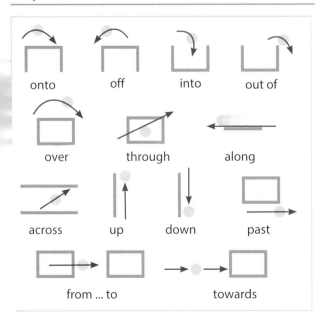

onto off into out of

over through along

across up down past

from ... to towards

- When we talk about a means of transport, we use the preposition *by*. *by car/bus/train/taxi/plane/boat* **BUT** *on foot*
- We do not use the preposition *by* when there is an article *(a/an/the)*, a possessive adjective (*my*, *your*, etc) or a possessive case before the means of transport. *on the bus* (NOT: ~~by the bus~~), *in your car* (NOT: ~~by your car~~), *on the two o'clock ferry*, *on the plane*, *in Susan's car*

Unit 3

Present perfect

Form: subject + *have/has* + past participle of the main verb

Affirmative	Negative
I/You/We/They **have**/**'ve visited**. He/She/It **has**/**'s visited**.	I/You/We/They **have not/haven't visited**. He/She/It **has not/hasn't visited**.
Interrogative	**Short answers**
Have I/you/we/they **visited**? **Has** he/she/it **visited**?	**Yes**, I/you/we/they **have**./ **No**, I/you/we/they **haven't**. **Yes**, he/she/it **has**./ **No**, he/she/it **hasn't**.

Use
We use the **present perfect**:
- for actions which **started in the past** and **continue** up to the **present**, especially with stative verbs such as *be*, *have*, *like*, *know*, etc. *Paul has been in Edinburgh for two years.* (= He came to Edinburgh two years ago and he is still here.)
- to talk about **a past action** which has a **visible** result in the **present**. *Adam has cut his hair and he looks different now.*
- for actions which happened at an **unstated time** in the **past**. The action is more important than the time it happened. *She has bought a new car.* (When? We don't know; it's not important.)
- with *today*, *this morning/afternoon/week*, *so far*, etc when these periods of time are not finished at the time of speaking. *He has written two letters today.* (The time period – 'today' – is not over yet. He may write another letter.)
- for **recently completed actions**. *They have just cleaned the room.* (The action is complete. The room is clean now.)
- for **personal experiences/changes** which have happened. *It's the first time they have travelled abroad.*

Grammar Reference

Time words/phrases used with the *present perfect*:
- *already* (normally in affirmative sentences)
  *You don't need to call Laura. I've **already** talked to her.*
- *yet* (normally in interrogative or negative sentences)
  *Have you seen the film **yet**? He hasn't called me **yet**.*
- *just* (normally in affirmative sentences to show that an action finished a few minutes earlier)
  *She has **just** finished her project.*
- *ever* (normally in affirmative and interrogative sentences) *This is the best book I've **ever** read. Have you **ever** been to Sweden?*
- *never* (negative meaning)
  *She has **never** tried sushi.*
  *Peter has **never** travelled by plane.*
- *for* (over a period of time)
  *He has worked as a teacher **for** five years.*
- *since* (from a starting point in the past)
  *She has been in Spain **since** last week.*
- *recently* (normally in affirmative or interrogative sentences)
  *They have **recently** bought a new house.*
  *Have you seen Lisa **recently**?*
- *so far* (normally in affirmative sentences)
  *We have done a great job **so far**.*

have gone (to)/have been (to)/have been in

- *Paul **has gone** to the gym.* (He's on his way to the gym or he's there now. He hasn't come back yet.)
- *Liz **has been** to France.* (She went to France but she isn't there now. She's come back.)
- *They **have been in** Wales for three weeks.* (They are still in Wales.)

Present perfect vs Past simple

Present perfect	Past simple
an action which happened at an **unstated time** in the past. *They **have arrived**.* (We don't know when.)	an action which happened at a **stated time** in the past. *They **arrived** yesterday.* (When? Yesterday. The time is mentioned.)
an action which started in the past and is still continuing in the present. *Mark **has lived** here since 2008.* (He still lives here.)	an action which started and finished in the past. *She **moved** here from Lisbon.* (She's not in Lisbon now.)

Present perfect continuous

Form: subject + *have/has been* + main verb *-ing*

Affirmative	Negative
I/You/We/They **have/'ve been working**. He/She/It **has/'s been working**.	I/You/We/They **have not/haven't been working**. He/She/It **has not/hasn't been working**.
Interrogative	**Short answers**
Have I/you/we/they **been working**? **Has** he/she/it **been working**?	**Yes**, I/you/we/they **have**./ **No**, I/you/we/they **haven't**. **Yes**, he/she/it **has**./ **No**, he/she/it **hasn't**.

Use

We use the **present perfect continuous**:
- to place **emphasis** on **the duration of an action** which started in the past and continues up to the present. *Charles **has been working** all day.*
- for an action that **started in the past** and lasted for some time. It may still be continuing or has finished, but its **results are visible in the present**. *Grace is tired. She's **been studying** since morning.*
- to express **anger, irritation, annoyance** or **criticism**. *Who **has been using** my laptop?* (annoyance)

Time words/phrases used with the *present perfect continuous*: since, for, how long (to place emphasis on duration)

Past perfect

Form: subject + *had* + past participle of the main verb

Affirmative	Negative
I/You/He, etc **had left**.	I/You/He, etc **had not/hadn't left**.
Interrogative	**Short answers**
Had I/you/he, etc **left**?	**Yes**, I/you/he, etc **had**./ **No**, I/you/he, etc **hadn't**.

We use the **past perfect**:
- for an action which **finished before another past action** or **before a stated time in the past**. *They **had finished** dinner by the time Mary arrived.* (past perfect [**had finished**] before another past action [**arrived**]) *The rainfall **had stopped** by midnight.* (before a stated time in the past [**by midnight**])
- for an action which **finished in the past** and whose **result was visible at a later point in the past**. *Emma was thrilled because she **had won** the contest.*

Note: The **past perfect** is the past equivalent of the **present perfect**. *There was no pizza left; Denise **had eaten** the last piece.* (present perfect: *There **is** no pizza left, Denise **has eaten** the last piece.*)

Time words used with the *past perfect*: before, already, after, for, since, just, till/until, by, by the time, never, etc

Past perfect continuous

Form: subject + *had been* + main verb -*ing*

Affirmative	Negative
I/You/He/She/It/We/They **had been swimming**.	I/You/He/She/It/We/They **had not/hadn't been swimming**.
Interrogative	**Short answers**
Had I/you/he, etc **been swimming?**	**Yes**, I/you/he/she/it/we/they **had**./ **No**, I/you/he/she/it/we/they **hadn't**.

We use the **past perfect continuous**:

- to put emphasis on the **duration** of an action which started and finished in the past, before another action or stated time in the past, usually with *for* or *since*. *I had been searching for two hours before I found the car keys.*

- for an action which **lasted for some time** in the past and whose **result was visible** in the past. *He had been studying for weeks, so the exam was easy for him.*

Note: The **past perfect continuous** is the past equivalent of the **present perfect continuous**. *Sheila was tired because she had been painting the house all day.* (present perfect continuous: *Sheila is tired because she has been painting the house all day.*)

Time words/phrases used with the *past perfect continuous*: for, since, how long, before, until, etc

The/–

The definite article is used with singular and plural nouns. *the apple – the apples*
We use *the*:

- with **nouns when we are talking about something specific**, that is, when the noun is mentioned for a second time or is already known. *She bought a pair of gloves yesterday. The gloves were made of leather.*

- with nouns which are **unique** *(the sun, the moon, the earth, etc).*

- before the names of **rivers** *(the Nile)*, **seas** *(the Mediterranean)*, **oceans** *(the Atlantic)*, **mountain ranges** *(the Alps)*, **deserts** *(the Sahara)*, **groups of islands** *(the Canary Islands)*, **countries** when they include words such as 'state', 'kingdom', etc *(the United Kingdom)* and nouns with **of** *(the Leaning Tower of Pisa)*.

- before the names of **musical instruments** *(the piano, the drums, etc).*

- before the names of **hotels** *(the Hilton Hotel)*, **theatres/cinemas** *(the Odeon)*, **ships** *(the Queen Mary)*, **organisations** *(the EU)*, **newspapers** *(the Times)* and **museums** *(the Museum of Modern Art).*

- before **nationalities** *(the Canadians)* and **families** *(the Robinsons).*

- before **titles when the person's name is not mentioned** *(the Queen, the President).*

- before the words **morning, afternoon** and **evening**. *He usually takes his dog for a walk in the morning.*

- with **adjectives** in the **superlative** form. *It's the best film I've ever seen.*

We don't use *the*:

- with **plural nouns when we talk about them in general**. *Dogs are faithful companions.*

- before **proper names**. *This is Ann. She comes from Ireland.*

- before the names of **countries** *(Spain)*, **cities** *(Seoul)*, **streets** *(Madison Avenue)*, **parks** *(Hyde Park)*, **mountains** *(Everest)*, **islands** *(Sicily)*, **lakes** *(Victoria)* and continents *(Europe).*

- before the names of **meals** *(breakfast, lunch,* etc*)* and **games/sports** *(tennis, basketball,* etc*). Swimming is a relaxing sport.*

- with the words **this/that/these/those**. *This car is mine.*

- with **possessive adjectives** or the **possessive case**. *That isn't my bag. It's Marsha's.*

- **before titles when the person's name is mentioned.** *Queen Elizabeth, Prince Charles* **BUT** *the Queen, the Prince*

- with the words **school, church, bed, hospital, prison** or **home** when we refer to the purpose for which they exist. *Mary goes to school every day.* (Mary is a student.) **BUT** *Mary's father wants to go to the school to ask Mary's teacher about her progress.* (Mary's father wants to go to the school as a visitor, not a student.)

- with **languages**. *I speak German.* **BUT** *The German language is difficult to pronounce.*

NOTE: We use *the* + **adjective** to refer to a group of people, usually with the following adjectives: *poor, rich, sick, old, dead, blind, young* etc. *The elderly usually like to advise the young.*

Unit 4

Future simple

Form: subject + *will* + main verb

Affirmative	Negative
I/You/He/She/It/We/They **will/'ll run.**	I/You/He/She/It/We/They **will not/won't run.**
Interrogative	**Short answers**
Will I/you/he/she/it/we/they **run?**	**Yes**, I/you/he/she/it/we/they **will**./ **No**, I/you/he/she/it/we/they **won't**.

Grammar Reference

Use

We use the **future simple**:

- for **on-the-spot decisions**.
  I'm so hungry. I'll order a pizza.

- for **predictions based on what we believe or imagine will happen** (usually with the verbs: *hope*, *think*, *believe*, *expect*, *imagine*, etc; with the expressions: *I'm sure*, *I'm afraid*, etc; with the adverbs: *probably*, *perhaps*, etc).
  I think John will be a great doctor one day.
  We will probably go to the cinema tonight.

- for **promises** (usually with the verbs *promise*, *swear*, etc) *I promise I'll email you every day.*; **threats** *If you do that again, I will tell the teacher.*; **warnings** *Don't touch that plate! You will get burnt.*; **hopes** *I hope I will pass the exams.*; **offers** *Don't worry! I'll help you.*

- for **actions/events/situations which will definitely happen** in the future and which **we cannot control**.
  Mark will be ten years old next week.

> **Time words/phrases used with the *future simple*:**
> tomorrow, the day after tomorrow, next week/month/year, tonight, soon, in a week/month/year, etc

---

be going to

Form: subject + verb *to be (am/is/are)* + *going to* + base infinitive of the main verb

Affirmative	I am/'m He/She/It **is**/**'s** We/You/They **are**/**'re**	**going to eat.**
Negative	I am not/ I'm not He/She/It **is not**/**isn't** We/You/They **are not**/**aren't**	**going to eat.**
Interrogative	**Am** I **Is** he/she/it **Are** we/you/they	**going to eat?**
Short answers	Yes, I am./No, I'm not. Yes, he/she/it **is.**/ No, he/she/it **isn't.** Yes, we/you/they **are.**/ No, we/you/they **aren't.**	

Use

We use *be going to*:

- to talk about **future plans** and **intentions**.
  John is going to study Chemistry. (He's planning to.)

- to make **predictions based on what we see or know**.
  Look at those clouds! It's going to rain tonight.

- to talk about **things we are sure about**, or **we have already decided to do** in the near future.
  They are going to buy a new car. (They have already decided to do it.)

Present simple/Present continuous (future meaning)

- We can use the **present simple** to talk about **schedules** or **timetables**.
  Classes start at 9:00.

- We use the **present continuous** for **fixed arrangements** in the near future.
  I'm meeting my boss in an hour.

Time clauses

- **Time clauses** are introduced by: *after*, *as*, *as soon as*, *before*, *by the time* (= before, not later than), *every time*, *just as*, *once*, *the moment (that)*, *until/till* (= up to the time when), *when*, *while*, etc.
  I'll call you as soon as I arrive at the airport.

- **Time clauses** follow the rule of the sequence of tenses.

Main clause	Time clause
present/future form	present form
I'll cook dinner before I go to the cinema. (NOT: ~~will go~~)	

Main clause	Time clause
past form	past form
He went out after he had finished his homework.	

- When the time clause precedes the main clause, a comma is used. When the time clause follows, no comma is used.
  After Mary finishes work, she goes to the gym.
  BUT *Mary goes to the gym after she finishes work.*

Note: We use future forms with '**when**' when it is used as a question word.
When will they deliver our new sofa?
(**Compare:** *I'll send you a postcard when I go to Brazil.* [time word])

Conditionals: types 0 & 1

Conditional clauses consist of two parts: the *if-clause* (hypothesis) and the **main clause** (result).
When the *if-clause* comes before the **main clause**, the two clauses are separated with a comma.
If the weather is bad, we'll stay in.
When the **main clause** comes before the *if-clause*, no comma is needed.
We'll stay in if the weather is bad.

	If-clause (hypothesis)	Main clause (result)
0 conditional: general truth or scientific fact	**if/when** + present simple	present simple
	*If you **exercise** regularly, you **keep** fit.*	
1st conditional: real situation, likely to happen in the present/ future	**if/when** + present simple	simple future, imperative, *can/ must/may*, etc + bare infinitive
	*If we **have** free time, we**'ll go** to the cinema.*	

Notes:
- With type 1 conditionals we can use *unless* + **affirmative verb** or *if* + **negative verb**. *Unless you study hard, you **won't pass** the exam.* (You won't pass the exam if you don't study hard.)
- We use *if* to show that something might happen, whereas we use *when* to show that something will definitely happen. *If I see her tomorrow, I **will give** her the book.* (= I might see her tomorrow) *When I see her tomorrow, I **will give** her the book.* (= I will definitely see her tomorrow)
- We do not normally use *will*, *would* or *should* in an *if*-clause. However, we can use *will* or *would* after *if* to make a polite request, or express insistence or uncertainty (usually with expressions such as *I don't know*, *I doubt*, *I wonder*, etc). In this case, *if* means *whether*. We can also use *should* after *if* to talk about something which is possible, but not very likely to happen. *If you **will fill** in this form, we **will offer** you our special discount.* (Will you please fill in this form? – polite request) *If you **will keep** disturbing the class I'll inform your parents.* (If you insist on disturbing ... – insistence) *I wonder if my sister **will remember** to pay the electricity bill.* (I wonder whether ... – uncertainty) *If your toothache **should get** worse, I will **take** you to the dentist.* (I don't really expect that your toothache will get worse.)

Unit 5

Future continuous

Form: subject + *will be* + main verb *-ing*

Affirmative	Negative
I/You/He/She/It/ We/They **will/'ll be moving**.	I/You/He/She/It/We/They **will not/ won't be moving.**
Interrogative	**Short answers**
Will I/you/he/she/it/ we/they **be moving?**	**Yes**, I/you/he/she/it/we/they **will**./ **No**, I/you/he/she/it/we/they **won't.**

We use the **future continuous:**
- for actions which will be **in progress** at a **stated future time**. *This time next week, they **will be flying** to Buenos Aires.*

- for actions which will **definitely happen** in the future as a result of a **routine** or **arrangement**.
  *She **will be having** lunch with her friends later.*
- when we **ask politely** about someone's **plans for the near future** (to see if they can do sth for us or because we want to offer to do sth for them).
  *Will you **be using** your laptop this evening?*

Future perfect

Form: subject + *will have* + past participle of the main verb

Affirmative	Negative
I/You/He/She/It/We/They **will/'ll have run.**	I/You/He/She/It/We/They **will not/won't have run.**
Interrogative	**Short answers**
Will I/you/he/she/it/we/ they **have run?**	**Yes**, I/you/he/she/it/we/they **will**./ **No**, I/you/he/she/it/we/they **won't.**

We use the **future perfect** for actions that will have **finished before a stated time in the future**.
*Jenny **will have completed** the project by October.*

> **Time words/phrases used with the *future perfect*:**
> before, by, by then, by the time, until/till, etc
> **Note:** *until/till* are normally used with future perfect only in **negative sentences**.

Unit 6

The passive

Form
We form the **passive** with the verb *to be* in the appropriate tense and the **past participle** of the main verb.
Study the table:

	Active	Passive
Present simple	*Ian builds houses.*	*Houses are built by Ian.*
Present continuous	*Ian is building houses.*	*Houses are being built by Ian.*
Past simple	*Ian built houses.*	*Houses were built by Ian.*
Past continuous	*Ian was building houses.*	*Houses were being built by Ian.*
Present perfect	*Ian has built houses.*	*Houses have been built by Ian.*
Past perfect	*Ian had built houses.*	*Houses had been built by Ian.*
Future simple	*Ian will build houses.*	*Houses will be built by Ian.*
Infinitive	*Ian has to build houses.*	*Houses have to be built by Ian.*
Modal verbs	*Ian can build houses.*	*Houses can be built by Ian.*

Grammar Reference

We use the **passive**:
- when the agent (the person/people doing the action) is **unknown**, **unimportant** or **obvious from the context**. *The wall was painted last week.* (We don't know who painted it.)
  Cheddar cheese is produced in England. (Who produces it is unimportant.)
  The criminals were arrested this morning. (It's obvious that the police arrested them.)
- when the **action** is **more important** than the **agent**, as in **news headlines**, **newspaper articles**, **advertisements**, **instructions**, **formal notices**, **processes**, etc. *Three people were injured in a car accident last night.*
- when we want to **avoid taking responsibility** for an action, or when we refer to an unpleasant event and we do not want to say who or what is to blame. *The dress has been ruined.*
- to **emphasise** the agent. *The novel was written by Charles Dickens.*
- to make statements **more formal** or **polite**. *The vase has been broken.* (More polite than saying "You broke the vase.")

Changing from the active into the passive:
- The **object** of the active sentence becomes the **subject** in the passive sentence.
- The active verb remains in the same tense but changes into the passive form.
- The **subject** of the active sentence becomes the **agent**, and is either introduced with the preposition **by** or is omitted.

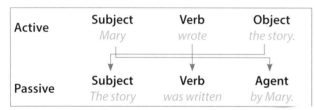

Active	Subject *Mary*	Verb *wrote*	Object *the story.*
Passive	Subject *The story*	Verb *was written*	Agent *by Mary.*

Only transitive verbs (verbs that take an object) can be changed into the passive. *The baby is sleeping soundly.* (intransitive verb; **no passive form**)

Note: Some transitive verbs (*have, fit* [= be the right size], *suit, resemble,* etc) cannot be changed into the passive. *The costume fits the actor perfectly.* (NOT: ~~The actor is fitted by the costume perfectly.~~)
- *Let* becomes *be allowed to* in the passive. *He lets me use his computer. I am allowed to use his computer.*
- We can use the verb *to get* instead of the verb *to be* in everyday speech, when we talk about things that happen by accident or unexpectedly. *The house got damaged by the storm.*
- *By* + **agent** is used to say who or what carries out an action. *With* + **instrument/material/ingredient** is used to say what the agent used. *The cake was made by my sister. It was made with chocolate.*

- The agent can be **omitted** when the subject is *they*, *(s)he*, *someone/somebody*, *people*, *one*, etc. *The flowers will be watered.* (= He will water the flowers.)
- The agent is **not omitted** when it is a **specific** or **important person**, or when it is **essential** to the meaning of the sentence. *The 'Mona Lisa' was painted by Leonardo da Vinci.*
- With verbs which can take two objects, such as *bring*, *tell*, *send*, *show*, *teach*, *promise*, *sell*, *read*, *offer*, *give*, *lend*, etc, we can form two different passive sentences. *Peter gave Mary a birthday present.* (active) *Mary was given a birthday present by Peter.* (passive, more common) *A birthday present was given to Mary by Peter.* (passive, less common)
- In passive questions with *who*, *whom* or *which*, we do not omit *by*. *Who wrote the story? Who was the story written by?*
- The verbs *hear*, *help*, *see* and *make* are followed by a bare infinitive in the active, but a *to*-infinitive in the passive. *She made him apologise.* (active) *He was made to apologise.* (passive)

Reflexive/Emphatic pronouns

I – myself	he – himself	we – ourselves
you –yourself	she – herself	you – yourselves
	it – itself	they – themselves

We use **reflexive pronouns**:
- with verbs such as *burn*, *cut*, *hurt*, *introduce*, *kill*, *look at*, *teach*, etc, or with prepositions, when the subject and the object of the verb are the same person. *Tom* (subject) *hurt himself* (object) *while he was playing tennis.*
- in the following expressions: *enjoy yourself* (have a good time), *behave yourself* (be good), *help yourself* (you are welcome to take sth if you want) *by yourself* (on your own). *Did you enjoy yourselves at the cinema?*
- We use **emphatic pronouns** to emphasise the subject or the object of a sentence. *The director herself chose the actors for the film.* (No one else chose them.)

Notes:
- We do not normally use reflexive pronouns with the verbs *concentrate*, *feel*, *meet* and *relax*. *She finds it difficult to relax.*
- Reflexive pronouns are used with the verbs *dress*, *wash* and *shave* when we want to show that someone did something with a lot of effort. *Although she had a broken arm, she managed to dress herself.*

Unit 7

Reported speech

Direct speech is the exact words someone said. We use quotation marks in direct speech.
Reported speech is the exact meaning of what someone said, but not the exact words. We do not use quotation marks in reported speech. The word '**that**' can either be used or omitted after the introductory verb (*say*, *tell*, etc).

Say – Tell
- *say* + **no personal object**
  John said (that) he felt tired.
- *say* + *to* + **personal object**
  John said to me (that) he felt tired.
- *tell* + **personal object**
  John told me (that) he felt tired.
- We use **say** + *to*-**infinitive**, but never *say about*. We use *tell sb/speak/talk about sth*.
  Dad said to be home by 10 o'clock.
  She told me/spoke/talked about her holiday adventures.

Say	hello, good morning/afternoon, etc, something/nothing, so, a few words, no more, for certain/sure, sorry, etc
Tell	the truth, a lie, a story, a secret, a joke, the time, the difference, one from another, someone one's name, someone the way, someone so, someone's fortune, etc
Ask	a question, a favour, the price, about someone, the time, around, for something/someone, etc

Reported statements

- In reported speech, personal/possessive pronouns and possessive adjectives change according to the meaning of the sentence. *Bob said, "I'm working hard."* (direct speech)
  Bob said (that) he was working hard. (reported speech)
- We can report someone's words either a long time after they were said (out-of-date reporting), or a short time after they were said (up-to-date reporting).

Up-to-date reporting
The tenses can either change or remain the same in reported speech.
Direct speech: *Lucy said, "I called my brother."*
Reported speech: *Lucy said that she called/had called her brother.*

Out-of-date reporting
The introductory verb is in the past simple, and the tenses change as follows:

Direct speech	Reported speech
Present simple → Past simple	
"I speak Chinese well."	*She said (that) she spoke Chinese well.*
Present continuous → Past continuous	
"Mum is talking on the phone."	*He said (that) Mum was talking on the phone.*
Present perfect → Past perfect	
"I have applied for a job."	*She said (that) she had applied for a job.*
Past simple → Past simple or Past perfect	
"I stopped eating junk food."	*He said (that) he stopped/had stopped eating junk food.*
Past continuous → Past continuous or Past perfect continuous	
"They were searching for the burglar all night."	*She said (that) they were searching/had been searching for the burglar all night.*
Will → Would	
"I will order a pizza for dinner."	*He said (that) he would order a pizza for dinner.*

- Certain words and time expressions change according to the meaning, as follows:

now	→	then, immediately
today	→	that day
yesterday	→	the day before, the previous day
tomorrow	→	the next/following day
this week	→	that week
last week	→	the week before, the previous week
next week	→	the week after, the following week
ago	→	before
here	→	there

- Verb tenses **change** in reported speech when we consider what the speaker said to be untrue.
  "Giraffes live in the desert." → He said that giraffes lived in the desert. (We know they don't.)
- Verb tenses can **either change or remain the same** in reported speech when reporting a **general truth** or **law of nature**.
  "More and more animals are becoming extinct," the article said. → The article said (that) more and more animals are/were becoming extinct.
- Verb tenses **remain the same** in reported speech:
  a) when the introductory verb is in the **present**, **future** or **present perfect**. *She says, "The weather is cold." She says the weather is cold.* b) in **type 2** and **3 conditionals**. *"If I lived in Sweden, I would take up skiing," Meg told me. Meg told me (that) if she lived in Sweden, she would take up skiing.*

Grammar Reference

Reported questions

- Reported questions are usually introduced with the verbs *ask*, *enquire*, *wonder*, or the phrase *want to know*.
- When the direct question begins with a question word (*who*, *where*, *how*, *when*, *what*, etc), the reported question is introduced with the same question word.
  "Who wrote the letter?" she asked. (direct question)
  She asked who had written the letter. (reported question)
- When the direct question begins with an auxiliary (*be*, *do*, *have*) or a modal verb (*can*, *may*, etc), then the reported question is introduced with *if* or *whether*.
  "Has Ryan paid the phone bill?" he asked. (direct question)
  He asked if/whether Ryan had paid the phone bill. (reported question)
- In reported questions, the verb is in the affirmative. The question mark and words such as *please*, *well*, *oh*, etc are omitted. The verb tenses, pronouns, possessive adjectives and time phrases change as in statements.
  "Where did you leave your glasses?" she asked me. (direct question)
  She asked me where I had left my glasses. (reported question)

Reported orders/instructions/commands/requests/suggestions

- **Reported orders/instructions/commands/requests/suggestions** are introduced with a special introductory verb (*advise*, *ask*, *beg*, *suggest*, etc) followed by a *to*-infinitive, an *-ing* form or a *that*-clause, depending on the introductory verb.
  "Turn off the tap," Mum told me. → *Mum told me to turn off the tap.* (command)
  "Be quiet, please," he told the class. → *He asked the class to be quiet.* (request)
  "Let's eat out tonight," she said. → *She suggested eating out that night.* (suggestion)
  "You'd better go to the dentist," he told me. → *He suggested that I (should) go to the dentist.* (suggestion)
- To report **orders** or **instructions**, we use the verbs *order* or *tell* + sb + (not) *to*-infinitive.
  "Don't leave any dirty plates in the sink," Mum told me. (direct order)
  Mum told me not to leave any dirty plates in the sink. (reported order)
  "Open your books," the teacher told us. (direct order)
  The teacher ordered us to open our books. (reported order)

Special Introductory Verbs			
Introductory verb	Direct speech		Reported speech
+ *to*-inf **agree** **demand** **offer** **promise** **refuse** **threaten** **claim**	*"OK, I'll help you paint the bathroom."* *"I want to see you now."* *"Would you like me to call your parents?"* *"I'll look after your children for the weekend."* *"No, I won't lend you my car."* *"Turn down the radio or I'll call the police."* *"I saw the burglar run away."*	→ → → → → → →	*She agreed to help me paint the bathroom.* *He demanded to see me immediately.* *He offered to call my parents.* *She promised to look after my children for the weekend.* *He refused to lend me his car.* *He threatened to call the police if I didn't turn down the radio.* *He claimed to have seen the burglar run away.*
+ sb + *to*-inf **advise** **allow/permit** **ask** **beg** **command** **encourage** **forbid** **instruct** **invite** **order** **remind** **urge** **warn** **want**	*"You shouldn't eat junk food."* *"You can use my laptop."* *"Please, sit down!"* *"Please, help me!"* *"Stand up!"* *"Go on, phone her!"* *"You mustn't enter the building."* *"Turn right at the corner of the street."* *"Will you come to the cinema?"* *"Sit down!"* *"Don't forget to lock the door."* *"Finish your work!"* *"Keep away from the animals!"* *"I'd like you to study harder."*	→ → → → → → → → → → → → → →	*He advised me not to eat junk food.* *She allowed/permitted me to use her laptop.* *He asked me to sit down.* *She begged me to help her.* *He commanded me to stand up.* *He encouraged me to phone her.* *He forbade us to enter the building.* *He instructed us to turn right at the corner of the street.* *She invited me to go to the cinema.* *He ordered me to sit down.* *He reminded me to lock the door.* *She urged me to finish my work.* *He warned us to keep away from the animals.* *He wanted me to study harder.*

Introductory verb	Direct speech		Reported speech
+ -ing form **accuse sb of** **apologise for**	*"You broke the vase."* *"I'm so sorry I forgot our anniversary."*	→ →	She **accused me of breaking** the vase. He **apologised for forgetting/having forgotten** their anniversary.
admit (to) **boast about** **complain to sb about**	*"Yes, I lied to her."* *"I am the best cook."* *"You always leave the door open!"*	→ → →	He **admitted (to) lying/having lied** to her. He **boasted about being** the best cook. She **complained to me about my** always **leaving** the door open.
deny **insist on** **suggest**	*"I didn't take your bag!"* *"You must tidy your room."* *"Let's invite George!"*	→ → →	She **denied taking/having taken** my bag. He **insisted on my/me tidying** my room. He **suggested inviting** George.
+ that-clause **agree** **boast**	*"Yes, it's a great idea."* *"I donate a lot of money to children's charities."*	→ → →	He **agreed that** it was a great idea. She **boasted that** she donated a lot of money to children's charities.
claim **complain** **deny** **exclaim** **explain** **inform sb**	*"I met a famous actress at the mall."* *"I have a terrible headache."* *"I didn't scratch your car!"* *"What a nice dress!"* *"The lift is out of order."* *"Mr Jones will see you in five minutes."*	→ → → → → →	He **claimed that** he had met a famous actress at the mall. He **complained that** he had a terrible headache. He **denied that** he had scratched my car. She **exclaimed that** it was a nice dress. He **explained that** the lift was out of order. He **informed me that** Mr Jones would see me in five minutes.
promise **suggest**	*"I will drive you to the airport."* *"You should take care of yourself."*	→ →	He **promised that** he would drive me to the airport. He **suggested that** I should take care of myself.
explain to sb + **how + to-infinitive**	*"This is how you make it."*	→	He **explained to me how to make** it.
wonder + where/ **what/why/** **how + clause** (when the subject of the introductory verb is not the same as the subject in the reported question)	*She asked herself, "Where is Joan?"* *He asked himself, "Why is Tom so sad?"* *He asked himself, "What is John's phone number?"* *He asked himself, "How is Linda?"*	→ → → →	She **wondered where** Joan was. He **wondered why** Tom was so sad. He **wondered what** John's phone number was. He **wondered how** Linda was.
wonder + **where/what/how** **+ to-inf or clause** (when the subjects are the same)	*She asked herself, "How can I fix it?"*	→	She **wondered how to fix** it. She **wondered how she could fix** it.

Grammar Reference

Unit 8

Conditionals: types 2 & 3

	If-clause (hypothesis)	Main clause (result)
2nd conditional: • imaginary, unreal, or highly unlikely situations in the present/future • advice	*If* + past simple	*would/could/might* + bare infinitive
	*If I **had** lots of money, I **would buy** a sports car.* (but I don't – unreal in the present) *If I **were** you, I **wouldn't trust** him.* (advice)	
3rd conditional: • unreal situations in the past • regrets • criticism	*If* + past perfect	*would/could/might* *have* + past participle
	*If he **hadn't missed** the bus, he **would have arrived** earlier.* *If Craig **had been** more careful, he **wouldn't have lost** his car keys.*	

Note: We can use *were* instead of *was* for all persons in the *if*-clause of type 2 conditionals. We use *if I were you* ... in the *if*-clause of type 2 conditionals when we want to give advice. *If I were/was you, I'd apply for the job.*

Wishes

We can use *wish/if only* to express a wish.

Wish/If only		Use
+ past simple/ past continuous	*I wish I **had** a bigger house.* (but I don't) *If only Jim **wasn't/weren't** working today.* (but he is)	to express what we would like to be different about a present situation
+ could + bare infinitive	*Karen wishes she **could dance** as well as Jenny does.*	to express regret in the present concerning lack of ability
+ past perfect	*I wish I **hadn't lied** to my best friend.* (but I did) *If only we **hadn't eaten** so much.* (but we did)	to express regret about something that happened or didn't happen in the past
+ subject + would + bare infinitive	*I wish you **would apologise** to your teacher.* *If only it **would stop** snowing.*	to express: • a polite imperative • a desire for a situation or a person's behaviour to change

Notes:
- **If only** is used in exactly the same way as *I wish*, but it is more emphatic or more dramatic.
  If only I had told him the truth!
- We can use *were* instead of *was* after *wish* and *if only*.
  I wish I were/was young again.

Question tags

- **Question tags** are short questions at the end of statements.
- We use them in speech **to confirm something**, or to find out if something is true or not.
- We form them with the **auxiliary** or **modal** verb from the main sentence and the appropriate subject pronoun. *We have a meeting later, **don't we**? You can drive a car, **can't you**?*

Use
- A positive statement takes a negative question tag.
  *She worked in a hospital, **didn't she**?*
- A negative statement takes a positive question tag.
  *There aren't enough chairs for everyone, **are there**?*
- When the verb of the sentence is in the present simple, we use *do (not)/does (not)* in the question tag.
  *She lives in Paris, **doesn't she**?*
- When the verb of the sentence is in the past simple, we use *did (not)*. *They went shopping, **didn't they**?*

Some verbs/expressions form question tags differently:

I am → aren't I?	I am the tallest, **aren't' I**?
Imperative → **will you/won't you?**	Close the door, **will you/won't you**?
Don't → **will you?**	Don't turn off the TV, **will you**?
Let's → **shall we?**	Let's play chess, **shall we**?
You've got → **haven't you?**	You've got a dog, **haven't you**?
You have (idiomatically) → **don't you?**	You have plenty of time, **don't you**?
This/That is → **isn't it?**	This is your jacket, **isn't it**?
No one → **do/did they**	No one called, **did they**?

Intonation
- When we are sure of the answer, the voice goes down in the question tag. *She'll take the bus, won't she?* (↘)
- When we are not sure of the answer and want to check information, the voice goes up in the question tag. *He's abroad, isn't he?* (↗)

Clauses of concession

Clauses of concession are used to express contrast. They are introduced with the following words/phrases:
- **but** – *Joe swam fast **but** he didn't manage to finish first.*
- **although/even though/though** + **clause** –
  Even though is more emphatic than **although**.
  Though is informal and is often used in everyday speech. It can also be put at the end of a sentence.

Although/Even though/Though she has lots of experience, she didn't get the job.
She didn't get the job *although/even though/though* she has lots of experience.
She has lots of experience. She didn't get the job, *though*.

- *in spite of/despite* + noun/-*ing form* –
  In spite of/Despite the heavy rain, the match continued.
  In spite of/Despite studying hard, he failed the exam.
- *in spite of/despite* + *the fact that* + clause –
  In spite of/Despite the fact that it is April, the weather is quite cold.
- *however/nevertheless* – A comma is always used after '*however/nevertheless*'.
  I set my alarm clock for 7:00 am. *However/Nevertheless*, it didn't go off.
- *while/whereas* – David has got dark hair *while/whereas* his sister has got fair.
- *yet* (formal)/*still* – It hadn't rained, *yet* it was rather humid. My grandfather is 75. *Still/Yet*, he is able to drive.
- *on the other hand* – She would like to take music lessons. *On the other hand*, she doesn't have much free time.

Unit 9

Infinitive

The *to-infinitive* is used:

- to express **purpose**. He went to the market *to buy* fresh fruit.
- after certain verbs that refer to the future (*agree, appear, decide, expect, hope, plan, promise, refuse*, etc). He hopes *to graduate* next year.
- after *would like, would prefer, would love*, etc to express a specific preference. I would like *to eat* pasta.
- after adjectives which describe feelings/emotions (*happy, glad, sad*, etc), express willingness/ unwillingness (*eager, reluctant, willing*, etc) or refer to a person's character (*clever, kind*, etc), and the adjectives *lucky* and *fortunate*. Bob is eager *to help* in any way he can.
- after *too/enough*. The food is too salty *to eat*.
- to talk about an unexpected event, usually with *only*. I went to Mark's house *only to find* he had already left.
- after *it* + *be* + **adjective/noun**. It was sad *to see* her go.
- in the expressions *to tell you the truth, to be honest, to sum up, to begin with*, etc. *To be honest*, I didn't know how to react.

The **infinitive without to** (bare infinitive) is used:

- after **modal verbs**. He could *play* the violin when he was young.
- after the verbs *let, make, see, hear* and *feel*. He made us *clean* the room. **BUT** we use the *to-infinitive* after *be made, be heard, be seen*, etc (passive form). We were made *to clean* the room.
- after *had better* and *would rather*. I had better *go* home now.

Note:

- *Help* can be followed by the *to-infinitive*, but in American English it is normally followed by the **infinitive without to**. She helped us (to) *move* the furniture.
- If two *to-infinitives* are linked by *and* or *or*, the *to* of the second infinitive can be omitted.
  I'd prefer *to stay* in and *watch* a film.

-*ing* form

The -*ing* form is used:

- as a **noun**. *Swimming* is a good form of exercise.
- after certain verbs: *admit, appreciate, avoid, consider, continue, deny, go* (for activities), *imagine, mind, miss, quit, save, suggest, practise, prevent*.
  He is considering *moving* to Japan.
- after *love, like, enjoy, prefer, dislike, hate* to express general preference. Sarah loves *sunbathing*. **BUT** for a specific preference (*would like/would prefer/would love*) we use *to-infinitive*.
  She'd like *to take* a long holiday.
- after expressions such as *be busy, it's no use, it's no good, it's (not) worth, what's the use of, can't help, there's no point (in), can't stand, have difficulty (in), have trouble*, etc. It's worth *visiting* the Pyramids.
- after *spend, waste* or *lose* (time, money, etc).
  He spends too much time *watching* TV.
- after the preposition *to* with verbs and expressions such as *look forward to, be/get used to, in addition to, object to, prefer to*. She is used to *getting* up early.
- after other **prepositions**.
  I'm tired *of waiting* for him.
- after the verbs *hear, listen to, notice, see, watch* and *feel* to describe an incomplete action. I heard her *singing*. (I heard part of it.) **BUT** we use the **bare infinitive** with these verbs to describe the complete action. I heard her *sing*. (I heard the whole thing.)

Forms of the infinitive		
	Active voice	**Passive voice**
Present	(to) write	(to) be written
Present continuous	(to) be writing	–
Perfect	(to) have written	(to) have been written
Perfect continuous	(to) have been writing	–

Forms of the -*ing* form		
	Active voice	**Passive voice**
Present	doing	being done
Perfect	having done	having been done

Grammar Reference

Forms of the infinitive/-*ing* form corresponding to verb tenses
present simple/*will* → **present infinitive/-ing form**
present continuous/future continuous → **present continuous infinitive**
past simple/present perfect/past perfect/future perfect → **perfect infinitive/-ing form**
past continuous/present perfect continuous/past perfect continuous → **perfect continuous infinitive**

Difference in meaning between the *to*-infinitive and the *-ing* form
Some verbs can take either the *to*-infinitive or the *-ing* form with a change in meaning.
• *forget* + *to*-infinitive = not remember *He forgot to turn off the lights.*
• *forget* + *-ing* form = not recall *I'll never forget touring the south of Italy.*
• *remember* + *to*-infinitive = not forget *Did you remember to lock the door?*
• *remember* + *-ing* form = recall *I don't remember seeing her at the meeting.*
• *mean* + *to*-infinitive = intend to *I mean to start a new life.*
• *mean* + *-ing* form = involve *Being a doctor means working long hours.*
• *regret* + *to*-infinitive = be sorry to (normally used in the present simple with verbs such as *say*, *tell* and *inform*) *I regret to say he isn't a reliable employee.*
• *regret* + *-ing* form = feel sorry about *She regrets buying such an expensive bag.*
• *try* + *to*-infinitive = attempt, do one's best *She tried to answer all the exam questions.*
• *try* + *-ing* form = do sth as an experiment *Try cutting down on sweets if you want to lose weight.*
• *stop* + *to*-infinitive = stop temporarily in order to do sth else *James stopped to get something to eat on the way home.*
• *stop* + *-ing* form = finish doing sth *Daisy stopped working and went home.*
• *would prefer* + *to*-infinitive (specific preference) *He would prefer to stay at home rather than go out for dinner.*
• *prefer* + *-ing* form (general preference) *I prefer skiing to snowboarding.*

Singular – Plural nouns

We use **singular verb forms** with:
- uncountable nouns: *butter*, *cheese*, *bread*, *air*, *gold*, *wood*, etc.
  There is some cheese left in the fridge.

- school/college subjects: *Maths*, *Geography*, *Physics*, etc.
  Physics involves a lot of theoretical study.
- amounts of money, distance, weight: *£10 is expensive. 50 kilometres is a long way. A kilo of meat is not enough.*
- games & sports: *football*, *billiards*, *dominoes*, etc.
  Dominoes is his favourite game.
- diseases: *measles*, *mumps*, *flu*, etc.
  Mumps is contagious.
- some other nouns: *news*, *advice*, *equipment*, *information*, *money*, *furniture*, *hair*, *homework*, *rubbish*, *jewellery*, *luggage*, etc. *His luggage was left on the platform.*

We use **plural verb forms** with:
- objects consisting of two parts: **items of clothing** (pyjamas, trousers, shorts, etc), **tools** (scissors, pliers, etc), **instruments** (binoculars, compasses, etc).
- group nouns: *family*, *team*, *crew*, *staff*, etc, when we mean the individuals that make up the group. However, we use singular verb forms when we refer to them as a unit. *The team are warming up for the match.* (We mean the individual members of the team.) *The team is ready to go on the field.* (We refer to them as a unit.)
- nouns such as: *cattle*, *clothes*, *congratulations*, *earnings*, *outskirts*, *people*, *police*, *premises*, *stairs*, *wages*, etc. *The police are on their way.*

Unit 10

Modals

Modal verbs:
- don't take -*s*, -*ing* or -*ed* suffixes.
- are followed by the bare infinitive (infinitive without *to*).
- come before the subject in questions and are followed by *not* in negations.
- don't have tenses in the normal sense. When followed by a **present infinitive**, they often refer to an action or state in the **present** or **future**. *You should wash your car more often.* When followed by a **perfect infinitive**, they often refer to an **action** or **state** in the **past**. *He should have washed his car before he left.*

Note: The forms of the infinitive are the following:

Present: (to) work **Present continuous:** (to) be working **Perfect:** (to) have worked **Perfect continuous:** (to) have been working

Obligation/Duty/Necessity (*must, have to, need to, should/ought to*)

- *Must* expresses a **duty/strong obligation** to do sth, and shows that sth is essential. We generally use *must* when the speaker has decided that sth is necessary to do. *You must return these books soon.* (**It's your duty. You are obliged to do it.**) *Jill must get more exercise.*

- *Need to/Have to* express **strong necessity/obligation**. *You **need to** enter your password twice to confirm it.* We usually use *have to* when somebody other than the speaker has decided that sth is necessary to do. *My teacher says I **have to** wear a uniform at school.* **(It's necessary. My teacher says so.)**
- *Had to* is the past form of both *must* and *have to*.
- *Should/Ought to* express a **duty/weak obligation**. *We **should** take care of the environment.* **(It's our duty.** – less emphatic than *must*)

> **Absence of necessity**
> *(don't have to/don't need to/needn't)*

- *Don't have to/Don't need to/Needn't:* **it isn't necessary** to do sth in the present/future.
  *She **doesn't have to** come with us if she doesn't want to. You **don't need to** cook; I've ordered a takeaway. You **needn't water** the plants tomorrow morning.*
- *Didn't need to/Didn't have to:* **it wasn't necessary** to do sth. We don't know if it was done or not.
  *Beth **didn't have to** employ more staff.* (We don't know whether she employed more staff or not.)
- *Needn't have + past participle:* **it wasn't necessary** to do sth, but it was done. An action happened in the past even though it wasn't necessary. *We **needn't have booked** a room; the hotel was half empty.* (but we did)

> **Permission/Prohibition**
> *(can, could, may, be allowed to, mustn't, can't)*

- *Can/Could/May* are used to **ask for/give permission**. *Can/Could/May I borrow your car?* **(Is it OK if ...?)** *May* and *could* are more formal than *can*.
- *Can/May* are used to **give permission**. *You can/may use my laptop.* (NOT: ~~You could use my laptop.~~)
- *Be allowed to* is used to ask/state what is **the rule**. *Are the students allowed to use dictionaries in the exam?*
- *Mustn't/Can't:* it is **forbidden** to do sth; it is **against the rules/law; you are not allowed to** do sth. *You **mustn't/can't** walk on the grass.*

> **Advice** *(should/ought to/must/shouldn't/ oughtn't to/mustn't)*

- *Should:* general advice – *Susan **should** try to eat less sweets.* **(It's my advice./I advise her to do so.)**
- *Ought to:* general advice – *You **ought to** follow the rules.* **(It's a good idea/thing to do.)**
- *Must:* strong advice – *You **mustn't** leave candles burning – it's dangerous!*

> **Possibility** *(can, could, may, might)*

- *Can + present infinitive:* general/theoretical **possibility**; not usually used for a specific situation. *An earthquake **can** be a difficult experience.* (general possibility – **It is theoretically possible.**)
- *Could/May/Might + present infinitive:* **possibility** in a specific situation. *She **might** see a doctor about her food allergies.* **(It is possible./It is likely./Perhaps.)**

Note: We can use *can/could/might* in questions but **not 'may'**. *Who **could** help me with my problem?*

- *Could/Might + perfect infinitive* refers to **sth in the past that was possible but didn't happen**. *I **could have** called you but I thought you were busy.* **(It was possible but I didn't do it.)**

> **Ability/Inability** *(can, could, was able to)*

- *Can('t)* expresses **(in)ability in the present/future**. *My mum **can** speak three languages.* **(She is able to ...)**
- *Could* expresses general repeated **ability in the past**. *I **could** play chess when I was 5.* **(I was able to ...)**
- *Was able to* expresses ability on a **specific occasion** in the **past**. *We **were able to** find cheap plane tickets.* **(We managed to ...)**
- *Couldn't/Wasn't able to* may be used to express inability in the past, repeated or specific. *Ryan **couldn't** run fast as a child.* **(wasn't able to; past repeated action)** *Peter **couldn't/wasn't able to** get to work early because of the heavy traffic.* **(didn't manage to; past single action)**

> **Offers/Suggestions**
> *(can, would, shall, could)*

- *Can* (offer): *Can I do anything to help?* **(Would you like me to ...?)**
- *Would* (offer): *Would you like me to cook dinner?* **(Do you want me to ...?)**
- *Shall* (offer): *Shall I help you tidy up?* **(What about helping ...?)**
- *Can/Could* (suggestion): *We **can** eat out tonight. We **could** spend our holiday in Italy.* **(Let's ...)**
- *Can/Could/Would* (request): *Can/Could/Would you help me create a blog?* **(Are you willing to ...?)**

> **Deductions** *(must, may/might/could, can't/couldn't*

- *Must:* **almost certain** that sth is/was **true** (positive logical assumption).
  *Jane **must** be exhausted; she has been working all day. They aren't talking to each other; they **must have argued.*** **(I'm almost sure that sth is/was true.)**
- *May/Might/Could:* maybe, it's possible.
  *She said she **may/might/could** call me later in the afternoon.*
  *Gary is late; he **may/might/could have** missed the bus.*
  (It is possible/it is likely/perhaps.)

Grammar Reference

- *Can't/Couldn't:* **be sure** that this is/was **impossible** (negative logical assumption).
  *It's boiling hot today; you **can't/couldn't** be cold.*
  *It **can't/couldn't have** been Susan you saw yesterday; she's still in Paris.* **(I'm sure that sth isn't/wasn't true.)**

• *Perhaps she **is** a good doctor.* • *I'm sure he **knows** her well.* • *It's likely that it **will** snow tomorrow.*	**present infinitive**	• *She **may be** a good doctor.* • *He **must know** her well.* • *It **may snow** tomorrow.*
• *It's possible that they **are visiting** us tomorrow.* • *It's likely that he **is moving** house next year.*	**present continuous infinitive**	• *They **could be visiting** us tomorrow.* • *He **may be moving** house next year.*
• *I'm sure she **didn't know** the answers.* • *It's likely the film **has finished** already.* • *Perhaps she **had left** the office.*	**perfect infinitive**	• *She **can't have known** the answers.* • *The film **might have finished** already.* • *She **may have left** the office.*
• *Perhaps she **was sleeping** when you called her.* • *Perhaps he **has been studying** hard.* • *I'm sure they **had been running**; they were out of breath.*	**perfect continuous infinitive**	• *She **may have been sleeping** when you called her.* • *He **may have been studying** hard.* • *They **must have been running**; they were out of breath.*

Unit 11

Comparatives/Superlatives (adjectives/adverbs)

- We use the **comparative** to compare one person or thing with another. We use the **superlative** to compare one person or thing with others of the same group. *Matt is **taller** than John. He's **the tallest** student in the class.*
- We often use *than* after a comparative.
  *My brother is **younger than** me.*
- We normally use *the* before a superlative. We can use *in* or *of* after superlatives. We often use *in* with places.
  *She's **the funniest** person in the office.*
  *She's **the most generous of** all my friends.*

Formation of comparatives and superlatives

Adjectives of **one syllable** take *-(e)r/-(e)st* to form their comparative and superlative forms.

Adjective	Comparative	Superlative
strong	strong**er** (than)	**the** strong**est** (of/in)
nice	nic**er** (than)	**the** nic**est** (of/in)

Adjectives of **one syllable** that end in **a single vowel + a single consonant** double the last consonant and add *-er/-est*.

Adjective	Comparative	Superlative
big	big**ger** (than)	**the** big**gest** (of/in)

Adjectives of **one** or **two syllables** ending in *-ly* or *-y*, drop the *-y* and add *-ier/-iest*

Adjective	Comparative	Superlative
ugly	ugl**ier** (than)	**the** ugl**iest** (of/in)
funny	funn**ier** (than)	**the** funn**iest** (of/in)

Adjectives of **two or more syllables** take *more/the most*

Adjective	Comparative	Superlative
expensive	**more** expensive (than)	**the most** expensive (of/in)
modern	**more** modern (than)	**the most** modern (of/in)

Note: *clever, common, cruel, friendly, gentle, narrow, pleasant, polite, quiet, shallow, simple, stupid* form their comparatives and superlatives either with *-er/-est* or with *more/the most*.
*friendly – friendlier/**more** friendly – **the** friendliest/**the most** friendly*

Adverbs

- Adverbs that have **the same form** as their adjectives *(hard, fast, free, late, high, early, low, deep, long, near, straight)* take *-er/-est*.
  low – lower – the lowest
- Adverbs formed by adding *-ly* to the adjective take *more* in the comparative and *the most* in the superlative form.
  *politely – **more** politely – **the most** politely*

Adverbs		Comparative	Superlative
adverbs having the same form as their adjectives add *-er/-est*	hard	harder	the hardest
early drops the *-y* and adds *-ier/-iest*	early	earlier	the earliest
two-syllable adverbs and those formed by adding *-ly* to their adjectives take **more/most**	often slowly	more often more slowly	the most often the most slowly

Irregular forms		
Adjective/Adverb	Comparative	Superlative
good/well	better	best
bad/badly	worse	worst
little	less	least
a lot of/much/many	more	most
far	farther/further	farthest/furthest

Notes:

- We can use *elder/eldest* for people in the same family but not in comparisons.
  My elder/eldest sister is an architect.
- *further/farther* (adv) = longer (in distance)
  His house is further/farther away than John's.
  further (adj) = more
  If you need any further information, please call me.

Study the examples:

- *very* + adjective/adverb:
  I'm very happy in my job.
- *much/a lot/even/a bit/a little/far/slightly* + comparative form of adjective/adverb:
  Helen feels slightly better today.
- *by far* + superlative form of adjective/adverb:
  Bill is by far the best player in the team.

Types of comparisons

- *as* + adjective + *as* (to show that two people or things are similar/different in some way). In negative sentences we use *not as/so ... as*. *Her hair is as soft as silk. The service is not as/so good as it used to be.*
- *less* + adjective + *than* (expresses the difference between two people or things). The opposite is *more ... than*. *This book is less interesting than that one.*
- *the least* + adjective + *of/in* (compares one person or thing with two or more people or things of the same group). The opposite is *the most ... of/in*. *He is the least likely of all to win the race.*
- comparative + *and* + comparative (to show that something is increasing or decreasing). *People are recycling more and more of their rubbish.*
- *the* + comparative ... , *the* + comparative (shows that two things change together, or that one thing depends on another thing). *The less you sleep, the more tired you get.*
- *the same as* *Hilary's dress was the same as mine.*
- *twice/three times/half* etc *as* + adjective + *as*
  She earns twice as much as me.
  The end of the film wasn't half as exciting as I had expected.
- *too* + adjective/adverb + *to*-infinitive (to show that something is more, or at a higher degree, than necessary). *Nick is too young to drive a car.*
- adjective/adverb + *enough* + *to*-infinitive (to show that there is as much of something as it is wanted, or at the necessary degree). *She is fast enough to win the race.*

Countable/Uncountable nouns

- **Countable nouns** are nouns that **we can count**. They have both singular and plural forms. We use *a/an* with **singular countable nouns**. *a carrot, an egg*
- **Uncountable nouns** are nouns which **we cannot count**. *some water* (NOT: ~~one water, two waters, etc~~) They usually have only singular forms. These include:
  food: *rice, butter, cheese, flour, sugar, salt,* etc
  liquids: *oil, juice, milk, coffee, tea, water,* etc
  materials: *plastic, iron, wood, glass,* etc
  sports: *rugby, volleyball,* etc
  subjects: *Geography, Science,* etc
  languages: *Italian, French,* etc
  abstract nouns: *information, love, advice,* etc
  other: *hair, money, luggage, news, rubbish,* etc
- We use *some* in the **affirmative** with either **countable nouns in the plural** or with **uncountable nouns**.
  I made some sandwiches. Have some tea.

Plurals

- Most nouns take *-s* to form the plural.
  book → books, pencil → pencils
- Nouns ending in *-s, -ss, -sh, -x* and *-o* take *-es* to form the plural. *bus → buses, glass → glasses, beach → beaches, fox → foxes, tomato → tomatoes*
- Some nouns ending in *-o* that come from other languages or are the short form of a word take only *-s*. *piano → pianos* (**BUT** *hero – heroes*), *photo → photos* (photograph)
- Nouns ending in a **vowel** + *-y* take *-s* in the plural. *boy → boys*
- Nouns ending in a **consonant** + *-y* drop the *-y* and take *-ies* in the plural. *berry → berries*
- Some nouns ending in *-f* or *-fe* drop the *-f* or *-fe* and take *-ves* in the plural. *scarf → scarves, life → lives*
- Some nouns have the same singular and plural forms. *aircraft → aircraft, deer → deer, fish → fish, sheep → sheep, trout → trout, salmon → salmon*

Irregular plurals: *woman → women, man → men, person → people, child → children, foot → feet, tooth → teeth, mouse → mice, goose → geese, ox → oxen, louse → lice*

Quantifiers

- We use *a/an* with singular countable nouns when we mention something for the first time. *Cathy has got a bicycle. The bicycle is red.*
- We use *a* before singular countable nouns which begin with a consonant sound *(a book, a car)*. We use *an* before singular countable nouns which begin with a vowel sound *(an umbrella, an hour)*.
- We don't use *a/an* with uncountable or plural nouns. In these cases we use *some* in affirmative sentences.
  There is some orange juice in the fridge. I've bought some oranges.

Grammar Reference

- We use *any* in interrogative and negative sentences with uncountable nouns and plural countable nouns. *Are there any cherries in the bowl? There aren't any oranges in the fridge.*

- We use *no* instead of *not any* in sentences to make them negative. *There is no coffee.* (= There isn't any coffee.)

- *Much* and *many* are usually used in negative or interrogative sentences. *Much* is used with uncountable nouns and *many* is used with countable nouns. *There isn't much milk. Is there much butter left? There aren't many biscuits. Are there many onions in the basket?*

- *Too many* is used with countable nouns and *too much* is used with uncountable nouns to show that there is more than the required quantity of something. *There are too many olives in the salad. There is too much salt in this soup.*

- *How much/many* is used in interrogative sentences. *How much milk do we want? How many tomatoes do we need?*

- *Enough* is used with countable and uncountable nouns in the affirmative, negative and interrogative to show that there is as much of something as required. *We've got enough eggs to make an omelette. We haven't got enough bread to make sandwiches. Have you got enough coffee?*

- *A couple of/Hundreds of/Three of* etc are used with countable nouns. They are normally used in affirmative sentences. The *of* is omitted when *a couple/hundred/plenty/three* etc are not followed by a noun. *We've got a couple of loaves. How many loaves have we got? A couple.*

- *A bit of* is used with uncountable nouns. It is normally used in affirmative sentences or interrogatives. The *of* is omitted when *a bit* is not followed by a noun. *We've got a bit of flour. Have we got a bit of sugar? We've got a bit.*

- *A lot of/Lots of/Plenty of* are used with both plural countable and uncountable nouns. They are normally used in affirmative sentences. The *of* is omitted when *a lot/lots/plenty* are not followed by a noun. *We've got a lot of/lots of food. There are plenty of sandwiches. Have we got many cheeseburgers? Yes, we've got lots.*

- *A few* means not many, but enough. It is used with plural countable nouns. *I have a few cherries. I can make a cherry pie.*

- *A little* means not much, but enough. It is used with uncountable nouns. *I have a little flour. I can make a cake.* Note: *few/little* mean hardly any, not enough and can be used with *very* for emphasis. *Few people like this dish as it is very spicy. I've got very little time this week, I'm busy at work.*

- *Several (of)* (= more than three but not many) is used with countable nouns. *We've got several apples in the fridge. Several of the apples have turned bad.*

- *Both* (= two) and *all* (= the whole quantity) are used with countable and uncountable nouns. *Both lemons and oranges are citrus fruits. Simon drank all the milk in the fridge.*

Partitives

- We cannot use *a/an* or a number before an uncountable noun. If we want to say how much of something there is, we use a phrase of quantity, called a **partitive**, followed by *of*. Partitives can be used with **uncountable nouns** or **plural countable nouns**. *a cup of coffee, a carton of milk, a tin of sardines, a bag of flour, a bottle of water, a can of cola, a packet of spaghetti, a glass of water, a slice of cheese, a bowl of cereal, a jar of jam, a tube of toothpaste, a pot of tea, a box of chocolates*

some/any/no/every & compounds

- *Some*, *any* and *no* are used with uncountable nouns and plural countable nouns.

	Affirmative	Interrogative	Negative
Countable/ Uncountable	some	any	no/not any
People	someone/ somebody everyone/ everybody	anyone/ anybody	no one/ not anyone nobody/ not anybody
Things	something/ everything	anything	nothing/not anything
Places	somewhere everywhere	anywhere	nowhere/ not anywhere

- *Some* and its compounds are used in interrogative sentences when we make an offer or a request. *Would you like some cake?* (offer) *Can someone help me with those bags?* (request)

- When *any* and its compounds are used in affirmative sentences, there is a difference in meaning. Study the following examples:
  a) *You can visit me any time you like.* (It doesn't matter when.)
  b) *Anyone/Anybody who witnessed the accident should contact the police.* (It doesn't matter who.)
  c) *You can buy anything you like for your birthday.* (It doesn't matter what.)
  d) *We can go anywhere you want for the weekend.* (It doesn't matter where.)

- *Every* is used with singular countable nouns. *Every student has a library card.*

- The pronouns *everyone/everybody, everything* and the adverb *everywhere* are used in affirmative, interrogative and negative sentences, and are followed by a singular verb. *Everything is going well. Everyone uses the stairs in our building.*

Unit 12

The causative

- We use *have* + object (thing) + past participle to say that we have arranged for someone to do something for us. *Carrie is having her house cleaned.* (She's not cleaning it herself.)
- Questions and negations in the causative are formed with *do/does* (present simple) or *did* (past simple) + *have* + object + past participle.
  When did he have his car serviced?

	Active	Passive
Present simple	He washes his car.	He has his car washed.
Present continuous	He is washing his car.	He is having his car washed.
Past simple	He washed his car.	He had his car washed.
Past continuous	He was washing his car.	He was having his car washed.
Future simple	He will wash his car.	He will have his car washed.
Future continuous	He will be washing his car.	He will be having his car washed.
Present perfect simple	He has washed his car.	He has had his car washed.
Present perfect continuous	He has been washing his car.	He has been having his car washed.
Past perfect simple	He had washed his car.	He had had his car washed.
Past perfect continuous	He had been washing his car.	He had been having his car washed.
Infinitive	He needs to wash his car.	He needs to have his car washed.
***-ing* form**	He keeps washing his car.	He keeps having his car washed.
Modal verbs	He should wash his car.	He should have his car washed.

- We also use **the causative form** to say that something unpleasant or unexpected happened to somebody. *She had her purse stolen last night.*
- We can use *get* instead of *have* only in informal conversation. *Gill should get the roof repaired.*
- *Make/Have* + object (person) + bare infinitive are used to express that someone causes someone else to do something, but the meaning is slightly different. *James made me type the letter.* (He insisted that I typed the letters.) *They had a gardener mow the grass.* (They asked him to mow the grass.)

- *Get* + object (person) + *to*-infinitive shows that someone persuades someone else to do something. *Sue got the caretaker to fix the door.* (She persuaded him to fix the door.)

Clauses of purpose

Clauses of purpose are used to explain why somebody does something.

We can express positive purpose using:
- *to* + infinitive
  They bought a bigger house to have more room.
- *in order (not) to/so as (not) to* + infinitive
  I went to the market early in order to/so as to buy some fresh fish.
- *so that/in order that* + *can/will* (present/future reference)
  She works hard so that/in order that she will have better career prospects.
- *so that/in order that* + *could/would* (past reference)
  He gave me directions so that/in order that I could find his house easily.
- *in case* + present tense (present/future reference)
  I'll write it down in case I forget it.
- *in case* + past tense (past reference)
  He took a torch in case there was no light in the attic.
  Note: *in case* is never used with *will* or *would*. *He took a map in case he got lost.* (NOT: *...in case he would get...*)
- *for* + noun (expresses the purpose of an action)
  She went to the bakery for some bread.
- *for* + *-ing* form (expresses the purpose of sth or its function)
  This is a knife for cutting meat.
- *with a view to* + *-ing* form
  They are saving up with a view to buying a new car.

We can express **negative purpose** using:
- *in order not to/so as not to* + infinitive
  She lied to him in order not to/so as not to make him angry.
  Note: We never use *not to* to express negative purpose.
- *prevent* + noun/pronoun (+ *from*) + *-ing* form
  Eating healthy prevents you from gaining weight.
- *avoid* + *-ing* form
  She took a taxi to work to avoid being late.
- *so that* + *can't/won't* (present/future reference)
  I'll invite her so that she won't feel lonely.
- *so that* + *couldn't/wouldn't* (past reference)
  She locked the door so that burglars couldn't get in.

Notes:
- **Clauses of purpose** should not be confused with **clauses of result**.
- **Clauses of purpose** are introduced with *so that/in order that*. *She moved to New York so that she could find a better job.* (this shows purpose)

Grammar Reference

- **Clauses of result** are introduced with *so/such ... that*. *It was such a lovely day that we went jogging in the park.* (this shows result)
- **Clauses of purpose** follow the rule of the sequence of tenses. *I'm going to buy an English dictionary so that my spelling will improve.* *She trained every day so that she could enter the competition.*

Clauses of result

Clauses of result are used to express result. They are introduced with the following words/phrases:

- *as a result/therefore/consequently/as a consequence* *The cinema was crowded. As a result/Therefore/ Consequently/As a consequence, we left.* OR *The cinema was crowded and as a result/ therefore/ consequently/as a consequence we left.*
- *such a/an* + **adjective** + **singular countable noun** + *that* *It was such a nice dress that she bought it.*
- *such* + **adjective** + **plural/uncountable noun** + *that* *They are such good students that they always get top marks.* *It was such bad weather that we stayed indoors.*
- *such a lot of* + **plural/uncountable noun** + *that* *She has such a lot of clothes that she can't store them all in her wardrobe. There was such a lot of traffic that I was late for work.*
- *so* + **clause** *It was raining so they didn't have a picnic.*
- *so* + **adjective/adverb** + *that* *She was so tired that she fell asleep on the sofa. He speaks so quickly that I can't understand him.*
- *so much/little* + **uncountable noun** + *that* *They had so much luggage that they couldn't carry it. She has so little food that she must be starving.*
- *so many/few* + **plural noun** + *that* *She had to write so many reports that it took her all day to finish. There were so few eggs that I couldn't make an omelette.*

Clauses of reason

Clauses of reason are adverbial clauses and are used to express the reason for something. They are introduced by:

- *because* *I took a break because I wasn't feeling well.*
- *as/since* (= because) *They spent the night in a hotel as/ since their flight was delayed.*
- *the/a reason for* + **noun/-ing form** + *is/was* + **noun/ -ing form** *The reason for him being late was the stormy weather.*
- *the/a reason why ... is/was* + **noun/-ing form/that-clause** *The reason why she left early is that she felt ill.*
- *because of/on account of/due to* + **noun** *She took the underground because of/on account of/due to the huge traffic jam.*

- *due to the fact that* + **clause** *She took the underground due to the fact that there was a huge traffic jam.*
- *now (that)* + **clause** *Now (that) we are on holiday, we can finally relax.*
- *for* = **because (in formal written style)** *He couldn't eat the food, for it was very spicy.*
  Note: a clause of reason introduced with **for** always comes after the main clause.

Determiners

every – each
- *Every* and *each* are used with singular countable nouns. We normally use *each* when we talk about two people or things. We use *every/each* when we talk about three or more people or things. *I was holding two bags in each hand so I couldn't open the door.* (NOT: *... in every hand ...*) *I enjoyed every/each page of this book.*
- *Every one* and *each (one)* can be followed by of. *Every one of the employees will be given ten days off.*
- We use *every* when we are thinking of people or things together, in a group, to mean 'all', 'everybody/ everything'. *Every student needs to study hard for the exam.* (all students) We use *each* when we are thinking of people or things separately, one at a time. *Each student was awarded a diploma.*
- We use *every* to show how often something happens. *I go to the gym every day.*
- We use *every*, but not *each*, with words and expressions such as *almost*, *nearly*, *practically* and *without exception*. *My best friend and I talk on the phone almost every day.* (NOT: *each day*)

Note:
- *each other* = one another *We see each other every weekend.*
- *every other* = alternate *Ron has a piano lesson every other day.*
- *another* = one more part from those already mentioned. **Another** can also be used with expressions of distance, money and time. *My digital camera broke and now I need to buy another one. In another three years, she will have bought a new house.*

both/neither – all/whole/none – either
- *Both* refers to two people, things or groups. It has a positive meaning and is followed by a plural verb. *Both hotels seem like good choices.*
- *Neither* refers to two people, things or groups, and has a negative meaning. *Neither of* + **plural noun phrase** can be followed by either a singular or plural verb in the affirmative. *Neither of the two films is/are interesting.* **BUT** *Neither music class is held on Friday.*

- **All** refers to more than two people, things or groups. It has a positive meaning and is followed by a plural verb. *All the trainers at the gym are great. All of them are very helpful.*
- **Both/All** can go:
  a) after the verb **to be**. *They are both/all good books.*
  b) after a modal/auxiliary verb, but before the main verb. *You should all/both train harder for the school marathon.*
- **Whole** is used with singular countable nouns. We use *a/the/this/my,* etc + *whole* + *noun.*
  Bob actually ate the whole pizza himself!
  ALSO: *Bob actually ate all the pizza himself!*
  We don't use *whole* with uncountable nouns. *She drank all the juice in the carton.* (NOT: ...the whole juice ...)
  All + *day/morning/week/year* = *the whole* + *day/ morning/week/year We had been working all day/the whole day.*
- **None of** refers to more than two people, things or groups, and has a negative meaning. It is used with nouns or object pronouns, and is followed by either a singular or plural verb.
  None of the girls plays/play tennis.
  BUT *'How many eggs have we got?' 'None.'*

- **Either** refers to two people, things or groups, and is followed by a singular countable noun.
  Either of + **plural noun phrase** can be followed by either a singular or plural verb.
  Either of the two hotels has/have a swimming pool.
  BUT *Either hotel has a swimming pool.*
  We can use *not ... either of* instead of *neither of. Either* can also be used at the end of a negative sentence.
  She has two bikes, but she doesn't use either of them.
  (= She has two bikes but she uses **neither of** them.)
  Steven doesn't like horror films and I don't either.
- **Both ... and ...** is followed by a plural verb.
  Both Jill and Jane like adventure films.
- **Neither ... nor/Either ... or** take either a singular or plural verb, depending on the subject which follows *nor* or *or.*
  Neither John nor Bill is willing to help. Either Tina or her parents are visiting Mary in the hospital.

Word List

Unit 1 –
In Character

1a

adventurous /əd'ventʃərəs/ (adj) = risk-taking

arched /ɑːtʃt/ (adj) = curved

bossy /'bɒsi/ (adj) = always telling others what to do

brain /breɪn/ (n) = the organ inside the head that controls the body and feelings

brave /breɪv/ (adj) = showing no fear

brighten up /ˌbraɪtn 'ʌp/ (phr v) = to make sth look newer and more pleasant

bushy /'bʊʃi/ (adj) = (of hair, beard, etc) very thick

calm /kɑːm/ (adj) = relaxed; not nervous

careful /'keəfəl/ (adj) = paying attention to what you are doing

charming /'tʃɑːmɪŋ/ (adj) = pleasant and attractive

cheerful /'tʃɪəfəl/ (adj) = joyful and enthusiastic

chubby /'tʃʌbi/ (adj) = a little fat in a pleasant way

clever /'klevə/ (adj) = intelligent

confident /'kɒnfɪdənt/ (adj) = sure of yourself and your abilities

cruel /kruːəl/ (adj) = heartless; causing suffering

curious /'kjʊəriəs/ (adj) = wanting to know more and always asking questions

curved /kɜːvd/ (adj) = slightly rounded

earlobe /'ɪələʊb/ (n) = the soft part at the bottom of the ear

elderly /'eldəli/ (adj) = old; past middle-aged

eyebrow /'aɪbraʊ/ (n) = the thin line of hair above each eye

famous /'feɪməs/ (adj) = well-known

feature /'fiːtʃə/ (n) = a part of your face

forehead /'fɒrɪd/ (n) = the part of the face above the eyebrows

friendly /'frendli/ (adj) = pleasant and kind

funny /'fʌni/ (adj) = humorous

generous /'dʒenərəs/ (adj) = willing to give

gentle /'dʒentl/ (adj) = calm and kind

honest /'ɒnɪst/ (adj) = always telling the truth

hooked /hʊkt/ (adj) = (of a nose) slightly curved

jealous /'dʒeləs/ (adj) = envious of others

judge /dʒʌdʒ/ (v) = to form an opinion about sb/sth

kind /kaɪnd/ (adj) = caring about other people

lazy /'leɪzi/ (adj) = unwilling to work or make an effort

lip /lɪp/ (n) = each of the two outer parts of the mouth

look after /lʊk 'ɑːftə/ (phr v) = to take care of sb/sth

look for /lʊk fə/ (phr v) = to try to find

look forward to /lʊk 'fɔːwəd tu/ (phr v) = to expect sth with pleasure

look up /ˌlʊk 'ʌp/ (phr v) = to try to find a word, name, etc in a reference book

middle-aged /ˌmɪdl 'eɪdʒd/ (adj) = between 45 and 65 years old

patient /'peɪʃənt/ (adj) = able to remain calm and not get easily annoyed

popular /'pɒpjələ/ (adj) = well-known and liked by many people

rectangular /rek'tæŋgjʊlə/ (adj) = (of a shape) having two short equal sides, two long equal sides and four right angles

reliable /rɪ'laɪəbəl/ (adj) = trustworthy

rude /ruːd/ (adj) = not polite

sensible /'sensəbəl/ (adj) = showing good judgment

serious /'sɪəriəs/ (adj) = sensible and not joking

sociable /'səʊʃəbəl/ (adj) = enjoying being with other people

tend /tend/ (v) = to be likely to do sth

thick /θɪk/ (adj) = (of eyebrows) not thin; bushy

violent /'vaɪələnt/ (adj) = using force; aggressive

1b

by nature (phr) = from birth

complicated /'kɒmplɪkeɪtɪd/ (adj) = involving many different parts; difficult to understand

crew /kruː/ (n) = a film team with special skills

fairy tale /'feəri teɪl/ (n) = a fantasy story for children

glossy /'glɒsi/ (adj) = (of a magazine) printed on shiny high-quality paper

physicist /'fɪzɪsɪst/ (n) = a scientist who studies energy, light, natural forces, etc

queue /kjuː/ (n) = a line of people waiting for sth

receptionist /rɪ'sepʃənɪst/ (n) = sb whose job is to welcome people in an office/building/hotel

reliable /rɪ'laɪəbəl/ (adj) = trustworthy

strict /strɪkt/ (adj) = tough with rules and discipline

update /ʌp'deɪt/ (v) = to revise; to improve

1c

accessories /ək'sesəriz/ (pl n) = additional outfit items such as hats, belts, jewellery, etc

achievement /ə'tʃiːvmənt/ (n) = an accomplishment

ankle sock /'æŋkəl sɒk/ (n) = a piece of clothing that covers the foot and the ankle

beachwear /'biːtʃweə/ (n) = pieces of clothing that we wear when we go swimming

belt /belt/ (n) = a long narrow piece of material worn around the waist

blouse /blaʊz/ (n) = a type of shirt for women and girls

bow tie /bəʊ 'taɪ/ (n) = an accessory worn around men's necks that looks like a butterfly

champion /'tʃæmpiən/ (n) = an athlete who has won first prize in a sports competition

cross-country skier /ˌkrɒs 'kʌntri ˌskiːə/ (n) = an athlete who skis across fields and the countryside

fair play /ˌfeə 'pleɪ/ (n) = following the rules in sport

footwear /'fʊtweə/ (n) = shoes, boots, trainers, etc

ideal /aɪ'dɪəl/ (n) = a moral standard or principle

inspiring (to sb) /ɪn'spaɪərɪŋ/ (adj) = making people want to try and achieve sth great

menswear /'menzweə/ (n) = clothing items for men

participate (in sth) /pɑː'tɪsɪpeɪt/ (v) = to take part in an activity

polka dot /'pɒlkə dɒt/ (n) = each of the dots of a clothes design

polo shirt /'pəʊləʊ ʃɜːt/ (n) = a T-shirt with a collar and two or three buttons

polo-neck /'pəʊləʊ nek/ (adj) = (of a jumper, etc) with a high neck that folds over

proudly /'praʊdli/ (adv) = feeling pleased about sth you have achieved

pullover /'pʊləʊvə/ (n) = a sweater

regularly /'regjʊləli/ (adv) = frequently

silk /sɪlk/ (adj) = (of clothes) made of a luxurious, delicate, soft type of cloth

skinny jeans /ˌskɪni 'dʒiːnz/ (pl n) = a pair of jeans with very narrow legs

sportswear /'spɔːtsweə/ (n) = clothing items worn when we do sports

stylish /'staɪlɪʃ/ (adj) = trendy and attractive

suffer (from sth) /'sʌfə/ (v) = to experience sth unpleasant

sweatshirt /'swetʃɜːt/ (n) = a loose piece of clothing for the upper part of the body

tailored suit /ˌteɪləd 'suːt/ (n) = a suit made to fit a specific person's body closely

tracksuit /'træksuːt/ (n) = the loose trousers and sweatshirt that we wear when we go jogging

waistcoat /'weɪskəʊt/ (n) = a sleeveless piece of clothing with buttons worn over a shirt

womenswear /ˈwɪmɪnzweə/
(n) = clothing items for
women

Culture 1

checked /tʃekt/ (adj) = (of a
cloth pattern) with squares
of different colours

clan /klæn/ (n) = a large family
group

cloth /klɒθ/ (n) = a material for
making clothes

clothing /ˈkləʊðɪŋ/ (n) = items
of clothes

date back (to) /ˌdeɪt ˈbæk/
(phr v) = to have existed
since a certain time

event /ɪˈvent/ (n) = an
organised occasion

folds /fəʊldz/ (pl n) = parts
of a piece of cloth which
overlap one another

funeral /ˈfjuːnərəl/ (n) = a
ceremony for burying a
dead person

ghillie brogues /ˌgɪli ˈbrəʊgz/
(pl n) = a type of traditional
Scottish shoes

hang /hæŋ/ (v) = to be
suspended from sth at a
high place

hose /həʊz/ (n) = a pair of
knee-high socks

kilt pin /ˈkɪlt pɪn/ (n) = a special
safety pin for holding a
Scottish tartan skirt in place

knee /niː/ (n) = the joint that
connects the upper and
lower parts of the leg

occasion /əˈkeɪʒən/ (n) =
an important event or
celebration

pattern /ˈpætən/ (n) = a design
on clothes

pleats /pliːts/ (pl n) = the folds
in a piece of clothing

pouch /paʊtʃ/ (n) = a small bag
made of cloth

put on /pʊt ˈɒn/ (phr v) = to
wear clothes/shoes

sporran /ˈspɒrən/ (n) = a men's
pouch hanging in front of
the Scottish kilt

unlike /ʌnˈlaɪk/ (prep) = being
different from sth

wedding /ˈwedɪŋ/ (n) = a
marriage ceremony

Unit 2 – Reading Time

2a

action and adventure /ˈækʃən
ənd ədˈventʃə/ (n) = a
book full of dangerous and
exciting situations

amusing /əˈmjuːzɪŋ/ (adj) =
entertaining

bestseller /ˌbestˈselə/ (n) = a
book that has sold a lot of
copies

biography /baɪˈɒgrəfi/ (n) =
a book about the life of a
famous person

break a code (phr) = to decode
a message

break down /ˌbreɪk ˈdaʊn/
(phr v) = (of cars, engines,
etc) to stop working

break into /ˈbreɪk ɪntə/
(phr v) = to get into a
building, etc to steal sth

break out /ˌbreɪk ˈaʊt/ (phr v) =
(of wars, fires, storms, etc)
to begin suddenly

break up /ˌbreɪk ˈʌp/ (phr v) =
1) (of schools) to stop
for holidays; 2) to end a
relationship

clever /ˈklevə/ (adj) = done
in a way that shows
skill, intelligence and
inventiveness

comedy /ˈkɒmədi/ (n) = a book
intended to be funny

complicated /ˈkɒmplɪkeɪtɪd/
(adj) = hard to understand;
involving lots of different
parts

confusing /kənˈfjuːzɪŋ/ (adj) =
unclear and difficult to
understand

crime /kraɪm/ (n) = a book
about a detective and the
way they solve a mystery

depressed /dɪˈprest/ (adj) =
sad and unable to enjoy
anything

difficult to read (phr) = (of a
book, etc) hard to follow or
understand

dull /dʌl/ (adj) = boring;
uninteresting

easy to read (phr) = (of a book,
etc) requiring little effort to
follow or understand

educational /ˌedjuˈkeɪʃənəl/
(adj) = informative; teaching
you sth

epic /ˈepɪk/ (n) = a book,
poem or film relating to
a long story about great
events, usually of historical
significance

exciting /ɪkˈsaɪtɪŋ/ (adj) =
thrilling

expert (at sth) /ˈekspɜːt/
(adj) = very knowledgeable
about sth

fantasy /ˈfæntəsi/ (n) = a book
based on imagination, not
facts

full of action (phr) = with plenty
of exciting events

health /helθ/ (n) = a book
or manual that provides
information about medicine
and well-being

history /ˈhɪstəri/ (n) = a book
on the past events of a
nation, etc

horror /ˈhɒrə/ (n) = a book
featuring scary situations
and characters

impossible to put down
(phr) = (of a book) so
interesting that you cannot
stop reading

interesting /ˈɪntrəstɪŋ/ (adj) =
that attracts your attention

look (at sth) /lʊk/ (v) = to
direct your eyes at sth

main /meɪn/ (adj) = leading

missing /ˈmɪsɪŋ/ (adj) = (of a
person) lost

mystery /ˈmɪstəri/ (n) = a book
that is about unsolved
crimes or puzzling events

original /əˈrɪdʒɪnəl/ (adj) = new;
innovative

powerful /ˈpaʊəfəl/ (adj) =
having a strong effect on
people

realistic /rɪəˈlɪstɪk/ (adj) =
seeming real

romance /rəʊˈmæns/ (n) = a
book about a love story

rule /ruːl/ (v) = to govern

scary /ˈskeəri/ (adj) =
frightening

science /ˈsaɪəns/ (n) = a book
on a subject such as
physics, chemistry, biology,
etc

science fiction /ˌsaɪəns
ˈfɪkʃən/ (n) = a book set
in an imaginary future,
involving science, space
and technology

secret code /ˌsiːkrət ˈkəʊd/
(n) = a system of words,
numbers, symbols, etc for
transmitting messages that
only certain people will be
able to reveal the hidden
meaning of

see /siː/ (v) = to become aware
of sth by using your eyes

serious /ˈsɪəriəs/ (adj) =
important

settle down /ˌsetl ˈdaʊn/
(phr v) = to sit on a sofa,
in an armchair, etc in a
comfortable position to
do sth

silly /ˈsɪli/ (adj) = not serious

spaceship /ˈspeɪsʃɪp/ (n) = a
vehicle that travels in space

textbook /ˈtekstbʊk/ (n) = a
book with facts about a
school subject

thriller /ˈθrɪlə/ (n) = an exciting
book about criminal
activities

throne /θrəʊn/ (n) = a king's or
queen's chair

totally /ˈtəʊtli/ (adv) =
completely

travel /ˈtrævəl/ (n) = a book
with relevant information
about a place intended for
tourists

unbelievable /ˌʌnbɪˈliːvəbəl/
(adj) = incredible; amazing

unlikely /ʌnˈlaɪkli/ (adj) = not
expected

watch /wɒtʃ/ (v) = to pay
attention to sb or sth for a
period of time

2b

blow /bləʊ/ (v) = (of the wind)
to move

breeze /briːz/ (n) = a light and
pleasant wind

crash (against sth) /kræʃ/ (v)
= (of waves) to hit sth with
great force in a way that
makes a lot of loud noise

get rough (phr) = (of the sea) to
start moving a lot in a violent
and unpredictable way

Word List

grab /græb/ (v) = to take hold of sth/sb suddenly

hang out /hæŋ 'aʊt/ (phr v) = to spend time relaxing somewhere with sb or by yourself

lower /'ləʊə/ (v) = to move sth downwards carefully

river bank /'rɪvə bæŋk/ (n) = the edge of the river where it meets the land

sail /seɪl/ (v) = to control a boat, ship, etc through water

sail /seɪl/ (n) = the piece of cloth on the mast of a boat/ ship which helps it to move forward when the wind blows

share (sth with sb) /ʃeə/ (v) = to have or use sth with sb else

shower /'ʃaʊə/ (n) = the act of bathing when you stand under a spray of water

sink /sɪŋk/ (v) = to disappear below the surface of water

wave /weɪv/ (n) = a large raised mass of water which moves across the surface of the sea

2c

amazed /ə'meɪzd/ (adj) = filled with great surprise

annoyed /ə'nɔɪd/ (adj) = angry about sth

bored /bɔːd/ (adj) = fed up

close to tears (phr) = about to cry

confused /kən'fjuːzd/ (adj) = unable to understand sth

disappointed /dɪsə'pɔɪntɪd/ (adj) = sad at not getting what you hoped for

embarrassed /ɪm'bærəst/ (adj) = feeling self-conscious or ashamed

forest /'fɒrɪst/ (n) = a large area of land covered with trees

joke /dʒəʊk/ (v) = to say sth amusing

miserable /'mɪzrəbəl/ (adj) = sad; unhappy

nervous /'nɜːvəs/ (adj) = filled with or showing anxiety

pull over /pʊl 'əʊvə/ (phr v) = to move a vehicle to the side of the road and stop it

relieved /rɪ'liːvd/ (adj) = no longer worried

scared /skeəd/ (adj) = frightened

shake /ʃeɪk/ (v) = to tremble

terrified /'terəfaɪd/ (adj) = very frightened

Culture 2

a link in the chain (idm) = each of the stages that make up a process or a series of events

circumstances /'sɜː kəmstənsɪz/ (pl n) = conditions which affect a situation

collection /kə'lekʃən/ (n) = a group of things put together

detective /dɪ'tektɪv/ (n) = an investigator of a crime, etc

finest /'faɪnɪst/ (adj) = (of clothes) most stylish

ignore /ɪg'nɔː/ (v) = to not pay attention to

intelligence /ɪn'telɪdʒəns/ (n) = cleverness

moustache /mə'stɑːʃ/ (n) = the hair that grows on a man's upper lip

popular /'pɒpjələ/ (adj) = liked by a lot of people; well-known

proper /'prɒpə/ (adj) = correct

rush /rʌʃ/ (v) = to move quickly towards sb/a place

tragedy /'trædʒədi/ (n) = a shocking or very sad event

unlock /ʌn'lɒk/ (v) = to open the lock of sth

Unit 3 – All around the world

3a

classic /'klæsɪk/ (adj) = traditional

come across /kʌm ə'krɒs/ (phr v) = to happen to see sth

early /'ɜːli/ (adj) = near the beginning of a time period

journey /'dʒɜːni/ (n) = the act of travelling from one place to another

old-fashioned /ˌəʊld 'fæʃənd/ (adj) = not modern

platform /'plætfɔːm/ (n) = a flat structure

railway track /'reɪlweɪ træk/ (n) = a railway line

rainforest /'reɪnfɒrɪst/ (n) = a forest in a tropical area where it rains a lot

reed boat /'riːd ˌbəʊt/ (n) = a boat made from a plant like tall marsh grass

reindeer sled /'reɪndɪə ˌsled/ (n) = a small snow vehicle pulled by an animal like a big deer

ride /raɪd/ (n) = a trip in a vehicle

run after /rʌn 'ɑːftə/ (phr v) = to chase sb/sth

run into /rʌn 'ɪntə/ (phr v) = to meet sb by chance

run out of /rʌn 'aʊt əv/ (phr v) = to have no more of sth

run over /rʌn 'əʊvə/ (phr v) = to hit sb/sth with a car, etc

set up /set 'ʌp/ (phr v) = to prepare the equipment that will be needed for an activity

shine /ʃaɪn/ (v) = to glow

toboggan /tə'bɒgən/ (n) = a type of sled without skis for sliding over snow or other slippery surface

travel /'trævəl/ (n) = the activity of going to places, usually far away

trip /trɪp/ (n) = a short journey; an excursion

uniform /'juːnɪfɔːm/ (n) = a special set of clothes that some people have to wear at work

wheel /wiːl/ (n) = each of the round objects under a vehicle for moving it

whizz /wɪz/ (v) = to move very fast, usually making a sound

zip-line tour /'zɪp laɪn ˌtʊə/ (n) = a visit to a forest, river, valley, etc hanging from a wire with special equipment

3b

award /ə'wɔːd/ (n) = a prize

customer /'kʌstəmə/ (n) = sb who buys goods or services from a shop, company, etc

destination /ˌdestɪ'neɪʃən/ (n) = the place to which sb is going

details /'diːteɪlz/ (pl n) = information

fairytale land (phr) = a very beautiful place

freeze /friːz/ (v) = (of water) to become ice

hurricane /'hʌrɪkən/ (n) = a severe storm moving over water

move forward /ˌmuːv 'fɔːwəd/ (phr v) = to leave sth behind and get on with life

no doubt (phr) = surely

reach /riːtʃ/ (v) = to arrive somewhere

since records began (phr) = since the time when people started collecting data on a subject

weaken /'wiːkən/ (v) = to become less strong

3c

arrivals /ə'raɪvəlz/ (pl n) = (at an airport) the place for passengers who have just got off the plane

baggage /'bægɪdʒ/ (n) = a passenger's bags and suitcases

baggage reclaim /'bægɪdʒ rɪˌkleɪm/ (n) = (at an airport) the place for passengers to collect their bags and suitcases after their flight

boarding pass /'bɔːdɪŋ pɑːs/ (n) = a passenger's card for getting on a plane

check-in /'tʃek ɪn/ (n) = (at an airport) the desk where passengers leave their baggage and collect their boarding pass

customs /'kʌstəmz/ (pl n) = the place where passengers' baggage is checked on entering a foreign country

deliver /dɪ'lɪvə/ (v) = to take sth to a person or place

departures /dɪ'pɑːtʃəz/ (pl n) = (at an airport) the place for passengers waiting to board a plane

duty-free /ˌdjuːti ˈfriː/ (n) = (at an airport) the place with shops where passengers can buy goods without tax

fantasy /ˈfæntəsi/ (n) = an imaginary situation; imagination

information /ˌɪnfəˈmeɪʃən/ (n) = facts and details about sb/sth

luggage /ˈlʌɡɪdʒ/ (n) = a passenger's bags and suitcases

luggage receipt number (phr) = the number of a baggage tag that a passenger is given at the check-in desk

passenger /ˈpæsəndʒə/ (n) = sb who travels on a bus, plane, etc

passport control /ˈpɑːspɔːt kənˌtrəʊl/ (n) = (at an airport) the place where authorities check passengers' passports

strap /stræp/ (n) = a narrow piece of material for fastening or carrying things

Culture 3

amusing /əˈmjuːzɪŋ/ (adj) = entertaining

at the bottom of sth (phr) = at the lowest part of sth

bold /bəʊld/ (adj) = (of colours) very strong

change /tʃeɪndʒ/ (v) = to get off one means of transport and onto another

confusing /kənˈfjuːzɪŋ/ (adj) = difficult to understand

curve /kɜːv/ (n) = a bend in a river, a road, a railway line, etc

diamond /ˈdaɪəmənd/ (n) = a shape with four sides and two sharp ends

line /laɪn/ (n) = a railway track

straight /streɪt/ (adj) = not curved

symbol /ˈsɪmbəl/ (n) = sth that represents a place or idea

underground railway /ˌʌndəɡraʊnd ˌreɪlweɪ/ (n) = a railway system under the earth's surface

Values A: Philanthropy

announce /əˈnaʊns/ (v) = to make a public statement about sth

borrow /ˈbɒrəʊ/ (v) = to take sth which you are expected to return at a later time

fortune /ˈfɔːtʃən/ (n) = a large amount of money and wealth

invest /ɪnˈvest/ (v) = to put money into sth

project /ˈprɒdʒekt/ (n) = a detailed study on sth in order to build or make it

Public Speaking Skills A

cheeky /ˈtʃiːki/ (adj) = rather impolite

confidently /ˈkɒnfɪdəntli/ (adv) = in a way that shows that you feel sure about your own abilities, ideas, etc

fairy /ˈfeəri/ (n) = a female imaginary creature with wings that has magical powers

independent spirit (phr) = sb who is confident and able to do things by himself/herself, and who doesn't rely on other people's opinions

nurse /nɜːs/ (n) = sb whose job is to look after sick people in a hospital

trunk /trʌŋk/ (n) = the body of the tree without its branches

Unit 4 – Hard Times

4a

active /ˈæktɪv/ (adj) = always enjoying doing things

afford /əˈfɔːd/ (v) = to have enough money to be able to do sth

anxious (about sth) /ˈæŋkʃəs/ (adj) = worried about sth

attract /əˈtrækt/ (v) = to cause people to come to a place

become unemployed (phr) = to lose my job

believe (in sb/sth) /bɪˈliːv/ (v) = to be certain that sb/sth is effective and reliable

bill /bɪl/ (n) = a piece of paper showing the money you owe for goods or services

cause /kɔːz/ (n) = the reason why sth happens

CV /ˌsi ˈviː/ (n) = a written statement of sb's education and work experience

day care /ˈdeɪ keə/ (n) = the supervision provided to babies/young children when their parents are at work

divorce /dɪˈvɔːs/ (n) = the end of a marriage by law

financial problem (phr) = lack of money

fundraising event /ˈfʌndreɪzɪŋ ɪˌvent/ (n) = an event for collecting money for a charity

give up /ˌɡɪv ˈʌp/ (phr v) = to stop hoping or trying

illness /ˈɪlnəs/ (n) = a disease

let sb go (phr) = to tell sb to leave their job

miserable /ˈmɪzərəbəl/ (adj) = very unhappy

miss /mɪs/ (v) = to be unable to take advantage of (an opportunity)

move house (phr) = to leave my present home and go to live in a different one

personal information (phr) = details about yourself such as name, address, date of birth, etc

pile up /ˌpaɪl ˈʌp/ (phr v) = to accumulate

positive attitude (phr) = feeling hopeful and confident that things will be OK

professional networking site (phr) = a website that connects people with potential employers

promotion /prəˈməʊʃən/ (n) = getting a more important position in your job

proud (of sth) /praʊd/ (adj) = very pleased about sth you have done

quit /kwɪt/ (v) = to leave a job

reason /ˈriːzən/ (n) = the fact why sth happens

retire /rɪˈtaɪə/ (v) = to stop working because of old age

separation /ˌsepəˈreɪʃən/ (n) = a husband and wife living separately

serious injury (phr) = suffering severe physical or mental harm

start a new job (phr) = to find a new job and begin to work there

take after /ˈteɪk ɑːftə/ (phr v) = to have the same appearance or character as sb

take exams (phr) = to sit examinations

take off /ˌteɪk ˈɒf/ (phr v) = 1) to remove clothes; 2) (of planes) to leave the ground

take over /ˌteɪk ˈəʊvə/ (phr v) = to gain control of sth

take up /ˌteɪk ˈʌp/ (phr v) = 1) to begin a hobby, sport, etc; 2) to fill (time, space)

think /θɪŋk/ (v) = to have a certain opinion about sb/sth

useful /ˈjuːsfəl/ (adj) = that can help or serve a purpose

volunteer /ˌvɒlənˈtɪə/ (v) = to offer to work without getting paid

4b

audience /ˈɔːdiəns/ (n) = a group of people watching a play, a film, a concert, etc

backpacking /ˈbækˌpækɪŋ/ (n) = travelling with little money and a bag on your back

change of plan (phr) = a different decision

crowd /kraʊd/ (n) = a large number of people together

dentist /ˈdentɪst/ (n) = the doctor who takes care of people's teeth

exhibition /ˌeksɪˈbɪʃən/ (n) = a public show of paintings, sculptures, photographs, etc

fall asleep (phr) = to start sleeping

fear (of sth) /fɪə/ (n) = the feeling of being afraid of sth

Word List

landing /ˈlændɪŋ/ (n) = (of a plane) returning to the ground

opening ceremony /ˌəʊpənɪŋ ˈserəməni/ (n) = a formal social event marking the beginning of sth

surgery /ˈsɜːdʒəri/ (n) = a doctor's office

take-off /ˈteɪk ɒf/ (n) = (of a plane) departure

text /tekst/ (v) = to send a message on a mobile phone

4c

anxiety /æŋˈzaɪəti/ (n) = worry; nervousness

avoid (doing sth) /əˈvɔɪd/ (v) = to choose not to do sth

breathe /briːð/ (v) = to let air into and out of the lungs

bug /bʌg/ (n) = a small insect

change /tʃeɪndʒ/ (v) = to make sth different

closed space (phr) = a place with blocked entry or exit

consider /kənˈsɪdə/ (v) = to take into account

control my fear (phr) = to be able to remain calm and not get afraid

damage /ˈdæmɪdʒ/ (v) = to cause harm to sth

deal with /ˈdiːl wɪð/ (phr v) = to try to solve a problem

develop /dɪˈveləp/ (v) = to start suffering from an illness

empty /ˈempti/ (v) = (of a place) to get abandoned

face my fears (phr) = to confront and overcome my fears of certain things

feel (terribly) sick (phr) = to be very ill

flying /ˈflaɪɪŋ/ (n) = travelling by air

focus (on sb/sth) /ˈfəʊkəs/ (v) = to give my attention to sb/sth

freeze /friːz/ (v) = to stop moving completely

freeze up /ˌfriːz ˈʌp/ (phr v) = to not be able to say sth because you feel uncomfortable

height /haɪt/ (n) = a high place

hurt /hɜːt/ (v) = to cause pain or injury to sb

metre /ˈmiːtə/ (n) = 100 centimetres

my hair stands on end (idm) = I feel extremely frightened

my hands sweat (phr) = my hands are covered with drops of liquid coming out through the skin

my heart beats faster (phr) = my heart moves more quickly than normal

my mouth goes dry (phr) = my mouth loses all its liquid (due to great fear)

pessimistic /ˌpesəˈmɪstɪk/ (adj) = thinking that only bad things will happen

phobia /ˈfəʊbiə/ (n) = an extreme and unreasonable fear

presentation /ˌprezənˈteɪʃən/ (n) = a piece of work that you show to other people

professional help (phr) = assistance from an expert

public speaking /ˌpʌblɪk ˈspiːkɪŋ/ (n) = the act of giving a speech to an audience

realise /ˈrɪəlaɪz/ (v) = to understand correctly

run a mile (idm) = to do my best to avoid sth

safety equipment /ˈseɪfti ɪˌkwɪpmənt/ (n) = all the clothes, tools, machines, etc necessary for protection

shake like a leaf (phr) = to tremble a lot (due to great fear)

smell /smel/ (v) = to give off a certain smell

stay /steɪ/ (v) = to remain in a place for some time

storm /stɔːm/ (n) = bad weather with lightning, thunder and heavy rain

sympathise (with sb) /ˈsɪmpəθaɪz/ (v) = to show that you can understand sb's bad feelings

tip /tɪp/ (n) = a piece of advice

wet /wet/ (v) = to cover or soak sth in water

Culture 4

brave /breɪv/ (adj) = courageous

bug /bʌg/ (n) = a small insect

creepy-crawly /ˌkriːpi ˈkrɔːli/ (n) = a small insect that can scare you

exciting /ɪkˈsaɪtɪŋ/ (adj) = very interesting

forget /fəˈget/ (v) = to not remember sth

giant /ˈdʒaɪənt/ (adj) = very big

highlight /ˈhaɪlaɪt/ (n) = the most interesting part of an event

host /həʊst/ (v) = to provide the place and facilities for an event

local /ˈləʊkəl/ (adj) = living in the area that we're talking about

rare /reə/ (adj) = scarce; unusual

sample /ˈsɑːmpəl/ (n) = a small amount of sth for testing

up close /ˌʌp ˈkləʊs/ (adv) = from a close distance

wonder /ˈwʌndə/ (v) = to ask myself about sth

Unit 5 – Citizen 2100

5a

alone /əˈləʊn/ (adj) = without anyone else

charging station /ˈtʃɑːdʒɪŋ ˌsteɪʃən/ (n) = a place that supplies electric power for recharging electric vehicles

come across /ˌkʌm əkrɒs/ (phr v) = to meet/find sb/sth by chance

come back /ˌkʌm ˈbæk/ (phr v) = to return

come into /ˈkʌm ɪntə/ (phr v) = to inherit

come over /ˌkʌm ˈəʊvə/ (phr v) = to visit

come round /ˌkʌm ˈraʊnd/ (phr v) = to visit

construct /kənˈstrʌkt/ (v) = to build sth

create /kriˈeɪt/ (v) = to generate sth

crowded /ˈkraʊdɪd/ (adj) = with too many people

deliver /dɪˈlɪvə/ (v) = to take sth to a particular place or person

drone delivery /ˈdrəʊn dɪˌlɪvəri/ (n) = bringing goods to sb's place using a small, remote-controlled aircraft

floating /ˈfləʊtɪŋ/ (adj) = that can stay on the surface of a liquid

improve /ɪmˈpruːv/ (v) = to make sth better

increase /ɪnˈkriːs/ (v) = to become bigger in amount

lonely /ˈləʊnli/ (adj) = sad because of being alone

perfect /ˈpɜːfɪkt/ (adj) = ideal

produce /prəˈdjuːs/ (v) = to make sth

provide (sth to sb) /prəˈvaɪd/ (v) = to supply sth to sb; to make sth available to sb

reduce /rɪˈdjuːs/ (v) = to make sth less in amount

self-driving bus (phr) = a large vehicle without a driver that can carry a lot of passengers

solar window /ˌsəʊlə ˈwɪndəʊ/ (n) = a window which has a panel to absorb the sun's rays and generate electric power

take up space (phr) = to occupy a certain amount of an area

3D-printed /ˌθriː ˈdiː ˌprɪntɪd/ (adj) = produced with the use of a machine in a three-dimensional form

traffic jam /ˈtræfɪk ˌdʒæm/ (n) = a big number of vehicles unable to move, or moving very slowly

transport /trænˈspɔːt/ (v) = to take people or goods from one place to another

vacuum tube train /ˌvækjuəm ˈtjuːb treɪn/ (n) = a high-speed train that travels on a magnetic track through a tunnel from which air has been removed

vertical farm (phr) = each portion of land for raising crops one on top of the other in a skyscraper

5b

install /ɪnˈstɔːl/ (v) = to put sth into position and make it ready for use

pick up /ˌpɪk ˈʌp/ (phr v) = to collect sb from a place in my car, etc

project-based /ˈprɒdʒekt ˌbeɪst/ (adj) = (of homework) mainly involving careful study and research of a specific subject

sales department /ˈseɪlz dɪˌpɑːtmənt/ (n) = the department of a firm in charge of selling its products or services

VR headset /ˌviː ˈɑː ˌhedset/ (n) = a device with which a user covers his/her eyes and its computer technology enables him/her to physically experience imaginary worlds

wish sb luck (phr) = to tell sb that you hope they will be successful

5c

advanced technology (phr) = cutting-edge machinery and equipment

affordable /əˈfɔːdəbəl/ (adj) = reasonably priced

body function /ˈbɒdi ˌfʌŋkʃən/ (n) = a series of operations that each organ of the body performs

contract /ˈkɒntrækt/ (n) = a written agreement between an employer and an employee

crime /kraɪm/ (n) = illegal activities in general punished by law

criminal /ˈkrɪmɪnəl/ (n) = sb who does sth illegal

cure /kjʊə/ (n) = a medicine or therapy that makes sb healthy again

disabled /dɪsˈeɪbəld/ (adj) = physically or mentally impaired

elderly /ˈeldəli/ (adj) = old

gain weight (phr) = to become heavier

health care /ˈhelθ keə/ (n) = the medical services of a country or region

heart disease /ˈhɑːt dɪˌziːz/ (n) = a medical condition in which the organ of the body that pumps blood does not work normally

medical attention (phr) = getting treatment from a doctor

monitor /ˈmɒnɪtə/ (v) = to keep track of sth

obesity /əʊˈbiːsəti/ (n) = the state of being unhealthily overweight

pollution levels (phr) = the amounts of harmful substances released in the air that cause harm to the environment

poverty /ˈpɒvəti/ (n) = the state of being extremely poor

regular /ˈregjʊlə/ (adj) = ordinary

soil /sɔɪl/ (n) = the top layer of the earth in which plants grow

space travel /ˈspeɪs ˌtrævəl/ (n) = a journey outside the Earth's atmosphere

suffer (from sth) /ˈsʌfə/ (v) = to experience pain or unpleasant emotions

surgery /ˈsɜːdʒəri/ (n) = an operation

wearable device /ˌweərəbəl dɪˈvaɪs/ (n) = a gadget such as a smart watch, etc that you can put on your wrist or other parts of your body

Culture 5

access (information, etc) /ˈækses/ (v) = to find and obtain sb's information, etc

alien /ˈeɪliən/ (n) = a creature from outer space

alien invasion /ˈeɪliən ɪnˌveɪʒən/ (n) = creatures from outer space entering another planet, such as the Earth, by force

attack /əˈtæk/ (v) = to use violence in order to do harm to a person or place

automatic door /ˌɔːtəmætɪk ˈdɔː/ (n) = a door that opens and closes by itself

clear /klɪə/ (adj) = easy to understand

latest /ˈleɪtəst/ (adj) = the most recent

military vehicle /ˌmɪlɪtəri ˈviːɪkəl/ (n) = any means of transport used by the armed forces

nuclear bomb /ˌnjuːkliə ˈbɒm/ (n) = an atomic or hydrogen bomb

predict /prɪˈdɪkt/ (v) = to make a guess about what will happen in the future

satellite /ˈsætəlaɪt/ (n) = an electronic device sent into space that moves round the Earth and is used for electronic communications

tap /tæp/ (v) = to hit sth lightly and repeatedly

task /tɑːsk/ (n) = an assigned job

virtual assistant /ˌvɜːtʃuəl əˈsɪstənt/ (n) = a digital assistant that responds to voice commands

voice-activated /ˈvɔɪs ˌæktɪveɪtɪd/ (adj) = (of a device) that can be controlled by oral commands

weapon /ˈwepən/ (n) = a gun, knife, bomb, etc used in fighting or a war

Unit 6 – The Big Screen

6a

act /ækt/ (v) = to perform in a film or play

action – adventure /ˈækʃən ədˈventʃə/ (n) = a film full of dangerous and exciting situations

adventure /ədˈventʃə/ (n) = an exciting or unusual activity

affect /əˈfekt/ (v) = to have an influence on sth/sb in some way

amusing /əˈmjuːzɪŋ/ (adj) = entertaining

animation /ˌænɪˈmeɪʃən/ (n) = a film with moving images

appear /əˈpɪə/ (v) = to first be shown

audience /ˈɔːdiəns/ (n) = a group of people gathered to watch a film, play, etc

blockbuster /ˈblɒkbʌstə/ (n) = a film that is very popular or successful

boring /ˈbɔːrɪŋ/ (adj) = uninteresting; dull

cartoon /kɑːˈtuːn/ (n) = a film in which the characters are drawn

catchphrase /ˈkætʃfreɪz/ (n) = a phrase which is often repeated by a person and becomes well-known

comedy /ˈkɒmədi/ (n) = a funny film

composer /kəmˈpəʊzə/ (n) = sb whose job is to write music

create /kriˈeɪt/ (v) = to make sth; to produce sth

crime /kraɪm/ (n) = a film that talks about the illegal activities of sb who breaks the law

demand /dɪˈmɑːnd/ (v) = to ask for sth enthusiastically

disgusting /dɪsˈgʌstɪŋ/ (adj) = very unpleasant; causing a strong dislike

do /duː/ (v) = to perform a task

documentary /ˌdɒkjuˈmentəri/ (n) = a film or TV programme that gives facts and information about a subject

drama /ˈdrɑːmə/ (n) = a serious film about social issues

enjoyable /ɪnˈdʒɔɪəbəl/ (adj) = pleasant

exciting /ɪkˈsaɪtɪŋ/ (adj) = very interesting; great

fantasy /ˈfæntəsi/ (n) = a film based on imagination, not facts

film-maker /ˈfɪlm ˌmeɪkə/ (n) = sb who makes movies

force /fɔːs/ (n) = the power used by Jedi knights in the film "Star Wars"

funny /ˈfʌni/ (adj) = that makes you laugh

galaxy /ˈgæləksi/ (n) = a large group of stars in the universe

give (sth) away /ˌgɪv əˈweɪ/ (phr v) = to ruin a surprise

give back /ˌgɪv ˈbæk/ (phr v) = to return sth

give in /ˌgɪv ˈɪn/ (phr v) = 1) to finally agree to what sb wants; 2) to stop fighting or competing

give up /ˌgɪv ˈʌp/ (phr v) = to stop doing sth you used to do regularly

horror /ˈhɒrə/ (n) = a film featuring scary situations and characters

interesting /ˈɪntrəstɪŋ/ (adj) = that attracts your attention

Word List

musical /ˈmjuːzɪkəl/ (n) = a film or play with a lot of singing and dancing

outdoors /ˌaʊtˈdɔːz/ (adv) = in the open air

outside /aʊtˈsaɪd/ (prep) = not in a building or room

planet /ˈplænɪt/ (n) = a large object in space that moves around the Sun or another star

play the role (of a character) (phr) = to portray sb in a film, etc

proudly /ˈpraʊdli/ (adv) = in a way that shows a sense of satisfaction for sth

prove /pruːv/ (v) = to show sb that sth is true

queue /kjuː/ (n) = a line of people waiting to enter a building, a bus etc

scary /ˈskeəri/ (adj) = that makes you feel frightened

sci-fi /ˌsaɪ ˈfaɪ/ (n) = a film set in an imaginary future, involving science, space and technology

sequel /ˈsiːkwəl/ (n) = a film, book or play that continues the story of a previous one

series /ˈsɪəriːz/ (n) = a collection of TV episodes which follow a group of characters in a story

space opera /speɪs ˌɒpərə/ (n) = a sci-fi film about space wars and melodramatic adventures

special effects /speʃəl ɪˈfekts/ (pl n) = images or sounds used in films with the help of technology to create an illusion

spectator /spekˈteɪtə/ (n) = sb who attends and views an event, usually a sports event

thriller /ˈθrɪlə/ (n) = an exciting film about criminal activities

western /ˈwestən/ (n) = a film with cowboys

6b

behave yourself (phr) = to act in a proper way

call off /kɔːl ˈɒf/ (phr v) = to cancel an activity

compose /kəmˈpəʊz/ (v) = to write a piece of music

corn syrup /ˈkɔːn sɪrəp/ (n) = glucose syrup

direct /dəˈrekt/ (v) = to give instructions to actors about what to do in a film or play

film set /ˈfɪlm set/ (n) = the enclosed area in which a scene of a film is shot including the scenery and all the movable objects used in it

present /prɪˈzent/ (v) = to formally give sth to sb in public, usually a prize or an award

usher /ˈʌʃə/ (n) = sb who shows people to their seats in a cinema or theatre

6c

cast /kɑːst/ (n) = the group of actors in a film or play

chat show /ˈtʃæt ʃəʊ/ (n) = TV or radio programme where famous people are invited and interviewed by a host

cookery programme /ˈkʊkəri ˌprəʊɡræm/ (n) = a TV show about food preparation

defeat /dɪˈfiːt/ (v) = to beat sb

disappearance /ˌdɪsəˈpɪərəns/ (n) = the fact that sb goes missing and it's impossible to find him/her

DIY programme /ˌdiː aɪ ˈwaɪ ˌprəʊɡræm/ (n) = a TV programme about making or repairing things on your own

documentary /ˌdɒkjuˈmentəri/ (n) = a TV programme that gives facts and information about a subject

experiment /ɪkˈsperɪmənt/ (n) = a scientific test

film /fɪlm/ (n) = a movie

game show /ˈɡeɪm ʃəʊ/ (n) = a TV programme in which contestants compete against each other in order to win prizes

imaginative /ɪˈmædʒɪnətɪv/ (adj) = having interesting ideas

news /njuːz/ (n) = a TV or radio programme about current events and recent happenings

original /əˈrɪdʒɪnəl/ (adj) = (of a script) that is not based on other works but rather on the writer's own ideas

plot /plɒt/ (n) = the story of a film or book

power /ˈpaʊə/ (n) = strength; the ability to control sb

reality show /riˈæləti ʃəʊ/ (n) = a TV programme that shows real people's daily lives

save /seɪv/ (v) = to protect sb/sth from danger

script /skrɪpt/ (n) = the written lines of a film or play

sitcom /ˈsɪtkɒm/ (n) = an amusing TV series in which the same characters appear in different situations

soap opera /ˈsəʊp ˌɒpərə/ (n) = a TV drama about the everyday lives of a group of ordinary people

spoil /spɔɪl/ (v) = to ruin a surprise about sth for sb

talented /ˈtæləntɪd/ (adj) = gifted; very good at doing sth

travel show /ˈtrævəl ʃəʊ/ (n) = a travel documentary with a host travelling to tourist destinations and providing information about them

universe /ˈjuːnɪvɜːs/ (n) = the planets, stars, galaxies, etc in space

wildlife programme /ˈwaɪldlaɪf ˌprəʊɡræm/ (n) = a film or TV programme that gives facts and information about plants and animals in nature

Culture 6

composer /kəmˈpəʊzə/ (n) = sb whose job is to write music

excitement /ɪkˈsaɪtmənt/ (n) = a thrilling sensation

orchestral performance (phr) = a large number of musicians playing many different musical instruments and led by a conductor

realise /ˈrɪəlaɪz/ (v) = to become aware of sth

showing /ˈʃəʊɪŋ/ (n) = a screening of a film

soundtrack /ˈsaʊndtræk/ (n) = the recorded background music of a film

take (sb somewhere) /teɪk/ (v) = to lead sb on an imaginary journey somewhere

theme /θiːm/ (n) = a recognisable melody played usually at the beginning or end of a film

typical /ˈtɪpɪkəl/ (adj) = normal

Values B: Self-confidence

deliver a speech (phr) = to give a speech that you have written earlier in front of an audience

dry up /ˌdraɪ ˈʌp/ (phr v) = to stop talking all of a sudden as you have no idea of what to say next

improve /ɪmˈpruːv/ (v) = to make sth better

lighten /ˈlaɪtən/ (v) = to make the expression on your face look less serious

material /məˈtɪəriəl/ (n) = facts and information used for an activity, such as when giving a public speech, etc

raise my voice (idm) = to speak in a louder voice

rush /rʌʃ/ (v) = to do sth very quickly; to hurry

tip /tɪp/ (n) = a piece of advice

Public Speaking Skills B

compete (against sb) /kəmˈpiːt/ (v) = to try hard to outdo sb

deep /diːp/ (adj) = great

drop out (of sth) /drɒp ˈaʊt/ (phr v) = to withdraw from a course of study at a university, etc

release /rɪˈliːs/ (v) = to launch a film, CD, etc for people to see or buy

run /rʌn/ (v) = to manage a company, an organisation, etc

Unit 7 –
Narrow Escapes

7a

alive /ə'laɪv/ (adj) = not dead

avalanche /'ævəlɑːntʃ/ (n) = a large amount of snow rolling down a mountainside

beat /biːt/ (v) = to hit sth

calm /kɑːm/ (adj) = relaxed; not nervous

cancel /'kænsəl/ (v) = to say that sth planned will not happen

conditions /kən'dɪʃənz/ (pl n) = circumstances

discover /dɪs'kʌvə/ (v) = to find sb/sth that you were looking for

earthquake /'ɜːθkweɪk/ (n) = a sudden violent movement of the Earth's surface

effort /'efət/ (n) = the physical activity required to achieve sth

explore /ɪk'splɔː/ (v) = to travel around a place to learn about it

explosion /ɪk'spləʊʒən/ (n) = a sudden violent burst of energy

fire /faɪə/ (n) = a blaze

flood /flʌd/ (n) = a large amount of water covering a dry area

gear /gɪə/ (n) = equipment

heavy snowfall (phr) = snow falling in large quantities

hit /hɪt/ (v) = (of a hurricane, earthquake, etc) to have a severe effect on sb/sth

ignore /ɪg'nɔː/ (v) = to not pay attention to sb/sth

injure /'ɪndʒə/ (v) = to cause physical harm to sb

knock (on sth) /nɒk/ (v) = to hit a door/window with your hand in order to attract the attention of the people inside

lava /'lɑːvə/ (n) = hot molten rock coming out of a volcano

meanwhile /'miːnwaɪl/ (adv) = while another thing is happening

narrow /'nærəʊ/ (adj) = small in width

promise /'prɒmɪs/ (v) = to give sb your word

put off /ˌpʊt 'ɒf/ (phr v) = to postpone

put on /ˌpʊt 'ɒn/ (phr v) = to cover part of one's body with clothes, shoes, etc

put out /ˌpʊt 'aʊt/ (phr v) = to stop a fire burning

put up /ˌpʊt 'ʌp/ (phr v) = to let sb stay in your house

recover /rɪ'kʌvə/ (v) = to become healthy again

rescue /'reskjuː/ (n) = the act of saving sb from harm or danger

rubble /'rʌbəl/ (n) = the pieces of a building that has collapsed or been destroyed

shake /ʃeɪk/ (v) = to make short quick movements

spread /spred/ (v) = to expand and cover a large area

strike /straɪk/ (v) = to hit sb/sth forcefully

supplies /sə'plaɪz/ (pl n) = food and equipment necessary for living

survive /sə'vaɪv/ (v) = to remain alive

thunderstorm /'θʌndəstɔːm/ (n) = bad weather with a lot of rain and thunder

tie /taɪ/ (v) = to fasten together with a knot

trap /træp/ (v) = to prevent sb from leaving a place

typhoon /ˌtaɪ'fuːn/ (n) = a very violent tropical storm

unhurt /ˌʌn'hɜːt/ (adj) = not injured

volcanic eruption /vɒlˌkænɪk ɪ'rʌpʃən/ (n) = a sudden explosion of a volcano

warning sign /ˌwɔːnɪŋ 'saɪn/ (n) = a message informing of danger

7b

board /bɔːd/ (v) = to get on a bus, plane, boat, etc

brand-new /ˌbrænd 'njuː/ (adj) = used for the first time

crew /kruː/ (n) = the people who work on a ship/plane

deck /dek/ (n) = a flat open surface on a ship

iceberg /'aɪsbɜːg/ (n) = a large mass of ice floating in the sea

lifeboat /'laɪfbəʊt/ (n) = a boat kept on a ship to be used in emergencies

on board (phr) = on a boat or plane

passenger /'pæsəndʒə/ (n) = sb travelling on a bus, plane, train, etc

snow chains /snəʊ tʃeɪnz/ (pl n) = a set of chains that help the car to move over snow safely

victim /'vɪktɪm/ (n) = sb injured or killed in an accident or attack

volcano /vɒl'keɪnəʊ/ (n) = a mountain out of which molten rock, ashes and gases burst

7c

ambulance service (phr) = the organisation that provides special vans for taking people to hospital in case of emergency

ankle /'æŋkəl/ (n) = the joint connecting the foot with the leg

burn /bɜːn/ (n) = an injury caused by fire or heat

carry out /ˌkæri 'aʊt/ (phr v) = to perform a task

cave rescue service (phr) = the expert organisation that helps injured, trapped or lost cave explorers

crime /kraɪm/ (n) = an illegal action

eyewitness /'aɪwɪtnəs/ (n) = sb who has seen a crime or accident happen

fire service /faɪə ˌsɜːvɪs/ (n) = the organisation responsible for putting out fires

giant /'dʒaɪənt/ (adj) = enormous; very big

government /'gʌvənmənt/ (n) = the group of people who rule a country

let in /ˌlet 'ɪn/ (phr v) = to allow sb/sth to enter

medical emergency (phr) = an unexpected critical condition of sb's health

mountain rescue service (phr) = the expert organisation that helps injured or lost people in the mountains

repair /rɪ'peə/ (n) = the act of fixing sth damaged

rip through /ˌrɪp 'θruː/ (phr v) = to destroy a place completely by moving forcefully through it

runway /'rʌnweɪ/ (n) = the long road in an airport where aeroplanes take off and land

rush (sb somewhere) /rʌʃ/ (v) = to take sb to a place very quickly

severe /sɪ'vɪə/ (adj) = very serious; extremely bad

speedboat /'spiːdbəʊt/ (n) = a fast motorboat

summit /'sʌmɪt/ (n) = the top of a mountain

suspiciously /sə'spɪʃəsli/ (adv) = in a way that causes sb to think that sth wrong is happening

the coastguard /ðə 'kəʊstgɑːd/ (n) = the organisation that helps swimmers and ships in danger and prevents crime at sea

the police /ðə pə'liːs/ (n) = the organisation that prevents crime and arrests criminals

Culture 7

blow up /ˌbləʊ 'ʌp/ (phr v) = to destroy sth with explosives

break out /ˌbreɪk 'aʊt/ (phr v) = to start all of a sudden

careless /'keələs/ (adj) = without paying attention

cure /kjʊə/ (n) = a remedy or a treatment for a disease

disaster /dɪ'zɑːstə/ (n) = a catastrophe; a sudden tragic event

guard /gɑːd/ (n) = sb whose job is to protect people, places, buildings, etc

gunpowder /'gʌnˌpaʊdə/ (n) = an explosive substance in the form of fine grains used in bombs and fireworks

Word List

high society /ˌhaɪ səˈsaɪəti/ (n) = the rich and powerful people who form the upper class of a society

knock down /ˌnɒk ˈdaʊn/ (phr v) = to completely destroy a building

put out /ˌpʊt ˈaʊt/ (phr v) = to stop sth from burning

royal court /ˌrɔɪəl ˈkɔːt/ (n) = the home of a king and queen

ruin /ˈruːɪn/ (n) = what is left of a damaged building, area, etc

spread /spred/ (v) = (of a disease) to affect more and more people

trade /treɪd/ (n) = the activity of buying and selling goods and services

Unit 8 – Learning & Earning

8a

banker /ˈbæŋkə/ (n) = sb who owns or manages a bank

breathing equipment /ˈbriːðɪŋ ɪˌkwɪpmənt/ (n) = devices that help you breathe underwater

carry off /ˌkæri ˈɒf/ (phr v) = to succeed in doing sth difficult

carry on /ˌkæri ˈɒn/ (phr v) = to continue doing sth

carry out /ˌkæri ˈaʊt/ (phr v) = to perform (a task)

cleaner /ˈkliːnə/ (n) – sb whose job is to clean buildings

contract /kənˈtrækt/ (n) = a legal agreement between two or more people

director /dəˈrektə/ (n) = sb whose job is to tell actors how to play their parts

earn /ɜːn/ (v) = to receive money from work

engineer /ˌendʒɪˈnɪə/ (n) = a scientist whose job is to design and build houses, machines, etc

farmer /ˈfɑːmə/ (n) = sb whose job is to grow crops and keep animals

flooding /ˈflʌdɪŋ/ (n) = water covering an area due to heavy rain

full-time /ˌfʊl ˈtaɪm/ (adv) = working the standard number of hours per week

hold my breath (phr) = to keep air inside my lungs without letting it out

indoors /ˌɪnˈdɔːz/ (adv) = inside a place

journalist /ˈdʒɜːnəlɪst/ (n) = a reporter

librarian /laɪˈbreəriən/ (n) = a professional who works in a library

life form /ˈlaɪf fɔːm/ (n) = a type of a living thing

mountain guide /ˈmaʊntɪn ˌgaɪd/ (n) = a professional who leads and instructs climbers

outdoors /ˌaʊtˈdɔːz/ (adv) = outside a place

overalls /ˈəʊvərɔːlz/ (pl n) = a one-piece garment for manual labour

oyster /ˈɔɪstə/ (n) = a type of shellfish

peak /piːk/ (n) = the top of a mountain

pearl diver /ˈpɜːl daɪvə/ (n) = sb whose job is to swim to the bottom of the sea in order to find and pick shells that have a valuable jewel inside

poisonous /ˈpɔɪzənəs/ (adj) = containing a substance that can cause death

possibility /ˌpɒsəˈbɪləti/ (n) = likelihood

publisher /ˈpʌblɪʃə/ (n) = sb or a company that produces books, magazines, newspapers, etc

pure /pjʊə/ (adj) = complete

receptionist /rɪˈsepʃənɪst/ (n) = sb whose job is to welcome and help in a hotel, office, hospital, etc

regular hours (phr) = normal working hours

responsible (for sth/sb) /rɪˈspɒnsəbəl/ (adj) = in charge of sth/sb

risky /ˈrɪski/ (adj) = dangerous

rockslide /ˈrɒkslaɪd/ (n) = a mass of rocks falling down a hillside

salary /ˈsæləri/ (n) = the money earned from a job in a month or year

shift /ʃɪft/ (n) = a part of a working day

snow goggles /ˈsnəʊ gɒgəlz/ (pl n) = a type of glasses for the protection of eyes when you are in a snowy place

speleologist /ˌspiːliˈɒlədʒɪst/ (n) = a scientist who explores and studies caves

surface /ˈsɜːfɪs/ (n) = the top of the sea

temporary /ˈtempərəri/ (adj) = not permanent

tiny /ˈtaɪni/ (adj) = very small

tricky /ˈtrɪki/ (adj) = confusing and difficult

uniform /ˈjuːnɪfɔːm/ (n) = a special set of clothes that some people have to wear to work

wages /ˈweɪdʒɪz/ (pl n) = the money earned from a job according to the number of hours, days or weeks that sb has worked

watch out for (sth) /ˌwɒtʃ ˈaʊt fə/ (phr v) = to look out for sth

well-paid /ˌwel ˈpeɪd/ (adj) = earning a lot of money

win /wɪn/ (v) = to get the first place in a game, competition, etc

8b

apply (for sth) /əˈplaɪ/ (v) = to ask for sth officially

be stuck (in sth) (phr) = to be trapped (in a bad situation)

bill /bɪl/ (n) = a piece of paper showing how much we should pay for goods or services

canteen /kænˈtiːn/ (n) = a cafeteria in a school, factory, etc

deadline /ˈdedlaɪn/ (n) = the time by which sth must be finished

deal with /ˈdiːl wɪð/ (phr v) = to interact with sb as part of your job

delete /dɪˈliːt/ (v) = to remove data from a computer

embarrassing /ɪmˈbærəsɪŋ/ (adj) = causing shame

pay /peɪ/ (n) = the money sb earns from their job

professional /prəˈfeʃənəl/ (adj) = expert in your job

project /ˈprɒdʒekt/ (n) = a piece of work about a subject assigned by sb

promotion /prəˈməʊʃən/ (n) = getting a more important position in your job

staff /stɑːf/ (n) = all the people who work at a place

training course /ˈtreɪnɪŋ kɔːs/ (n) = a period of study in which you acquire the skills for a specific job

8c

advanced /ədˈvɑːnst/ (adj) = at a higher, more difficult level

antisocial /ˌæntɪˈsəʊʃəl/ (adj) = not allowing you to meet and spend time with other people

certificate /səˈtɪfɪkət/ (v) = a document proving that you've completed a course of study or training

closely /ˈkləʊsli/ (adv) = in a way that shows a strong connection between two or more people

course /kɔːs/ (n) = a series of lessons

degree /dɪˈgriː/ (n) = a qualification given on completion of a university course

demanding /dɪˈmɑːndɪŋ/ (adj) = very difficult

experience /ɪkˈspɪəriəns/ (n) = knowledge and skill gained by doing sth regularly

humanity /hjuːˈmænəti/ (n) = all the people in general

lecturer /ˈlektʃərə/ (n) = a university teacher of the lowest rank

lose a patient (phr) = (of a doctor) to not be able to prevent a patient from dying

marine biologist /məˌriːn baɪˈɒlədʒɪst/ (n) = a scientist who studies the sea and the organisms living in it

mark /mɑːk/ (n) = a grade for school work

personal trainer /ˌpɜːsənəl ˈtreɪnə/ (n) = a physical education instructor who helps individuals become f...

142

porter /ˈpɔːtə/ (n) = a hotel employee who carries guests' luggage

qualification /ˌkwɒlɪfɪˈkeɪʃən/ (n) = a particular skill in or knowledge of a subject; a diploma or degree

qualify /ˈkwɒlɪfaɪ/ (v) = to obtain knowledge and abilities to do a job

script /skrɪpt/ (n) = the written text of a play, film, TV series, etc

security guard /sɪˈkjʊərəti ɡɑːd/ (n) = sb whose job is to protect a building and its people

set up /ˌset ˈʌp/ (phr v) = to prepare the necessary equipment for an activity

shot /ʃɒt/ (n) = the particular position in which a cameraman films sb/sth

stressful /ˈstresfəl/ (adj) = causing worry and anxiety

surgeon /ˈsɜːdʒən/ (n) = a doctor who performs operations on patients

training /ˈtreɪnɪŋ/ (n) = practice

Culture 8

affect /əˈfekt/ (v) = to have a consequence on sth

attack /əˈtæk/ (v) = to use violence against sb/sth

ceremony /ˈserəməni/ (n) = a formal event to celebrate sth

disease /dɪˈziːz/ (n) = an illness

employ /ɪmˈplɔɪ/ (v) = to give sb a job

injury /ˈɪndʒəri/ (n) = physical damage to the body

keep track of (phr) = to monitor sb/sth

lift (sb/sth up) /lɪft/ (v) = to take sb/sth to a higher place

look after /ˈlʊk ɑːftə/ (phr v) = to take care of sb/sth

measure /ˈmeʒə/ (v) = to find the size, degree, length, width, etc of sth

occasion /əˈkeɪʒən/ (n) = a special event

preserve /prɪˈzɜːv/ (v) = to protect

prison /ˈprɪzən/ (n) = the place where criminals are kept

riverbank /ˈrɪvəbæŋk/ (n) = each of the two edges of a river where it meets the land

rowing boat /ˈrəʊɪŋ bəʊt/ (n) = a small boat that sails on water with long wooden poles

swan /swɒn/ (n) = a large white bird with a long neck that lives on rivers and lakes

weigh /weɪ/ (v) = to measure how heavy sb/sth is

Unit 9 – Want to play?

9a

an element of (risk, etc) (phr) = an amount of risk, etc

ask for trouble (phr) = to behave in a way that it is likely to cause problems

attack /əˈtæk/ (v) = to use violence to hurt sb

beat /biːt/ (v) = 1) to defeat sb in a game or competition; 2) (of the heart) to make regular sounds and movements

competition /ˌkɒmpəˈtɪʃən/ (n) = an organised event where the participants perform a specific task and try to win first place

deal with /ˈdiːl wɪð/ (phr v) = to handle sth

earn /ɜːn/ (v) = to get money for doing work

energy /ˈenədʒi/ (n) = the ability and strength to do active physical things

experience /ɪkˈspɪəriəns/ (n) = sth that I do or happens to me

experience /ɪkˈspɪəriəns/ (v) = to feel or be affected by sth

face /feɪs/ (v) = to control sth

fairly /ˈfeəli/ (adv) = reasonably; more or less

forget /fəˈget/ (v) = to not remember sth

gain /ɡeɪn/ (v) = to get (a point in a game, etc)

hang (off sth) /hæŋ/ (v) = to be suspended from sth

hide (sth away) /haɪd/ (phr v) = to keep sth out of sight

instructor /ɪnˈstrʌktə/ (n) = sb who teaches a sport

prize /praɪz/ (n) = an award for having done well in a competition

proper /ˈprɒpə/ (adj) = right; suitable

reply /rɪˈplaɪ/ (n) = an answer to sth; a response to sth

risk /rɪsk/ (n) = possible harm

sales results (phr) = the final number of sold products

situation /ˌsɪtʃuˈeɪʃən/ (n) = the conditions at a certain time

take a call (phr) = to accept a phone call

take a chance (phr) = to do sth that involves some kind of risk in the hope of a positive outcome

take a look (at sth) (phr) = to look at sth with attention; to examine sth carefully

take my mind off sth (idm) = to make myself forget about sth that causes concern, etc for a little while

to the limit (phr) = to the extreme

turn down /ˌtɜːn ˈdaʊn/ (phr v) = 1) to refuse to accept; 2) to decrease volume, power, etc

turn into /ˌtɜːn ˈɪntə/ (phr v) = to change into

turn on /ˌtɜːn ˈɒn/ (phr v) = to switch on

turn off /ˌtɜːn ˈɒf/ (phr v) = to switch off

turn up /ˌtɜːn ˈʌp/ (phr v) = to increase volume, power, etc

whizz /wɪz/ (v) = to move very fast, usually making a sound

win /wɪn/ (v) = to gain a victory; to get first place in a race or competition

win (sth) /wɪn/ (v) = to get sth as the result of a competition

9b

annual /ˈænjuəl/ (adj) = yearly

cancel /ˈkænsəl/ (v) = to decide that sth planned will not happen

due to (sth) /ˈdjuː tu/ (prep) = because of sth

lift /lɪft/ (v) = to pick sth up

session /ˈseʃən/ (n) = a period of time when you do a particular activity such as a sport, attending a lesson, etc

toe /təʊ/ (n) = each of the five separate parts at the end of the foot

9c

burn calories (phr) = to lose some weight by doing a sport, exercising, etc

common /ˈkɒmən/ (adj) = happening often

course /kɔːs/ (n) = an area for playing golf

court /kɔːt/ (n) = an area where some sports are played, such as tennis, basketball, badminton, volleyball, etc

depend on /dɪˈpend ɒn/ (phr v) = to be determined by sth

discount /ˈdɪskaʊnt/ (n) = a reduction in the original price of sth

encourage /ɪnˈkʌrɪdʒ/ (v) = to give sb the courage to do sth

field /fiːld/ (n) = an area of grass where people play football, baseball, cricket, etc

flexible /ˈfleksəbəl/ (adj) = able to change easily to suit any new purpose, conditions, etc

give up /ˌɡɪv ˈʌp/ (phr v) = to stop making an effort to achieve sth

independent /ˌɪndɪˈpendənt/ (adj) = not controlled and free to do as you wish

membership /ˈmembəʃɪp/ (n) = the state of being part of a club, organisation, etc

pitch /pɪtʃ/ (n) = an area for playing football, cricket, etc

rink /rɪsk/ (n) = a place where you can ice-skate

speed /spiːd/ (n) = the rate at which sth moves

suit /suːt/ (v) = to be right for sb

teamwork /ˈtiːmwɜːk/ (n) = working together in a group

143

Word List

track /træk/ (n) = a piece of circular ground used for cycling, running, jogging, etc

Culture 9

drawer /drɔː/ (n) = a container that you slide in and out to keep things in

earliest /ˈɜːliəst/ (adj) = the first ever

except (that) /ɪkˈsept/ (conj) = apart from the fact that

fast and furious (phr) = speedy and with a lot of energy

in total (phr) = as a sum

record /ˈrekɔːd/ (n) = written and stored information about sth in a file, etc

score /skɔː/ (v) = to win points in a game

shape /ʃeɪp/ (n) = the outline of an object

shaped /ʃeɪpt/ (adj) = (of an object) that has a particular outline

social /ˈsəʊʃəl/ (adj) = relating to activities that we do with other people in public

swing /swɪŋ/ (v) = to move sth in a wide circle quickly

Values C: Appreciation

appreciate /əˈpriːʃieɪt/ (v) = to respect and be grateful to sb for sth

facial expression /ˌfeɪʃəl ɪkˈspreʃən/ (n) = a gesture on the face expressing a feeling

frown /fraʊn/ (n) = the expression you make by bringing the eyebrows together to show anger, annoyance, etc

grateful /ˈɡreɪtfəl/ (adj) = thankful

have sb in mind (idm) = to think of sb

old-fashioned /ˌəʊld ˈfæʃənd/ (adj) = not modern; no longer in use

personal /ˈpɜːsənəl/ (adj) = intimate

pick (sth) up /ˌpɪk ˈʌp/ (phr v) = to take sth in your hands

Public Speaking Skills C

admit /ədˈmɪt/ (v) = to accept that sth is true

attitude /ˈætɪtjuːd/ (n) = a way of thinking and acting

emotional /ɪˈməʊʃənəl/ (adj) = causing strong feelings

farewell speech /ˌfeəˈwel spiːtʃ/ (n) = a short talk to say goodbye

get my hands on sth (idm) = to make sth my own

persuasive /pəˈsweɪsɪv/ (adj) = convincing

rare /reə/ (adj) = not common

can't stand the cold (phr) = I can't bear low temperatures or cold weather

Unit 10 – Tech world

10a

app /æp/ (n) = a specialised software program downloaded onto a mobile phone

awesome /ˈɔːsəm/ (adj) = very impressive

bring (sb sth) /brɪŋ/ (v) = to get and give sth to sb

connect (sth to sth) /kəˈnekt/ (v) = to join a device to a software program

cook dinner (phr) = to prepare an evening meal

designer /dɪˈzaɪnə/ (n) = sb who makes plans for machines

device /dɪˈvaɪs/ (n) = an appliance

do DIY (phr) = to make or repair things on your own

do the ironing (phr) = to make clothes smooth with an electrical appliance

do the laundry (phr) = to wash your clothes

do the vacuuming (phr) = to clean the floors, etc by hoovering

feed the pet (phr) = to give food to a domestic animal

get across /ˌɡet əˈkrɒs/ (phr v) = to communicate

get along (well) with /ˌɡet əˈlɒŋ wɪð/ (phr v) = to have a friendly relationship with sb

get by /ˌɡet ˈbaɪ/ (phr v) = to have enough (money, food, etc) to survive

get off /ˌɡet ˈɒf/ (phr v) = to exit a train, bus, etc

get on /ˌɡet ˈɒn/ (phr v) = to enter a train, bus, etc

get on (well) with /ˌɡet ˈɒn wɪð/ (phr v) = to have a friendly relationship with sb

get over /ˌɡet ˈəʊvə/ (phr v) = to recover from an illness, shocking event, etc

high-definition /ˌhaɪ defɪˈnɪʃən/ (adj) = (of a camera, etc) that has a higher resolution than a standard camera, etc

household item /ˈhaʊshəʊld ˌaɪtəm/ (n) = an object used within a house

lay the table (phr) = to prepare a table for a meal by putting plates, glasses and cutlery in the right place on it

maid /meɪd/ (n) = a woman whose job is to do sb else's housework

make the bed (phr) = to tidy the sheets and covers on a bed after sleeping

mop /mɒp/ (n) = a stick with a wet cloth fixed at one end that is used for cleaning the floor

mop the floor (phr) = to clean the floor with a stick that has a wet cloth fixed at one end

serve /sɜːv/ (v) = to offer food or drink to sb

serve meals (phr) = to offer food and drinks to sb at home, at a restaurant, etc

share /ʃeə/ (v) = to provide sb else with sth that I have

take /teɪk/ (v) = to obtain sth; to receive sth

take (sth to sb) /teɪk/ (v) = to give sth to sb at a different location

technology /tekˈnɒlədʒi/ (n) = new machines and gadgets

trade show /ˈtreɪd ʃəʊ/ (n) = an exhibition at which specific industry products are put on display so that people can see and buy them

vacuum cleaner /ˈvækjuəm ˌkliːnə/ (n) = an appliance used for cleaning floors and carpets, removing dust, etc

water the plants (phr) = to pour water onto flowers and trees

10b

bill /bɪl/ (n) = a piece of paper showing how much you should pay for goods or services

borrow /ˈbɒrəʊ/ (v) = to take sth which you are expected to return at a later time

hard drive /ˈhɑːd draɪv/ (n) = the part of the computer where you store your data and files

install /ɪnˈstɔːl/ (v) = to put a program into a computer and make it ready for use

membership fee /ˈmembəʃɪp fiː/ (n) = an amount of money that people have to pay in order to join a club or group

memory /ˈmeməri/ (n) = the amount of space that a computer, a mobile phone, etc has for storing information

scan /skæn/ (v) = to produce a digital representation of a document, picture, etc with the use of a device that can read data

social media account /ˌsəʊʃəl ˈmiːdiə əˌkaʊnt/ (n) = registering at a website on the Internet that helps people communicate

10c

activation code /ˌæktɪˈveɪʃən kəʊd/ (n) = a series of numbers or letters sent by a bank via a text message that provides access to a customer's account online

blog entry /ˈblɒɡ entri/ (n) = sth that you write on an online shared diary

chat /tʃæt/ (v) = to talk to sb in a friendly and informal way on the Internet

instant messaging service /ˌɪnstənt ˈmesɪdʒɪŋ ˌsɜːvɪs/ (n) = a service that offers online text messages and chat functions

interest /ˈɪntrəst/ (n) = a hobby or an activity that you enjoy doing

landline /ˈlændlaɪn/ (n) = a phone connection that works with a wire as opposed to a mobile phone

log in /ˌlɒg ˈɪn/ (phr v) = to access an online account by using your password and username

online banking /ˌɒnlaɪn ˈbæŋkɪŋ/ (n) = accessing your bank account and making your transactions electronically through a bank's website

password /ˈpɑːswɜːd/ (n) = a group of letters and/or numbers or other characters that allows you to access a computer system, an online bank account, etc

PIN /pɪn/ (n) = a personal identification number for accessing your online bank account

post /pəʊst/ (n) = a message on a social networking site

set up (a bank account) /set ˈʌp/ (phr v) = to make all the necessary arrangements in order to have access to your bank account on the Internet

tweet /twiːt/ (n) = a message written on "Twitter", a social networking site

user-friendly /ˌjuːzə ˈfrendli/ (adj) = easy to use

video chat /ˈvɪdiəʊ tʃæt/ (v) = to communicate with sb with the use of a web camera on a computer or smartphone via the Internet

vlog /vlɒg/ (n) = a video blog

Culture 10

amount (of time) /əˈmaʊnt/ (n) = a length of time

chance /tʃɑːns/ (n) = an opportunity to do sth

decade /ˈdekeɪd/ (n) = a period of ten years

dial /ˈdaɪəl/ (n) = a disc on an older telephone that has holes with numbers which you turn in a circular direction to make a phone call

display /dɪˈspleɪ/ (v) = to show sth

earliest /ˈɜːliəst/ (adj) = the first ever

gramophone /ˈgræməfəʊn/ (n) = an antique record player

grow up (with sth) /ˌgrəʊ ˈʌp/ (phr v) = to have sth within your surroundings from childhood to adulthood

handle /ˈhændl/ (v) = to touch sth with your hands; to pick sth up and have it in your hands

invent /ɪnˈvent/ (v) = to create sth that hasn't existed before

rotary phone /ˈrəʊtəri ˌfəʊn/ (n) = an old-fashioned device for making phone calls with a circular dial

step back in time (idm) = to go back to an older time in history

throughout /θruːˈaʊt/ (prep) = during the whole period of sth

various /ˈveəriəs/ (adj) = different

Unit 11 – Food for Thought

11a

bake /beɪk/ (v) = to cook bread, cakes, pies, etc in the oven

choice /tʃɔɪs/ (n) = a number of things to choose from

course /kɔːs/ (n) = each of the parts of a meal (starter, main course, dessert, etc)

cucumber /ˈkjuːkʌmbə/ (n) = a long thin vegetable with a hard green skin and a juicy flesh, eaten in salads

desert /ˈdezət/ (n) = a large area of land with almost no water or trees

dessert /dɪˈzɜːt/ (n) = sweet food eaten after the main meal

disgusted /dɪsˈgʌstɪd/ (adj) = feeling a strong sense of distaste for sth

dish /dɪʃ/ (n) = a particular type of cooked food

dough /dəʊ/ (n) = a mixture of flour and water that is used to make bread, biscuits, pies, etc

filling /ˈfɪlɪŋ/ (adj) = (of food) that makes your stomach feel full

filling /ˈfɪlɪŋ/ (n) = food that is put inside things such as pastry, etc

fry /fraɪ/ (v) = to cook in a pan with hot oil or fat

garlic /ˈgɑːlɪk/ (n) = a small plant like an onion with a very strong taste and smell used for cooking

gravy /ˈgreɪvi/ (n) = a warm brown sauce made from the juice that comes from cooked meat mixed with flour and water

grilled /grɪld/ (adj) = cooked by using very strong heat directly next to, above or below food

ignore /ɪgˈnɔː/ (v) = to pay no attention to sth/sb

keep away from /ˌkiːp əˈweɪ frəm/ (phr v) = to stop sb/ yourself going near sb/sth

keep off /ˌkiːp ˈɒf/ (phr v) = to not walk on sth

keep on /ˌkiːp ˈɒn/ (phr v) = to continue doing sth

keep out /ˌkiːp ˈaʊt/ (phr v) = to not allow sb to enter

keep up with /ˌkiːp ˈʌp wɪð/ (phr v) = to move at the same speed as sb/sth

meal /miːl/ (n) = the food you eat on different occasions, such as breakfast, lunch or dinner

nutritious /njuːˈtrɪʃəs/ (adj) = (of food) providing things that people need in order to be healthy

pastry /ˈpeɪstri/ (n) = a mixture of flour, fat and water that is cooked, usually to cover or contain other food

pitta /ˈpɪtə/ (n) = a round flat bread that comes from the Middle East and you can fill with food

plate /pleɪt/ (n) = a round dish where you put your food to eat it

receipt /rɪˈsiːt/ (n) = a piece of paper that you get after paying for sth

recipe /ˈresɪpi/ (n) = a list of the ingredients and instructions on how to make a certain type of food

salty /ˈsɔːlti/ (adj) = tasting of salt

sauce /sɔːs/ (n) = a food dressing

seconds /ˈsekəndz/ (pl n) = an additional serving of food

silkworm /ˈsɪlkwɜːm/ (n) = a hairless white caterpillar that makes a thread used to manufacture a smooth, soft fabric

snack /snæk/ (n) = a small amount of food eaten between meals

sour /saʊə/ (adj) = having a sharp taste like lemon or vinegar

spicy /ˈspaɪsi/ (adj) = having a flavour of spice; having a burning taste

street food /ˈstriːt fuːd/ (n) = ready-to-eat meals sold at a public place by a vendor

sweet /swiːt/ (adj) = tasting like sugar

toothpick /ˈtuːθpɪk/ (n) = a thin piece of wood for cleaning your teeth

topping /ˈtɒpɪŋ/ (n) = sth you put on top of food to make it taste better

trust /trʌst/ (v) = to have faith in sth

tzatziki /tsəˈtsiːki/ (n) = a Greek sauce or dip made by mixing yoghurt, chopped cucumber, salt, garlic, olive oil and dill or mint

upright grill (phr) = a vertical appliance with two parallel metal bars or wires where you place meat to roast it

vendor /ˈvendə/ (n) = sb who sells things from a small stall or cart that is placed at a public place

11b

bag (of sth) /bæg/ (n) = a container used for carrying things in, such as sugar, flour, etc

bar (of sth) /bɑː/ (n) = a long thin piece of sth such as chocolate, soap, etc

145

Word List

bread roll /bred rəʊl/ (n) = a long or round-shaped piece of bread for one person

bunch (of sth) /bʌntʃ/ (n) = a number of flowers, grapes, bananas, etc held together

cabbage /ˈkæbɪdʒ/ (n) = a large round vegetable with thick green, white or purple leaves

can (of sth) /kæn/ (n) = a closed, small, metal container for drinks such as cola, beer, etc

cook /kʊk/ (n) = a chef

head (for sth) /hed/ (v) = to go towards a place

herb /hɜːb/ (n) = a plant whose leaves are used in cooking to add flavour to food, or as a medicine

lamb /læm/ (n) = the meat of a young sheep eaten as food

level /ˈlevəl/ (n) = each of the floors of a building

lift /lɪft/ (n) = an elevator

nightspot /ˈnaɪtspɒt/ (n) = a place that opens at night for entertainment purposes

path /pɑːθ/ (n) = a long strip of ground which people walk along to get from one place to another

shelf /ʃelf/ (n) = a thin piece of wood/metal horizontally fixed to a wall or in a frame for holding objects

shepherd's pie /ˌʃepədz ˈpaɪ/ (n) = a traditional English dish of minced meat covered with mashed potato

spice /spaɪs/ (n) = an aromatic substance from parts of plants used to add flavour to food

spinach /ˈspɪnɪdʒ/ (n) = a vegetable with large dark, green leaves that people eat as food

the shopping experience of a lifetime (idm) = the greatest experience you will ever have when you go shopping

tin (of sth) /tɪn/ (n) = a closed metal container in which food such as peas, beans, tuna, etc can be preserved for a long period of time

transform (into sth) /trænsˈfɔːm/ (v) = to change from sth to sth else

turkey /ˈtɜːki/ (n) = the meat of a large farm bird related to the chicken

11c

apology /əˈpɒlədʒi/ (n) = sth that you say or write to express that you are sorry for having done sth wrong

be entitled to sth (phr) = to have been given the right to get sth

bill /bɪl/ (n) = a piece of paper showing the money you owe for goods or services

change /tʃeɪndʒ/ (n) = the money you get back when you pay for sth with more money than it costs

change tables (phr) = to get a different table at a restaurant, etc from the one that was initially offered to you

complaint /kəmˈpleɪnt/ (n) = a statement or expression of annoyance or dissatisfaction with sb or sth

constant /ˈkɒnstənt/ (adj) = continuous; never-ending

credit card /ˈkredɪt kɑːd/ (n) = a small plastic card for charging goods or services now and paying later

demand /dɪˈmɑːnd/ (v) = to ask for sth very strongly

frustrating /frʌˈstreɪtɪŋ/ (adj) = annoying

full refund (phr) = the return of all the money paid for goods or services because they were of poor quality, etc

manager /ˈmænɪdʒə/ (n) = sb who is head of a business, such as a restaurant, etc

money-off coupon (phr) = a piece of printed paper which allows sb to pay less for sth

note /nəʊt/ (n) = money in paper form

order /ˈɔːdə/ (n) = the food/drink you've requested in a restaurant, etc

prompt reply (phr) = a fast response

regular /ˈreɡjələ/ (adj) = (of a customer) who often visits a place

replacement /rɪˈpleɪsmənt/ (n) = a product that takes the place of another one due to bad quality, etc

sincerely /sɪnˈsɪəli/ (adv) = honestly

sth is past its sell-by date (phr) = (of a drink or food item) it is after the recommended date that it should stay on the shop shelf

Culture 11

annual /ˈænjuəl/ (adj) = yearly

delicious /dɪˈlɪʃəs/ (adj) = tasty

food critic /ˈfuːd krɪtɪk/ (n) = an expert in tasting and analysing a wide selection of food dishes at a restaurant, etc and then presents the findings to the public in a magazine, etc

fun /fʌn/ (adj) = enjoyable

grounds /ɡraʊndz/ (pl n) = the land that belongs to a castle, mansion, hospital, etc

outdoor /ˈaʊtdɔː/ (adj) = outside

promote /prəˈməʊt/ (v) = to try to increase the popularity of sth

raise (money, etc for sth) /reɪz/ (v) = to collect (money, etc for sth)

sample /ˈsɑːmpəl/ (v) = to try (food or drink to see what they taste like)

sink my teeth into sth (idm) = to become involved in sth with a lot of enthusiasm

stall /stɔːl/ (n) = a large table at an open market where products are sold

taste /teɪst/ (n) = a flavour

workshop /ˈwɜːkʃɒp/ (n) = a short seminar with practical work on sth

Unit 12 – Earth, our Home

12a

air pollution /ˈeə pəˌluːʃən/ (n) = harmful substances released into the atmosphere

break up /ˌbreɪk ˈʌp/ (phr v) = to split sth into smaller parts

bucket /ˈbʌkɪt/ (n) = a container with a handle for carrying water, sand, etc

clean /kliːn/ (adj) = not dirty

clear /klɪə/ (adj) = 1) not confusing; 2) (of the sky) without clouds

cutting down trees (phr) = the act of cutting trees so that they fall down on the ground

earn /ɜːn/ (v) = to receive money from your work

forest fire /ˈfɒrɪst faɪə/ (n) = a blaze in a wooded area

go off /ˌɡəʊ ˈɒf/ (phr v) = 1) to leave the place where you were; 2) (of electrical devices) to stop operating

go on /ˌɡəʊ ˈɒn/ (phr v) = 1) to continue; 2) to happen

go out /ˌɡəʊ ˈaʊt/ (phr v) = (of a fire/a light) to stop burning/shining

goat /ɡəʊt/ (n) = an animal we keep for its milk and meat

join in /ˌdʒɔɪn ˈɪn/ (phr v) = to get involved in an activity which others have started doing

lack of rain (phr) = a shortage of rain

little /ˈlɪtl/ (adj) = of a very small amount

look after /ˈlʊk ɑːftə/ (phr v) = to take care of sb

nearby /ˈnɪəbaɪ/ (adj) = located a short distance away

packaging /ˈpækɪdʒɪŋ/ (n) = a container or wrapping material in which products are sold

pick up /ˌpɪk ˈʌp/ (phr v) = to take sth in your hands

prove /pruːv/ (v) = to show that sth is true

receive /rɪˈsiːv/ (v) = to be given sth

refugee camp /ˌrefjʊˈdʒiː kæmp/ (n) = a place where people who have escaped their country can stay temporarily

rubbish /ˈrʌbɪʃ/ (n) = useless things thrown away

spoil /spɔɪl/ (v) = to damage sth; to make sth worse

staff /stɑːf/ (n) = a group of people who work for a company, factory, etc

support myself (phr) = to earn my living

wages /ˈweɪdʒɪz/ (pl n) = daily or weekly payment for your work

war /wɔː/ (n) = armed fighting between countries

water pollution /ˈwɔːtə pəˌluːʃən/ (n) = harmful substances released into water sources

12b

bottle bank /ˈbɒtl bæŋk/ (n) = a container for recycling glass bottles

car fumes /kɑː fjuːmz/ (pl n) = gases released from cars into the air

carbon footprint /ˈkɑːbən ˈfʊtprɪnt/ (n) = how much carbon dioxide each person produces

climate /ˈklaɪmət/ (n) = the typical weather conditions in a place

dry up /ˌdraɪ ˈʌp/ (phr v) = to lose all water and become completely dry

emergency /ɪˈmɜːdʒənsi/ (n) = an unexpected serious situation that needs immediate action

install /ɪnˈstɔːl/ (v) = to set up a piece of equipment and make it ready to use

LED bulb /led bʌlb/ (n) = a modern electronic device for producing light, more economical than conventional bulbs

light bulb /laɪt bʌlb/ (n) = a round-shaped glass container that produces light through electricity

recycling centre /ˌriːˈsaɪklɪŋ ˌsentə/ (n) = a place where used materials are processed so as to be reused

service /ˈsɜːvɪs/ (v) = to examine and maintain a car/machine

traffic jam /ˈtræfɪk ˌdʒæm/ (n) = too many vehicles that move very slowly

vegetarian /ˌvedʒəˈteəriən/ (n) = sb who never eats meat or fish

12c

buy /baɪ/ (v) = to give money in order to get sth

jar /dʒɑː/ (n) = a glass container with a top

plant /plɑːnt/ (v) = to put seeds in the ground so that they can grow into trees, flowers, etc

plugged in /ˌplʌgd ˈɪn/ (pp) = (of an appliance) connected to a supply of electricity

rubbish tip /ˈrʌbɪʃ tɪp/ (n) = the area where rubbish from cities and towns is dropped

spare (time) /speə/ (v) = to give your time to sb, especially when it's inconvenient for you

take part in (phr) = to get involved in sth with other people

take turns (phr) = two or more people do sth one after the other

tin /tɪn/ (n) = a metal container for food and drinks

turn off /ˌtɜːn ˈɒf/ (phr v) = to stop the water running from a tap

waste /weɪst/ (n) = unwanted substances and materials

wrap /ræp/ (v) = to put cloth, paper, plastic, etc around sth

Culture 12

ashore /əˈʃɔː/ (adv) = on the land at the edge of an ocean, lake or river

clean /kliːn/ (adj) = not dirty

curious /ˈkjʊəriəs/ (adj) = interested to know

divide /dɪˈvaɪd/ (v) = to separate into parts or groups

exhibition /ˌeksɪˈbɪʃən/ (n) = an event in which pieces of art are shown to the public

giant /ˈdʒaɪənt/ (adj) = extremely large

go on /ˌgəʊ ˈɒn/ (phr v) = to continue doing sth

increase /ɪnˈkriːs/ (v) = to become bigger or larger

jellyfish /ˈdʒelifɪʃ/ (n) = a sea creature with a transparent body that can sting people

mammal /ˈmæməl/ (n) = an animal that has babies and feeds them on its milk

octopus /ˈɒktəpəs/ (n) = a sea creature with eight legs and a soft head

pile /paɪl/ (n) = a number of things one on top of the other

puffin /ˈpʌfɪn/ (n) = a black and white seabird with a coloured beak

remind (sb of sth) /rɪˈmaɪnd/ (v) = to make sb remember sth

sculpture /ˈskʌlptʃə/ (n) = work of art made by carving stone, marble, wood, etc

set up /ˌset ˈʌp/ (phr v) = to start an organisation, business, etc

Values D: Caution

argue (with sb) /ˈɑːgjuː/ (v) = to disagree with sb expressing your views

bitter /ˈbɪtə/ (adj) = being angry about a past event/ experience

cyberspace /ˈsaɪbəspeɪs/ (n) = the Internet

deal with /ˈdiːl wɪð/ (phr v) = to handle sth

electronic data (phr) = information in a digital form

embarrassed /ɪmˈbærəst/ (adj) = ashamed

encourage /ɪnˈkʌrɪdʒ/ (v) = to give sb confidence to do sth

fake /feɪk/ (adj) = not real

ignore /ɪgˈnɔː/ (v) = to take no notice of sb

mean /miːn/ (adj) = not kind; cruel

nasty /ˈnɑːsti/ (adj) = horrible; very bad

offensive /əˈfensɪv/ (adj) = rude and upsetting

suspicious /səˈspɪʃəs/ (adj) = not trusting people, and careful when dealing with them

ugly /ˈʌgli/ (adj) = not beautiful

upsetting /ʌpˈsetɪŋ/ (adj) = causing worry and anger

watch out for sth /ˌwɒtʃ ˈaʊt fə/ (phr v) = to be careful in order to avoid sth

Public Speaking Skills D

communication tool /kəˌmjuːnɪˈkeɪʃən tuːl/ (n) = any piece of equipment for contacting people

constantly /ˈkɒnstəntli/ (adv) = all the time

gain access (phr) = to be able to use a smartphone, a computer, etc

hack /hæk/ (v) = to gain illegal access to sb's data

harm /hɑːm/ (n) = damage

lift /lɪft/ (n) = an elevator

message notification /ˈmesɪdʒ nəʊtɪfɪˌkeɪʃən/ (n) = the short sounds on your mobile phone informing you that you have a text message

pick (sth) up /ˌpɪk ˈʌp/ (phr v) = to take sth in your hands

CLIL A
Literature

be fond of (doing) sth (phr) = to like (doing) sth very much

current /ˈkʌrənt/ (n) = a continuous flow of water in a particular direction

depth /depθ/ (n) = the distance between the upper and lower surface of sth

Word List

flat /flæt/ (adj) = (of the sea) having a straight level surface without waves

gently /ˈdʒentli/ (adv) = softly and carefully

harbour /ˈhɑːbə/ (n) = a small port

head (for sth) /hed/ (v) = to go towards a place

hill /hɪl/ (n) = a high area of land that is lower than a mountain

row /rəʊ/ (v) = to move a boat through the water using oars

shore /ʃɔː/ (n) = the land next to the sea, lake, etc

steadily /ˈstedɪli/ (adv) = at a constant pace

wish (sb/sth to do sth) /wɪʃ/ (v) = to want sb/sth to do sth

CLIL B
Film studies

brain /breɪn/ (n) = the organ inside your head which controls your body and the way you act

depth /depθ/ (n) = the distance from the front to the back of an object

dimensions /daɪˈmenʃənz/ (pl n) = the length, width and height of sth

display /dɪˈspleɪ/ (v) = to show sth on a screen

flat /flæt/ (adj) = (of a computer/ TV) having a slim light screen without any curves at the edges and with very sharp and clear images

float /fləʊt/ (v) = to move gently in the air

length /leŋθ/ (n) = the measurement that shows how long sth is

lens /lenz/ (n) = a thin curved piece of glass or plastic attached to a camera, telescope or pair of glasses that makes images smaller, bigger, etc

mixture /ˈmɪkstʃə/ (n) = a combination of two or more different things

possible /ˈpɒsəbəl/ (adj) = able to be done

slightly /ˈslaɪtli/ (adv) = a little bit

stand for /ˈstænd fə/ (phr v) = to mean sth

trick into /ˈtrɪk ˌɪntu/ (phr v) = to deceive sb into doing sth

version /ˈvɜːʃən/ (n) = a form of sth which is similar to, but not exactly the same as, its original form

width /wɪdθ/ (n) = the measurement that shows the extent of sth from one side to another

CLIL C
Science

build up /ˌbɪld ˈʌp/ (phr v) = to accumulate over a period of time

epicentre /ˈepɪsentə/ (n) = the point on the Earth's surface directly above the centre of an earthquake

fault line /ˈfɔːlt laɪn/ (n) = the place on the Earth's surface where a long crack is formed when two tectonic plates have moved past each other and an earthquake occurs

focus /ˈfəʊkəs/ (n) = the place underneath the Earth's surface at which an earthquake occurs

layer /ˈleɪə/ (n) = a thin flat area, usually lying above or below another

pressure /ˈpreʃə/ (n) = the force which is put onto sth

release /rɪˈliːs/ (v) = to let sth flow out

rise up /ˌraɪz ˈʌp/ (phr v) = to move upwards

seismic wave /ˌsaɪzmɪk ˈweɪv/ (n) = a vibration that travels through the Earth caused by an earthquake, explosion, etc

shake /ʃeɪk/ (v) = (of a part of land) to vibrate; to tremble

smooth /smuːð/ (adj) = having an even surface

surface /ˈsɜːfɪs/ (n) = the outer top part or layer of sth

tectonic plate /tekˌtɒnɪk ˈpleɪt/ (n) = each of the rock parts of the Earth's crust

CLIL D
Geography

acid /ˈæsɪd/ (n) = a chemical substance that can burn sth or dissolve other substances

break down /ˌbreɪk ˈdaʊn/ (phr v) = to separate into the substances that sth is made up of

calcite /ˈkælsaɪt/ (n) = a white or colourless mineral that is a major component of marble, limestone, etc

carbon dioxide /ˌkɑː bən daɪˈɒksaɪd/ (n) = a colourless gas that is produced by the decomposition of organic substances and when people/animals breathe out

carbonic acid /kɑːˌbɒnɪk ˈæsɪd/ (n) = a colourless chemical substance that is formed by dissolving carbon dioxide in water

create /kriˈeɪt/ (v) = to produce sth

dolomite /ˈdɒləmaɪt/ (n) = a type of white mineral that is used to produce marble and cement

drop (of sth) /drɒp/ (n) = a very small amount of liquid

enter /ˈentə/ (v) = to go into a place

erosion /ɪˈrəʊʒən/ (n) = the process in which soil or rock is worn away by wind, water, etc

explore /ɪkˈsplɔː/ (v) = to go around a place to discover what is there

form /fɔːm/ (v) = to make sth

glacier /ˈglæsiə/ (n) = a large slowly-moving body of ice

gypsum /ˈdʒɪpsəm/ (n) = a white or colourless mineral used to produce plaster or cement

hit (against sth) /hɪt/ (v) = to strike against sth

karst cave /ˈkɑːst keɪv/ (n) = a large hole in the side of a hill, cliff or mountain that is made of rocks such as limestone, marble or gypsum

limestone /ˈlaɪmstəʊn/ (n) = a kind of rock that contains calcium used as a building material

melted /ˈmeltɪd/ (adj) = changed from a solid to a liquid form

mineral /ˈmɪnərəl/ (n) = a substance, such as salt, gold, etc which is naturally made in rocks and in the Earth

pile /paɪl/ (n) = a number of things lying one on top of the other

tiny /ˈtaɪni/ (adj) = extremely small

Pronunciation

Vowels

a	/eə/	care, rare, scare, dare, fare, share
	/eɪ/	name, face, table, lake, take, day, age, ache, late, snake, make
	/æ/	apple, bag, hat, man, flat, lamp, fat, hand, black, cap, fan, cat, actor, factor, manner
	/ɔ:/	ball, wall, call, tall, small, hall, warn, walk, also, chalk
	/ɒ/	want, wash, watch, what, wasp
	/ə/	alarm, away, America
	/ɑ:/	arms, dark, bar, star, car, ask, last, fast, glass, far, mask
e	/e/	egg, end, hen, men, ten, bed, leg, tell, penny, pet, bell, pen, tent
i	/ɪ/	in, ill, ink, it, is, hill, city, sixty, fifty, lip, lift, silly, chilly
	/ɜ:/	girl, sir, skirt, shirt, bird
	/aɪ/	ice, kite, white, shine, bite, high, kind
o	/əʊ/	home, hope, bone, joke, note, rope, nose, tone, blow, know, no, cold
	/ɒ/	on, ox, hot, top, chop, clock, soft, often, box, sock, wrong, fox
	/aʊ/	owl, town, clown, how, brown, now, cow
oo	/ʊ/	book, look, foot
	/u:/	room, spoon, too, tooth, food, moon, boot
	/ʌ/	blood, flood
	/ɔ:/	floor, door
u	/ɜ:/	turn, fur, urge, hurl, burn, burst
	/ʌ/	up, uncle, ugly, much, such, run, jump, duck, jungle, hut, mud, luck
	/ʊ/	pull, push, full, cushion
	/j/	unique, union
y	/aɪ/	sky, fly, fry, try, shy, cry, by

Consonants

b	/b/	box, butter, baby, bell, bank, black
c	/k/	cat, coal, call, calm, cold
	/s/	cell, city, pencil, circle
d	/d/	down, duck, dim, double, dream, drive, drink
f	/f/	fat, fan, first, food, lift, fifth
g	/g/	grass, goat, go, gold, big, dog, glue, get, give
	/dʒ/	gem, gin, giant
h	/h/	heat, hit, hen, hand, perhaps BUT hour, honest, dishonest, heir
j	/dʒ/	jam, just, job, joke, jump
k	/k/	keep, king, kick
l	/l/	lift, let, look, lid, clever, please, plot, black, blue, slim, silly

m	/m/	map, man, meat, move, mouse, market, some, small, smell, smile
n	/n/	next, not, tenth, month, kind, snake, snip, noon, run
p	/p/	pay, pea, pen, poor, pink, pencil, plane, please
q	/kw/	quack, quarter, queen, question, quiet
r	/r/	rat, rich, roof, road, ready, cry, grass, bring, fry, carry, red, read
s	/s/	sit, set, seat, soup, snow, smell, glass, dress, goose
	/z/	houses, cousin, husband
t	/t/	two, ten, tooth, team, turn, tent, tool, trip, train, tree
v	/v/	veal, vet, vacuum, vote, arrive, live, leave, view
w	/w/	water, war, wish, word, world
y	/j/	youth, young, yes, yacht, year
z	/z/	zoo, zebra, buzz, crazy

Diphthongs

ea	/eə/	pear, wear, bear
	/ɪə/	ear, near, fear, hear, clear, year, dear
	/i:/	eat, each, heat, leave, clean, seat, neat, tea
	/ɜ:/	earth, pearl, learn, search
ee	/i:/	keep, feed, free, tree, three, bee
	/ɪə/	cheer, deer
ei	/eɪ/	eight, freight, weight, vein
	/aɪ/	height
ai	/eɪ/	pain, sail, tail, main, bait, fail, mail
ie	/aɪ/	die, tie, lie
ou	/ʌ/	tough, touch, enough, couple, cousin, trouble
	/aʊ/	mouse, house, round, trout, shout, doubt
oi	/ɔɪ/	oil, boil, toil, soil, coin, choice, voice, join
oy	/ɔɪ/	boy, joy, toy, annoy, employ
ou	/ɔ:/	court, bought, brought
au	/ɔ:/	naughty, caught, taught

Double letters

sh	/ʃ/	shell, ship, shark, sheep, shrimp, shower
ch	/tʃ/	cheese, chicken, cherry, chips, chocolate
ph	/f/	photo, dolphin, phone, elephant
th	/θ/	thief, throne, three, bath, cloth, earth, tooth
	/ð/	the, this, father, mother, brother, feather
ng	/ŋ/	thing, king, song, sing
nk	/ŋk/	think, tank, bank

Rules of punctuation

Capital letters

A capital letter is used:

- to begin a sentence. *It is cold today.*
- for days of the week, months and public holidays.
  Sunday, August, May Day Bank Holiday
- for names of people and places.
  This is Paul and he's from New York.
- for people's titles.
  Mr and Mrs Jones, Dr Miller, Prince William, etc.
- for nationalities and languages.
  She is Mexican.
  Can you speak Spanish?
  Note: The personal pronoun **I** is always a capital letter.
  Jenny and I are friends.

Full stop (.)

A full stop is used to end a sentence that is not a question or an exclamation.

Sue is away on holiday. She's in Brazil.

Comma (,)

A comma is used:

- to separate words in a list.
  There's lettuce, tomatoes, cucumber and olives in the salad.
- to separate a non-essential relative clause (i.e. a clause giving extra information which is not essential to the meaning of the main clause) from the main clause.
  Mary, who has moved here, is a teacher.
- after certain joining words/transitional phrases (e.g. **in addition to this**, **moreover**, **for example**, **however**, **in conclusion**, etc).
  For example, I like playing tennis and swimming.
- when a complex sentence begins with an **if-clause** or other dependent clauses.
  If Bob isn't there, ask for Ann.
  Note: No comma is used, however, when they follow the main clause.
- to separate questions tags from the rest of the sentence.
  It's hot, isn't it?
- before the words **asked**, **said**, etc when followed by direct speech.
  Max said, "It was late to call them."

Question mark (?)

A question mark is used to end a direct question.

What time does Sheila arrive?

Exclamation mark (!)

An exclamation mark is used to end an exclamatory sentence (i.e. a sentence showing admiration, surprise, joy, anger, etc).

He's so tall!
What a nice dress!

Quotation marks (" ", ' ')

- Double quotes are often used in direct speech to report the exact words someone said.
  "Nora called for you," Mark said to me.
- Single quotes are used when you are quoting someone in direct speech (nested quotes).
  "She got up, shouted 'I'm late' and ran out of the room," Bob said.

Colon (:)

A colon is used to introduce a list.

To make an omelette we need the following: eggs, milk, butter, cheese, salt and pepper.

Semicolon (;)

A semicolon is used to join two independent clauses without using a conjunction.

We can go to the aquarium; Tuesdays are quiet there.

Brackets ( )

Brackets are used to separate extra information from the rest of the sentence.

The Taj Mahal (built between 1622 and 1653) is in India.

Apostrophe (')

An apostrophe is used:

- in short forms to show that one or more letters or numbers have been left out.
  She's (= she is) *sleeping now.*
  This restaurant opened in '99. (= 1999)
- before or after the possessive **-s** to show ownership or the relationship between people.
  Charlee's dog, my dad's sister (singular noun + **'s**)
  the twins' sister (plural noun + **'**)
  the children's balls (irregular plural + **'s**)

American English – British English Guide

American English	British English
A	
account	bill/account
airplane	aeroplane
anyplace/anywhere	anywhere
apartment	flat
B	
bathrobe	dressing gown
bathtub	bath
bill	banknote
billion=thousand million	billion=million million
busy (phone)	engaged (phone)
C	
cab	taxi
call/phone	ring up/phone
can	tin
candy	sweets
check	bill (restaurant)
closet	wardrobe
connect (telephone)	put through
cookie	biscuit
corn	sweetcorn, maize
crazy	mad
D	
desk clerk	receptionist
dessert	pudding/dessert/sweet
downtown	(city) centre
drapes	curtains
drugstore/pharmacy	chemist's (shop)
duplex	semi-detached
E	
eggplant	aubergine
elevator	lift
F	
fall	autumn
faucet	tap
first floor, second floor, etc	ground floor, first floor, etc
flashlight	torch
French fries	chips
front desk (hotel)	reception
G	
garbage/trash	rubbish
garbage can	dustbin/bin
gas	petrol
gas station	petrol station/garage
grade	class/year
I	
intermission	interval
intersection	crossroads
J	
janitor	caretaker/porter
K	
kerosene	paraffin
L	
lawyer/attorney	solicitor
line	queue
lost and found	lost property
M	
mail	post
make a reservation	book
motorcycle	motorbike/motorcycle
movie	film
movie house/theater	cinema
N	
news-stand	newsagent
O	
office (doctor's/dentist's)	surgery
one-way (ticket)	single (ticket)
overalls	dungarees

American English	British English
P	
pants/trousers	trousers
pantyhose/nylons	tights
parking lot	car park
pavement	road surface
pedestrian crossing	zebra crossing
(potato) chips	crisps
public school	state school
purse	handbag
R	
railroad	railway
rest room	toilet/cloakroom
S	
sales clerk/sales girl	shop assistant
schedule	timetable
shorts (underwear)	pants
sidewalk	pavement
stand in line	queue
store, shop	shop
subway	underground
T	
truck	lorry, van
two weeks	fortnight/two weeks
V	
vacation	holiday(s)
vacuum (v.)	hoover
vacuum cleaner	hoover
vest	waistcoat
W	
with or without (milk/cream in coffee)	black or white
Y	
yard	garden
Z	
(pronounced, "zee")	(pronounced, "zed")
zero	nought
zip code	postcode

Grammar

He just went out./ He has just gone out.	He has just gone out.
Hello, is this Steve?	Hello, is that Steve?
Do you have a car?/ Have you got a car?	Have you got a car?

Spelling

aluminum	aluminium
analyze	analyse
center	centre
check	cheque
color	colour
honor	honour
jewelry	jewellery
practice(n,v)	practice(n)
	practise(v)
program	programme
realize	realise
tire	tyre
trave(l)ler	traveller

Expressions with prepositions and particles

different from/than	different from/to
live on X street	live in X street
on a team	in a team
on the weekend	at the weekend
Monday through Friday	Monday to Friday

Irregular Verbs

Infinitive	Past	Past Participle	Infinitive	Past	Past Participle
be /biː/	was /wɒz/	been /biːn/	learn /lɜːn/	learnt (learned) /lɜːnt (lɜːnd)/	learnt (learned) /lɜːnt (lɜːnd)/
bear /beə/	bore /bɔː/	born(e) /bɔːn/	leave /liːv/	left /left/	left /left/
beat /biːt/	beat /biːt/	beaten /ˈbiːtən/	lend /lend/	lent /lent/	lent /lent/
become /bɪˈkʌm/	became /bɪˈkeɪm/	become /bɪˈkʌm/	let /let/	let /let/	let /let/
begin /bɪˈgɪn/	began /bɪˈgæn/	begun /bɪˈgʌn/	lie /laɪ/	lay /leɪ/	lain /leɪn/
bite /baɪt/	bit /bɪt/	bitten /ˈbɪtən/	light /laɪt/	lit /lɪt/	lit /lɪt/
blow /bləʊ/	blew /bluː/	blown /bləʊn/	lose /luːz/	lost /lɒst/	lost /lɒst/
break /breɪk/	broke /brəʊk/	broken /ˈbrəʊkən/			
bring /brɪŋ/	brought /brɔːt/	brought /brɔːt/	make /meɪk/	made /meɪd/	made /meɪd/
build /bɪld/	built /bɪlt/	built /bɪlt/	mean /miːn/	meant /ment/	meant /ment/
burn /bɜːn/	burnt (burned) /bɜːnt (bɜːnd)/	burnt (burned) /bɜːnt (bɜːnd)/	meet /miːt/	met /met/	met /met/
burst /bɜːst/	burst /bɜːst/	burst /bɜːst/	pay /peɪ/	paid /peɪd/	paid /peɪd/
buy /baɪ/	bought /bɔːt/	bought /bɔːt/	put /pʊt/	put /pʊt/	put /pʊt/
can /kæn/	could /kʊd/	(been able to /bɪn ˈeɪbəl tə/)	read /riːd/	read /red/	read /red/
			ride /raɪd/	rode /rəʊd/	ridden /ˈrɪdən/
catch /kætʃ/	caught /kɔːt/	caught /kɔːt/	ring /rɪŋ/	rang /ræŋ/	rung /rʌŋ/
choose /tʃuːz/	chose /tʃəʊz/	chosen /ˈtʃəʊzən/	rise /raɪz/	rose /rəʊz/	risen /ˈrɪzən/
come /kʌm/	came /keɪm/	come /kʌm/	run /rʌn/	ran /ræn/	run /rʌn/
cost /kɒst/	cost /kɒst/	cost /kɒst/			
cut /kʌt/	cut /kʌt/	cut /kʌt/	say /seɪ/	said /sed/	said /sed/
			see /siː/	saw /sɔː/	seen /siːn/
deal /diːl/	dealt /delt/	dealt /delt/	sell /sel/	sold /səʊld/	sold /səʊld/
dig /dɪg/	dug /dʌg/	dug /dʌg/	send /send/	sent /sent/	sent /sent/
do /duː/	did /dɪd/	done /dʌn/	set /set/	set /set/	set /set/
draw /drɔː/	drew /druː/	drawn /drɔːn/	sew /səʊ/	sewed /səʊd/	sewn /səʊn/
dream /driːm/	dreamt (dreamed) /dremt (driːmd)/	dreamt (dreamed) /dremt (driːmd)/	shake /ʃeɪk/	shook /ʃʊk/	shaken /ˈʃeɪkən/
			shine /ʃaɪn/	shone /ʃɒn/	shone /ʃɒn/
drink /drɪŋk/	drank /dræŋk/	drunk /drʌŋk/	shoot /ʃuːt/	shot /ʃɒt/	shot /ʃɒt/
drive /draɪv/	drove /drəʊv/	driven /ˈdrɪvən/	show /ʃəʊ/	showed /ʃəʊd/	shown /ʃəʊn/
			shut /ʃʌt/	shut /ʃʌt/	shut /ʃʌt/
eat /iːt/	ate /eɪt/	eaten /ˈiːtən/	sing /sɪŋ/	sang /sæŋ/	sung /sʌŋ/
			sit /sɪt/	sat /sæt/	sat /sæt/
fall /fɔːl/	fell /fel/	fallen /ˈfɔːlən/	sleep /sliːp/	slept /slept/	slept /slept/
feed /fiːd/	fed /fed/	fed /fed/	smell /smel/	smelt (smelled) /smelt (smeld)/	smelt (smelled) /smelt (smeld)/
feel /fiːl/	felt /felt/	felt /felt/			
fight /faɪt/	fought /fɔːt/	fought /fɔːt/	speak /spiːk/	spoke /spəʊk/	spoken /ˈspəʊkən/
find /faɪnd/	found /faʊnd/	found /faʊnd/	spell /spel/	spelt (spelled) /spelt (speld)/	spelt (spelled) /spelt (speld)/
fly /flaɪ/	flew /fluː/	flown /fləʊn/			
forbid /fəˈbɪd/	forbade /fəˈbeɪd/	forbidden /fəˈbɪdən/	spend /spend/	spent /spent/	spent /spent/
forget /fəˈget/	forgot /fəˈgɒt/	forgotten /fəˈgɒtən/	stand /stænd/	stood /stʊd/	stood /stʊd/
forgive /fəˈgɪv/	forgave /fəˈgeɪv/	forgiven /fəˈgɪvən/	steal /stiːl/	stole /stəʊl/	stolen /ˈstəʊlən/
freeze /friːz/	froze /frəʊz/	frozen /ˈfrəʊzən/	stick /stɪk/	stuck /stʌk/	stuck /stʌk/
			sting /stɪŋ/	stung /stʌŋ/	stung /stʌŋ/
get /get/	got /gɒt/	got /gɒt/	swear /sweə/	swore /swɔː/	sworn /swɔːn/
give /gɪv/	gave /geɪv/	given /ˈgɪvən/	sweep /swiːp/	swept /swept/	swept /swept/
go /gəʊ/	went /went/	gone /gɒn/	swim /swɪm/	swam /swæm/	swum /swʌm/
grow /grəʊ/	grew /gruː/	grown /grəʊn/			
			take /teɪk/	took /tʊk/	taken /ˈteɪkən/
hang /hæŋ/	hung (hanged) /hʌŋ (hæŋd)/	hung (hanged) /hʌŋ (hæŋd)/	teach /tiːtʃ/	taught /tɔːt/	taught /tɔːt/
			tear /teə/	tore /tɔː/	torn /tɔːn/
have /hæv/	had /hæd/	had /hæd/	tell /tel/	told /təʊld/	told /təʊld/
hear /hɪə/	heard /hɜːd/	heard /hɜːd/	think /θɪŋk/	thought /θɔːt/	thought /θɔːt/
hide /haɪd/	hid /hɪd/	hidden /ˈhɪdən/	throw /θrəʊ/	threw /θruː/	thrown /θrəʊn/
hit /hɪt/	hit /hɪt/	hit /hɪt/			
hold /həʊld/	held /held/	held /held/	understand /ˌʌndəˈstænd/	understood /ˌʌndəˈstʊd/	understood /ˌʌndəˈstʊd/
hurt /hɜːt/	hurt /hɜːt/	hurt /hɜːt/			
keep /kiːp/	kept /kept/	kept /kept/	wake /weɪk/	woke /wəʊk/	woken /ˈwəʊkən/
know /nəʊ/	knew /njuː/	known /nəʊn/	wear /weə/	wore /wɔː/	worn /wɔːn/
			win /wɪn/	won /wʌn/	won /wʌn/
lay /leɪ/	laid /leɪd/	laid /leɪd/	write /raɪt/	wrote /rəʊt/	written /ˈrɪtən/
lead /liːd/	led /led/	led /led/			